Protocol in Sri Ramcharitmanas

Other Books by the Author

1. Protocol in Srimad Bhagvat
2. मानस में शिष्टाचार
3. श्रीमद भागवत में शिष्टाचार

Protocol in Sri Ramcharitmanas

Devi Dayal Aggarwal

Foreword by

Dr. Karan Singh

1998

Kaveri Books

New Delhi-110002

ISBN 81–7479–019–5

Published by : Rakesh Goel
Kaveri Books
4697/5-21A, Ansari Road,
New Delhi- 110002 (India).
Tel : 3288140, Fax : (011) 7198902

Laser Typesetting by : **Delite Printers**, Delhi.
Tel. : 7182133

PRINTED IN INDIA

Dr. Karan Singh
Member of Parliament
(Rajya Sabha)

सत्यमेव जयते

3, Nyaya Marg
Chanakyapuri
New Delhi - 110021

Foreword

As geological excavations continue to reveal new facets of past civilisations; classical texts also yield fresh semantic dimensions when subjected to close and continuous study. Shri D.D. Aggarwal, who has been in Govt. service for long and is well-conversant with protocol at high levels, is breaking new ground by concentrating on this subject in Ramcharitmanas. As far as I am aware, no scholar so far has paid attention to this thematic concern of Tulasidas. Shri Aggarwal seeks to demolish the British contention that India lacked even primary concepts of protocol before their arrival.

'Protocol in Ramcharitmanas' centres around the multiple levels of protocol discernible in Tulasi's celebrated work. Protocol, in simple terms, relates to hierarchical order as well as code of conduct prevailing in a particular society at a specific period. Its violation is looked upon as sacrilegious and punishable.

On the cosmic level, God is the most supreme. It is He who regulates the lives of all living organisms. Sage Vasistha consoles Bharat at King Dasratha's death, saying :

सुनहु भरत भावी प्रबल, विलखि कहेउ मुनिनाथ,
हानि लाभु जीवनु मरनु जसु अपजसु विधि हाथ।

At a number of places in 'Ramcharitmanas', the cosmological order is indicated by the tripartite concepts of Swarga, Prithvi and Naraka.

How strictly protocol was observed by King Janaka is evident from the seating plan at Sita's Swayamvara. All present on the occasion were provided seats according to their social status.

कहि मृदु वचन विनीत तिन्ह बैठारे नर नारि,
उत्तम मध्यम नीच लघु निज निज थल अनुहारि।

Diplomatic protocol too was conscientiously followed. When Hanuman ransacked the beautiful Ashok Vatika and even slayed one of the sons of Ravana, he was spared capital punsihment, keeping in view the following tenet of protocol :

नीति विरोध न मारिअ दूता।

In fact, the whole 'Ramcharitmanas' can be re-interpreted on the basis of protocol alone. Bali and Ravana were killed by Rama primarily because they broke the social norms sanctified by a long tradition.

Shri Aggarwal is to be commended on his fresh and interesting apprcach to the great epic 'Ramcharitmanas'.

Karan Singh

1 December 1997

Preface

Protocol is considered to be something given by the West to all countries, particularly India which was considered as a backward country. In fact India has never been backward, it has been branded to be so by the Britishers, who ruled India for a couple of centuries and prior to that Mohammedans tried to annihilate the Hindu culture and way of life. Having gone through Ramcharitmanas, I found that the modern ethics of protocol like order of precedent, immunities to ambassadors, international relations, laws of war, laws of peace, international agreements and their sanctity, the institutions of Emperor and Vassals etc., these all were available in our Ram period itself as propounded in Manas.

Raja Janak, at the time of Sita swayambar, had made arrangements for all to sit in a system similar to modern concept of order of precedent —

कहि मृदु बचन विनीत तिन्ह बैठारे नर नारि,

उत्तम, मध्यम नीच लघु निज निज थल अनुहारि।

Here the people have been made to sit in order of precedent according to their capability and not by dint of their varan— Brahmin, Kshatriya, Vaish, Shudra etc. Further, like the present concept of appointment of a returning officer/election officer to manage the show of an election, Raja Janak had appointed Shatanand. He at first announced the conditions of swayambar leaving no ambiguity like—

बोले बंदी बचन वर सुनहु सकल महिपाल,

पन विदेह कर कहहिं हम भुजा उठाई विसाल।

This is how the conditions of swayambar were announced in the sabha further emphasizing that one, who is able to throw arrow by the dhanush would be acceptable to Sita as her husband—

सोइ पुरारि कोदंड कठोरा, राज समाज आज जोइ तोरा,

त्रिभुवन जय समेत बैदेही, बिनहि विचार बरइ हठि तेही।

Anyone amongst the rajas, who broke the dhanush, would be able to marry Sita without any further consideration. After this, all rajas tried their luck but could not even move the dhanush. Then Ram broke the dhanush but Sita did not automatically go and garland Ram but went to him only after the overall incharge of the swayambar, Shatanand, having satisfied himself that the conditions of swayambar had been met, ordered Sita to go and garland Ram—

सतानंद तब आयसु दीन्हा, सीता गमन राम पहिं कीन्हा।

Further, Sita garlanded Ram and accepted him as her husband in the presence of all rajas, who confirmed the marriage. The marriage was further solemnised as per social protocol by Janak inviting Dasrath and performing all ceremonies of saptpadi etc. as required even today to make the marriage a perfect and recognisable act. In the marriage too all social protocols had been observed by both sides such as Raja Janak first inviting Dasrath for marriage, receiving Dasrath and his marriage party, arranging their stay and considering himself as inferior to the father of the groom etc.

Similarly, when Ram met Sugreeva, an agreement was executed between the two rajas before fire (fire being considered as a sacred witness for all such actions recognised by both sides)—

तब हनुमंत उभय दिसि की सब कथा सुनाइ,

पावक साखी देह करि जोरी प्रीति दृढ़ाई।

This is nothing but the agreement of modern days. Further, Bharat having come to take back Ram from forests to become Awadh Raja, Ram did not disappoint him and it appears Ram had been accepted as the overall raja of Awadh and Bharat only ruled as his lieutenant for the period of 14 years, Ram remained in forests. The paduka given by Ram to Bharat was nothing but the authority given by Ram to Bharat to rule in his absence. Bharat had put that authority on singhasan and ruled. Taking orders from paduka is nothing but ruling according to the provisions of letter of authority which must have been quite detailed one like present constitution.

After Ravan had expelled Vibheeshan from Lanka, he took refuge under Ram. An agreement was at that time too executed between them, according to which in exchange of Vibheeshan helping Ram, Ram would make him raja of Lanka. This agreement was executed taking water in hand thereby showing that the legal formality of evidence/witness was fulfilled with each such agreement executed. Subsequently, when Ravan was killed, Ram did not straight-away call for Sita. He executed first job first. Since after Ravan was killed, there was no raja of Lanka and the kingdom could not be left without a raja for a single day as it could invite anarchy, invasion etc., so, Ram first arranged for Vibheeshan's coronation. Then too he first sent Hanuman to go and check the intention of Sita and afterwards only he called for Sita. Even today if a government is not able to obtain vote of confidence and the Prime Minister resigns, he is asked to look after the government affairs for the time being till alternative government is formed meaning thereby that there cannot be a kingdom without a ruler for a single day.

There were set rules of war according to which the battles were fought like one person fighting with another one person. If one wants to fight with dhanush-ban, the other also fights with dhanush-ban. If one fights with sword, the other too is obliged to fight with sword and so on. These laws of war were exhibited during the battles with Ravan, Bali etc. There were also laws of peace. These have been demonstrated in the topic of Ram Rajya where the raja and praja used to follow all religious and vedic tenets as a result of which rains were in time, there were no famines, no ailments etc. The kings used to rule in a democratic way. They had Council of Ministers, advisers etc. and the guru was the prime adviser. There is mention of such councils existing in Awadh and Lanka. Before deciding to coronate Ram as yuvraj, Raja Dasrath had checked up the position from guru and the Council of

Ministers. Similarly, Ravan too (a very autocrat) had been shown as discussing the matter pertaining to the conduct of war with Ram in his darbar/sabha which comprised of elders, his brothers, sons etc., showing that democracy was in fall play in those days of monarchy, although in a limited way.

Awadh/Mithila were big monarchies headed by Chakravarty rajas and there were smaller rajas under them. These smaller rajas used to contribute to monarch some annual sums like Bali was a raja under overall rajya of Awadh. The purpose of Ashwamedh Yagya (Ram had conducted so many) was to show the force by the Chakravarty raja to his vassals. This is like the concept of vassals of present days.

There were ambassadorial immunities existing at that time. That is why when Ravan had ordered Hanuman, to be killed, who had destroyed Ashok Vatika and killed his son, Vibheeshan checked him saying—

नीति विरोध न मारिअ दूता।

Meaning thereby that there was some law on the subject according to which the ambassador/representative of a raja could not be killed by another raja, where such representative had been deputed inspite of the grave criminality having been done. This is as per modern international laws.

Ramcharitmanas, apart from political protocols, also depicts social procotol indicating the protocolic relations and behaviour amongst father and son, brothers, husband and wife, raja and praja, between friends (as Ram and Sugreeva), master and servant (Ram and Nishadraj). The ties of varan/ashram were also social protocols observed in those days. There is a mention that people of all varans were conducting themselves as per religious tenets due to which there were no quarrels/crimes amongst them.

Besides social and political protocol as is enunciated in modern age, Manas also demonstrates the spiritual protocol meaning thereby the relation of Ishwar and Jeeva (ईश्वर-जीव सम्बन्ध), control of the universe by almighty God. To provide confirmation to such ethics, the poet has managed to get them addressed by competent persons only e.g. through Ram, Shiv, Vashisth etc. like after Dasrath's death Vashisth calmed down Bharat saying—

सुनहु भरत भावी प्रबल, बिलखि कहेउ मुनिनाथ,
हानि लाभु जीवनु मरनु जसु अपजसु विधि हाथ।

Further the God–creature relations had been told by Ram himself to Lakshman and again to Bharat. Such protocol has been amply demonstrated in Uttar Kand in Ram's meeting with his brothers, rishis etc. and further in dialogue between Garud and Kagbhusand.

Even a protocol existed between the gods themselves. That is why the earth, having been annoyed by the rakshashas, had first approached Inder to relieve her of such anarchy and Inder took her to Brahma etc. Similarly, when Ram had defeated Ravan, all gods including Inder, Brahma, Shiv had gone to praise Ram. Ram himself too was the incarnation of Vishnu but neither he himself, nor through Brahma or Shiv, re-enlivened the vanaras etc., killed in the war with Ravan but found the proper person for such jobs i.e. Inder. Ram, therefore, requested Inder to re-enliven them as they had laid their lives for the sake of gods only. This shows that there was the modern concept of "Through Proper Channel" existing at that time also. This is also demonstrated when in a meeting where Ram was sitting with all his brothers and Hanuman, Bharat wanted certain clarifications from Ram. He rather than asking it straight-away from Ram, requested Hanuman to ask Ram for his sake—

जोरि पानि कह तब हनुमंता, सुनहु दीनदयाल भगवंता।
नाथ भरत कछु पूछन चहहीं, प्रश्न करत मन सकुचत अहहीं।

This clearly demonstrates the concept of 'Through Proper Channel' and 'Division of Labour' where each person had been assigned a task and he had to be approached for getting that job done by the overall master.

The poet has kept up the protocol — political, social, religious, spiritual to the maximum and I have not been able to find any breach of such a protocol anywhere. There have, however, been some instances where it seemed protocol had been breached but when it is read in conjunction with the provision at other places and historical, circumstantial position, the alleged breach of protocol has been eradicated e.g. at the time of Sita swayambar, when individually the rajas could not move the dhanush, a couplet is written—

नृप सहस दस एक ही बारा, लगे उठावन टरहिं न टारा।

Here the questions arose that—

(1) How could there be ten thousand (सहस दस) rajas as interpreted by various pandits in India?

(2) How could so many get hold of the dhanush to pick it up?

(3) How the overall incharge of swayambar allowed, so many to try to break the dhanush as in case they were successful in their mission then how Sita could accept them all as her husbands?

But this doubt gets redressed if we interpret it that after individually the rajas failed to move the dhanush, suddenly (सहस i.e. सहसा) ten rajas got up and tried to move the dhanush but they too failed in their attempt. Now ten rajas sitting nearby can think of such an attempt and since they suddenly got up and made effort to pick up the dhanush, and failed, they did not give any time to the overall administrator of the show to check them and the problem was solved when they went back unsuccessful in their attempt. So the breach of rule/protocol was avoided in this way.

In the end I would indicate that the book has been written by me for my own devotion, pleasure and satisfaction and not for any other consideration whatsoever. Some vernaclar words have been used in the book and glossary of the same has been brought out at the end for proper understanding.

Devi Dayal Aggarwal

Contents

Introduction

After having ruled over India for a couple of centuries, English have started claiming that India was a backward country and only they had taught them protocol/manners/etiquete/discipline. They, however, forget that when they landed in India for trade purposes, they had noted a kind of protocol existing in the darbars of Akbar/Jahangir/Shahjahan etc. There was, however, some indiscipline in the army due to lethargy etc. and taking advantage of the same, they created a gulf in various kings/kings and commanders etc. and became rulers of India.

Leaving aside the time of mughals etc., we go back to Ramayan kal or Mahabharat kal and find that protocol was at its height. In Ram kal there was protocol amongst raja-praja, father-son, brother-and-brother, mother and son, king and king, king and his vassals, king and ambassadors besides international relations and abiding by international law, laws of war, laws of peace, agreements amongst kings etc. For this purpose, I will restrict myself to Ramcharitmanas and will try to express to my understanding the existence of protocol—national, international, social and spiritual supported by the excerpts from Manas. What to speak of protocol existing in India in Ram kal, we find protocol existing in the realm of almighty too. In Uttar Kand, Kagbhushand has indicated that when during the childhood of Ram, he had gone to see his leela in Ayodhya, he had entered Ram's abdomen through his mouth and he saw there many Vishnus, Brahmas, Shivas, and other gods and goddesses but only one Ram. This shows Ram as supreme followed by Brahma, Vishnu and Shiv—incharges of their respective departments of creation, bearing up and annihilation—followed further by Inder, Surya,

Ashwinikumars etc. and then by their ganas. In this way the realm of God is a well organised institution and each incharge had been discharging his duty without interfering in others' affairs. It is clear from the fact that when Jayant (son of Inder) had bitten Sita, Ram had thrown an arrow to kill him. He had gone to all gods for protection but none was prepared to protect him against Ram, not even his father Inder. He had to go back to Ram and begged to be excused. Similarly, when Sati (Shiv's Rani) had some doubt about the bonafides of Ram and went to test him as Sita at the time when Sita had been kidnapped by Ravan and Ram had been wandering about in jungle in search of Sita, Shiv, when came to know that Sati had become Sita, the wife of his God Ram, he separated himself from her. This shows that there is a comprehensive set of protocol existing in our gods too.

Coming to the start of the universe after the annihilation of the universe, only one left was Manu, who helped in creation of universe. In Indian mythology, protocol starts from here itself. This led to Satya Yug. We do not have much facts about that Yug but from vedas and shastras, which are the creation of that time, we find these books full of all ethics of protocol, relations — social, national, international, laws of war and peace, law of vassalage etc. During this period the kings and others were faithful to each other. They cared for their words. Harishchander left his rajya when Vishwamitra asked for it and very religiously led his further life till he was owned again by Vishwamitra, who after testing his truthfulnes handed over the kingdom to him. Satyug was followed by Treta Yug or Ram Kal. In this period we find Ramcharitmanas the epic of that period full of protocol in respect of all relations—ruler and the ruled, father and son, brothers amongst themselves, husband-wife, master and servant, even God and his bhakta. This we will see in detail while going through Manas in detail.

In Duapur, protocol as per Shastras was followed and whenever it was not followed, the breacher knew that the protocol was otherwise. Kans caused havoc to his people as he had always a fear of Krishan causing his death. Duryodhan knew when he tried to uncloth Dropadi that he was doing a wrong thing and at that time Pandavas although sitting there could not object to his actions as they had lost Dropadi in gambling to Kauravas, who were free to behave, in any way they liked, with her. In Mahabharat although the battle was being fought as per rules, Abhimanyu was overpowered and killed by several rulers. Subsequently, Pandavas ruled India according to the tenets of Vedas and Shastras. There is mention of Yudhister having held darbars/ashwamedh yagya etc. in which we see the institutions of overall king (Chakravarti Raja) and small vassals under him. After Pandvas we come to rule of various rajas like Raja Bhoj, Bharat etc. but we do not have much written about them.

In about 6th century B.C. when Alexander invaded India, Puru was defeated and when Alexander asked him what behaviour be meted out with him, he said as is done by one king with another in the situation. This indicated that some canons of international relations were available and followed at that time too. This was followed by Mauryas. Chanakya Niti is the great creation of this time. The kings were governed by some ethics and inter-relations as well. They knew how to behave with their bureaucrats, the governors and others. Then came the Rajput period where small rajas had been fighting amongst themselves and taking advantage of the same, Mohd. Gouri invaded and defeated Prithviraj and started the Yavankal in India. Muslims ruled India for over 600-700 years. They had their own Islamic laws/rules to be followed. They were, however, influenced by the Hindu laws as well. The Yavan period was followed by English, who ruled for about 200 years and gave to India their own system of law/protocol etc. which is prevalent even on date. The modern concept of protocol includes the international law, international relation, relation between ruler and ruled, relation between employer and employee, law of war, law of peace, social laws for maintenance of law and order etc. This protocol, however, does not speak of social protocol and spiritual protocol as we find in Ramcharitmanas besides the protocol to be followed in wars, international relations with ambassadors etc. When Hanuman went to Sri Lanka in search of Sita and was caught there, the question under consideration was as to what punishment should be awarded to him. Generally the advisers spoke of killing him but Vibheeshan told—

नीति विरोध न मारिये दूता।

It means that the killing of ambassador would be against the law on the subject indicating that there must have been laws dealing with the immunities of ambassadors and international relations. At other places too there is mention of the ambassadors (दूत) speaking frankly and conveying without any fear to tell the message he was carrying from his king and the other king listened to the same without any harm to the messenger.

In ancient India, protocol in one form or the other did exist. It is evident from the varan and ashram institutions by Manu. Under these institutions, people had been divided into various categories according to their functions. Brahmins, considered to be bereft from worldly wealth had been those who were read and who taught others. Kshatriyas were there to fight and secure the kingdom and to administer law and order. Vaishyas were there for trade and agriculture and Shudras to do service to these three categories. The people in these varans had been destined to do their jobs religiously. These were main divisions but there were instances where according to one's capacity and capability one could cross over to other category. Vishwamitra being a kshatriya had by virtue of his tapasya become a rishi. Nishadraj, a shudra had become a chief and later a Rambhakta. That is why in Sita swayambar, the arrangement for seating of people had been made according to their capability—

उत्तम, मध्यम, नीच, लघु, निज निज थल अनुहारि।

Here the people were made to sit not according to their varna but according to their capability. This also shows that some order of precedence, as in present days, did exist at that time according to which people at various functions had been categorised. Further, there were also rules according to which the raja dealt with the visitors to his kingdom. At the time of Sita swayambar, Raja Janak had gone to receive Vishwamitra when he came to know that the rishi had come. He brought the rishi with Ram and Lakshman to rajmahal to stay comfortably after he came to know that Ram and Lakshman are rajkumars from Oudh. In swayambar again, the entire proceedings were as per laid protocol.

Although the people had been divided into varans, each one had equal right in the governance. Ram had separated Sita on the allegation by a washerman, who was a shudra. The institution of castes is in existence even today and the constitution has given equality to all irrespective of cast, creed and religion. Some such practice was in existence in Ram kal as well. Further in Ram kal everyone had been given right to be a Rambhakta. Not to speak of human beings, even vanaras and Jatayu had been accepted as Rambhaktas. It was only in later period that brahmins excluded shudras from bhakti and from reading the religious books and visiting temples. This had led to casteism and eventual disruption in the administration. English may be called responsible for this as they had fully exploited the "Divide and Rule" policy while ruling over India. That everyone had been given equal right is also clear from the fact that on return of Lav and Kush to Awadh, Ram had asked for the opinion of all the people as to whether Sita tyaga was called for or not. Although on this question all were unanimous in being excused for projecting allegation of infidelity on Sita on account of her having stayed with Ravan for several months, Sita gave up her life and then only Lav and Kush had been accepted as successors to the throne. Persons from every varan did respect the persons of other varans as per their capability. Vishwamitra although a kshatriya did not fight with the rakshasas, who had been causing disturbance in the worship but had come to Dasrath to take Ram and Lakshman, as he knew that the job of fighting with rakshashas was that of existing kshatriyas and not of rishis. Further, on each occasion, Dasrath had himself been consulting Vashisth before any important job was done. Vaishyas had been doing the trade and cultivation. They used to give a part of their products to raja to enable him to administer law and order and secure the kingdom from foreign invaders by maintaining army etc. Further, there is a mention that in Awadh, vaishyas had been running shops and had been selling things at nominal profit, which would indicate that there might be some economic constraints laid by the raja to govern trade; to take taxes from public in the form of rajbhag; and to cleverly and honestly utilise that money in doing their job. In Ram rajya it is said none was ill.

It may not be that nobody ever was ill but the hospitalisation must be available of very good standard because of which everyone, when ill, was treated. Lakshman, when unconcious because of Meghnad's attack, had been cured even when on death-bed. Such were the medicines available at that time and mention of these medicines is also available in our shastras. In the realm of God also Ashwanikumars are said to be the gods of medicines etc. All these rules were existing at that time as is evident from or Vedas and Shastras.

The purpose of my writing is to bring out that the concept of protocol existing in Ram kal based on what is indicated in Ramcharitmanas and whatever has been said above is to be seen keeping in view the time/environ existing when Manas was written. There was rule of Mughals. In Mohammedan period, Hindu ladies were not allowed to go out of the houses, as on going out, there was risk of their being kidnapped. Consequently, they were not adequately educated and their mental faculties had not been developed as a result of which Tulsidas was forced to write—

ढोल, गंवार, शूद्र, पशु, नारी, सकल ताड़ना के अधिकारी।

The women had been brought to this condition that is why we had to suffer as half of the population was just downtrodden and of not much use to society. Such things, which appear to be against protocol, had to be mentioned in Manas because of the restraints of time and environ otherwise in Manas there is no breach of protocol anywhere as per modern standard as well as according to the concept of Hinduism and whatever is written in Vedas and Shastras. In fact Tulsidas had studied all existing shastras before he started writing Manas and had made Manas a treasure of Hindu religion, social order and international relations. In Manas, Tulsidas had selected a character for speaking on any matter, as Ram had himself said at several places about bhakti such as Navada Bhakti to Sabri, Brahm-jiv bhed to Lakshman/Bharat etc. If these discourses had been imparted by someone else, people may not have believed. Giving consolation, teaching all shastras was the job of gurus that is why on Ram having gone to forests, Guru Vashisth told Bharat to compromise to the situation as—

हानि-लाभु, जीवनु-मरनु, जसु-अपजसु, विधि हाथ।

Let us now see what is in store in Ramcharitmanas in the light of the modern concept of protocol. In modern days protocol is by and large applied on formal occasions e.g. national functions, international seminars, relations between a state and ambassadors of other states etc. and do not provide anything about social protocol such as relation between father and son, wife and husband, brother and brother, amongst friends and so on or about spiritual protocol like God and devotees relations, gods intra and inter relations. As these are available in ample in Manas, I have tried to find some in these respects also and have tried to highlight the same in this book. I have also derived how far the institution of varan/ashram propounded by Manu is reflected in Manas. It is observed that in India, whenever and wherever the institutions of varan/ashram have been followed, there had been peace and whenever these were not followed the law and order started shattering. In Ram kal, the very existence of rakshasas was void of varan/ashram which led to battle between Ram and rakshasas. In Mahabharat, Karan's capability had not been recognised by the society which led to acrimosity amongst Kauravas and Pandvas and resulted in ultimate Mahabharat. In Rajput period also these were not followed, and Mohammedans were successful in invading and conquering India. Subsequently English too ruled over India because of the non-fulfilment of obligations cast upon the people by Manu's institutions. During medieval period the pandits had forbidden shudras from reading religious books. Even women had been deprived of taking any part in religious functions etc. It might be because of the influence or Muslims on Hindu fanatics. Even amongst Hindus, shaivites considered themselves aloof from vaishnavites, Ram bhaktas considered themselves different from Krishan bhaktas and so on. Therefore, there was need of someone who could bring about change in the mind of the people in this regard and bring Hindus at a common platform. Tulsidas's Ramcharitmanas written exactly at that time in 16th century A.D. brings out a compromise of all situations. He made Ram to say—

(i) "शिवद्रोही मम दास न होई"

(ii) "तुलसी मस्तक तब नवै धनुष बाण लो हाथ।"

In (i) Ram had himself said that one has to be devotee to both Ram and Shiv and he has been shown worshipping Shiv at Rameshwaram and Shiv worshipping Ram, the very basis of Manas. Similarly, in (ii) above, Tulsidas being Ram devotee did not recognise Krishan as his Lord when he visited a Krishan temple alongwith his cousin who was Krishan devotee. But same Krishan took dhanush-ban, the symbol of Ram and then Tulsidas had to accept Ram and Krishan as same and subsequently wrote Geetawali containing devotional songs on Krishan. He made everyone eligible to read religious books and become God's devotee. What to speak of human beings, he made Jatayu as a Rambhakat and the chapter on Kagbhusand and Garud is entirely to show that all creatures are free to worship Ram. He also made Sabri, a lady, as devotee of Ram to vindicate the feeling that even women are entitled to worship God and read religious books. It is Ram himself, who told Sabri about navadha bhakti. All such relations between God and his devotees have been explained by Ram himself in Manas and the religious discourses or the discourses for the consumption of society have been propounded by sadhus/gurus such as on Bharat's arrival in Awadh after Ram had left for forests, he was very much disturbed. In such a situation it is Guru Vashist who said—

सुनहु भरत भावी प्रबल बिलखि कहेउ मुनिनाथ,
हानि-लाभु, जीवनु-मरनु, जसु-अपजसु विधि हाथ।

In this way Manaskar has kept in mind which thing is to be talked about by whom as a matter of protocol and for inspiring belief in public.

Although all these things were available in our vedas and shastras but as already indicated the pandits had made monopoly on their teachings and these were not understood by the public at large. Tulsidas by writing the same in Hindi after having studied all shastras, Manas became handy for the laymen to understand and practise. Today Manas is common and available in every Hindu house.

1

Bal Kand

In Ramcharitmanas protocol starts right from the beginning itself. According to the tenets of Hindu religion, every job is started with Dev pooja. The first shaloka in Manas is about worship of Saraswati, the Goddess of knowledge and then Ganesh, the first amongst Gods, then come Shiv and Parvati and Guru, then Ram and Sita. Tulsidas has taken Ram as the controller of entire universe. Then Tulsidas says that he has studied various puranas and shastras, vedas, and other books relevant in writing Manas. He says he has written Manas for his satisfaction. After saying all this the poet starts writing Manas. He starts with worshipping Ganesh as is done in the beginning of any job in Hindus, then Vishnu, Shiv, Guru, then Brahmins, Prayag (where he wrote this book), then the wicked and mischievous as these persons can spoil any job being done by others. Such persons, therefore, have to be kept in good humour. Then the poet worships Saints and others. He worships saints as they give courage, and good thoughts. Modern ethics of protocol do not recognise the non-saints or wicked persons worthy of being taken cognizance of but in Manas appropriate recognition is given to them also so that atleast they will not cause any annoyance while doing the job. According to the poet nobody is good or bad character it is thinking which makes them so. After that the poet worships gods, rakshasas, human beings, animals, birds etc. and seeks everyone's cooperation in writing Manas. He worships everyone as he sees Ram in each one—

सीय-राममय सब जग जानी
करउं प्रनाम जोरि जुग पानी।

The poet thinks that he is not capable of writing Manas but this job can be done only if all the above help him. Like any great man, Tulsidas presents himself as very weak in intelligence, writing etc. and says that his book may not be worth anything except that it speaks of Ram-nam, which is the sole base of this writing and people may atleast read Ram-nam while going through this book. That is sufficient and serves the purpose of the writer. The writer at first prepares the reader for going through this book so that he gets the benefit of the contents of this book. The poet worships the ancestor poets, who have written on God and his doings so that they may bestow on the writer of Manas, the required capability. Not only the ancestor poets but the existing and poets to be are also recognised by the poet as atleast all of them speak about "God and His Doings". While wishing to poets, the Manaskar thought it correct to separately send his wishes for Valmiki, the earliest writer of Ramayan. Then he worships the vedas and shastras. Then Brahma, being number one in Gods, then the smaller gods, brahmins and pandits separately meaning thereby that he would have taken brahmin as by birth and pandits by function like Vishwamitra. Then he worships Saraswati (the Goddess of learning), Ganga, then Shiv and Parvati, whom he considered as his guru, father and mother and who could be helpful in writing Ramcharitmanas as Shiv had been the master, sewak and friend of Ram. He then worships Awadh including Saryu river, the people of Awadh, the raja of Awadh (Dasrath) and his queens, then Sita's father Janak with his people, then Bharat, Lakshman, Shatrughan. All this had been done in a system. After the brothers the poet comes to Hanuman, Sugreev, Jamvant, Angad, then others, human beings, animals, birds etc., who had been devotees of Ram, then the rishis and munis, then comes the turn of Sita followed by Ram and his name. He considered Ram name greater than Ram himself and so has been placed above Ram. Modern protocol does not provide for such spiritual themes. Tulsidas starts writing

Ramcharitmanas after worshipping Ram. According to spiritual protocol, all devotional jobs are done after remembering the almighty (इष्ट). So Tulsidas also starts writing (Manas) after remembering Ram in the samvat year 1631 (1570 AD), Chaitra month and date ninth. This also happens to be the birth day of Sri Ram.

Tulsidas starts after worshipping Ram, Shiv and Parvati. Here itself the poet has tried to finish the differences in shaivites and vaishnavites existing at that time. He has started writing the biography of Ram after remembering Shiv and Parvati. Also as already indicated, he has mentioned Shiv as Ram's swami, sevak and sakha. Shiv worships Ram so Ram is Shiv's swami. Ram also worships Shiv as he proved by installing Shivling at Rameshwaram. Both being swamis of each other becomes friends. Tulsidas, therefore, after worshipping Shiv and Parvati and after remembering Ram mentions about meeting of Yagvalkya and Bhardwaj munis. Yagvalkya muni used to come to Prayag in Magh and this time when he came, he went to Bhardwaj ashram after taking bath in Prayagraj. Other munis following him had left, Bhardwaj requested him for telling the Ram katha. While making this request, Bhardwaj had to follow the requisite protocol of touching Yagvalkya's feet, making him sit on a stage, and after doing necessary puja, archana, started telling about some doubts in Manas saying that one does not get clearance unless such doubts are got cleared by the competent guru. He asked which particular Ram had been worshipped by Shiv and others-out of one of Dasrath's sons, or some other Ram. Yagvalkya could know the intention of Muni Bhardwaj that he wanted to hear from Yagvalkya the entire Ramkatha. He then started telling Ramkatha. To give the katha proper recognition even Yagvalkya did not tell of his own but referred to a talk betwecn Shiv and Parvati and said that he would only repeat the same. Who should tell what and at which time is the protocol Tulsidas has maintained in entire Manas.

"कहउँ सो मति अनुहारि अब उमा संँभु-सवांद"

Once, when in Tretayug, Shiv had gone to the ashram of

Agast muni to listen to Ramkatha alongwith his queen Sati. Agast muni had told entire Ramkatha and on return Shiv saw Ram in the forest wandering in search of Sita. Having seen Ram, it was necessary for Shiv, who was Ram's devotee, to say bye to him as per swami-bhakta protocol but thinking that Ram had accepted incarnation in-cognito and his openly saying him bye could leave Sati to make out who Ram was. He, therefore, on meeting Ram only said "Jay Sachidanand" and proceeded further without actually meeting him. But even then Sati developed doubt as to why Shiv, who is the overall Lord of universe, should say Jai to an ordinary man who was wandering in forests in search of his wife. But Shiv would not say so to any ordinary man, particularly when he addressed him as 'Sachidananda'. If it were Lord Vishnu then why like ordinary person he should wander in forests in search of his wife, he would know where she could be. She also thought at the same time that Shiv could not be wrong also. She, therefore, ultimately expressed her doubt about his being Vishnu's incarnation. Shiv told her the entire background but Sati would not feel satisfied. Ultimately, Shiv told her to test the fact. Sati became Sita in-cognito to test whether it was actual Ram or just a human being. Ram, however, recognised Sati in Sita's shape and asked why she alone, without Shiv, was in the forest. Sati became perplexed but then Ram would not leave on that and he created a situation in which Sati saw entire universe—all worshipping Ram, who was only one while all other gods were many in number including Shiv and Brahma. When she came out of the perplexion, she went to Shiv and told him she had believed Shiv and did not test Ram. Shiv then could know the entire happening by virtue of his power and when he came to know that it was Sati who became Sita to test Ram, he took a vow not to hereafter accept her as his wife since she had become Sita, the wife of his God, Ram. According to spiritual protocol no one can treat the wife of God as his wife. Shiv's thinking was proclaimed by Akashwani. Sati became suspicion that Shiv had known all that she had done and became frightened. On reaching Kailash, Shiv did not treat Sati as his wife as per proclamation. They lived in this way of separation for many years when one day Sati saw many gods going to his father Daksha's house to participate in a yagya. Sati also aked Shiv to allow her to go to her father's house but Shiv forbade her from going there as they had not received the invitation and according to all ethics of protocol, one should not go till formally invited particularly when Shiv and Daksh were not on cordial terms.

यदपि मित्र प्रभु पितु गुर गेहा, जाइअ बिनु बोलेहुँ न सन्देहा।
तदपि विरोध मान जहँ कोई, तहाँ गएं कल्याण न होई।

Shiv told her many times not to insist on going there but she under the influence of what was in store for her insisted on going there and she did go there. Shiv had sent a few of his followers to accompany Sati. Sati was not welcomed by anyone in her father's house except to some extent by her mother. This shows that all can afford to be non-cordial with someone including father, brother, and sisters but mother will still have some affection for the ward. When Sati saw that her husband had not been accorded the respect he deserved in that yagya, she burnt herself to death. Shiv followers destroyed the arrangement for yagya. When Shiv came to know of it, he sent some more of his followers not to permit the yagya to take place. While dying, Sati had prayed the almighty to make her Shiv's devotee in the next birth too. This establishes two of Hindu dharam's bases — one the theory of rebirth (even gods are not above it) and the other the last wish of the dying man is generally fulfilled in the next birth. Also in the next birth the gender of the person does not change. So Sati was born as Parvati on the rebirth in the house of Himalayas. Narad told her about Shiv being her husband if she worshipped him. Sati had done great tapasya and so was married to Shiv. Narad Muni telling Himalaya about the good and bad things in the life of Parvati confirms the institution of jyotish in Hindus. Correct calculations in jyotish lead to correct conclusions and whatever is written in bhagya cannot be changed by anyone —

कह मुनीस हिमवंत सुनु जो विधि लिखा लिलार,

देव दनुज नर नाग मुनि कोउ न मेटनिहार।

While explaining the bad things in Parvati's groom, e.g. he would be jogi, nude, half clad, without parents, without any good features etc. but all these bad elements existed only in Shiv and if Parvati marries Shiv, then all these bad elements would appear tolerable—

समरथ कहुं नहिं दोषु गोसाईं, रवि पावक सुरसरि की नाईं।

Even today the dacoits and goondas become MPs and ministers and people, forgetting all their past bad deeds start following them. Having known the fate through astrologers, the same could not be changed and then the people compromise with fate. In all religions, fate is recognised as a must, so in Hindus too. This gives consolation to the aggrieved persons too. Himalaya consoled Maina saying:—

प्रिया सोचु परिहरहु सबु सुमिरहु श्री भगवान,

पारवतिहि निरमयउ जेहिं सोइ करिहि कल्यान।

Parvati then tells her parents her decision to involve herself in tapasya and tells that tapasya is supreme in universe as anything can be achieved by tapasya. This again the poet tells through Parvati, the wife of almighty Shiv. Whatever position has been achieved by anyone, it is through tapasya only. Even Brahma, Vishnu and Mahesh conduct themselves through tapasya only.

On one side Parvati started tapasya to achieve Shiv as her husband and after a long tapasya she heard akashvani saying her tapasya had been recognised and she will get Shiv as her husband, on the other Shiv, after Sati had killed herself in Daksha's Yagya, had started tapasya of his Lord Ram. Ram came to Shiv having been pleased with his tapasya and requested him to now stop this renouncement and marry Parvati, who had done tapasya to have him. As already indicated, Ram and Shiv are the worshippers of each other as also the followers of each other. Therefore, Ram even when he appeared before Shiv having been pleased with his devotion did not order him to marry Parvati as any overall Lord could do in respect of his devotee but only requested Shiv to marry Parvati. He said:—

अब बिनती मम सुनहु शिव जौं मो पर निज नेहु
जाइ विवाहहु सैलजहि यह मोहि माँगें देहु।

Shiv also, though not in favour of marrying now, told Ram that he being his overall Lord, his desire could not be left unfulfilled. This is respect for each other and shows the protocol existing even in gods.

Even after the tapasya, Parvati had undertaken to have Shiv as her husband, Shiv did not just agree to accept it and sent Saptrishi to test her devotion for him but Saptrishi were convinced of her determination to have only Shiv as her husband. They went back and apprised Shiv of her determination. Shiv was happy to know and as per protocol worshipped Ram, his God, who had requested Shiv for marrying Parvati.

At the same time Tarakasur had been annoying the gods. They all went to Brahma to get him eliminated. Brahma told the gods to request Kamdev to make Shiv indulge in Kam and marry Parvati. Subsequently, the son born of this union would be able to kill Tarakasur. Accordingly, all gods went and prayed Kamdev to do the job. This involved his death but still Kamdev agreed to do the job for the benefit of all gods as according to the then existing protocol in Hindu dharma—

और "श्रुति कह परम धरम उपकारा"
"पर हित लागि तजइ जो देही, सतंत संत प्रससंहि तेही।"

There was nothing better than sacrificing one's life for the sake of others' benefit. Immediately, Kamdev influenced his effect on universe and

जे सजीव जग अचर चर नारि पुरुष अस नाम,
ते निज निज मरजाद तजि भए सकल बस काम।

Even the non-creature were feeling Kamdev's effect—

और लता निहारि नवहिं तरु साखा,
संगम करहि तलाब तलाई।

But Shiv was not affected by Kam as a result of which Kamdev disturbed his samadhi by throwing arrows from bow. Shiv opened his third eye having been disturbed and Kamdev was burnt. Kamdev's wife became unconcious after knowing the fate of her husband. She came to Shiv and begged to be pardoned. Shiv told her that henceforth Kamdev will have his effect without having the body himself. Then all gods went to Shiv and prayed for his being married with Parvati. Shiv agreed for marriage. Great munis were called to tell the correct day of marriage. All good deeds ware done in Hindu dharam according to jyotish after finding good days for doing such jobs. Marriage is a great job in our life and has to be fixed on an auspicious day so that it comes out successful. So a day was fixed and bride's parents were apprised of the day. Also, it is necessary to tell the bride side of the day of marriage so that they prepare themselves to receive the marriage party and also tell the groom's side if still there was some reservation. Then the bride's parents invite the groom side for the marriage formally. On such occasions good omens take place to indicate that the job would successfully be done. Shiv called all his followers to join the marriage party. His followers included Bhoot, Pisach, etc. who in appearance seemed were fearful. Now protocol requires the marriage party to be received at some distant place from bride's house. So some elder people went for the reception but all came back running after seeing the fearful marriage party. This may also be the purpose to receive the marriage party in advance so that all ill doings of the groom's side could be known before actually the marriage party arrives and marriage takes place. Some people, who knew Shiv's character was like that, accompanied the marriage party to bride's house. Then there is a system to have groom's 'arti' so that the groom could be seen thoroughly before the marriage. This is done by bride's mother. Seeing the groom's unpleasant dress etc., she became unconcious. Then she was made to understand Shiv fully. Parvati also made her mother understand that the husband and other good and bad characters in him have to be as these are destined.

दुख, सुख, जो लिखा लिलार हमरें जाब जहँ पाउब तहीं।

All felt satisfied after Narad muni told the epic of Sati, who now became Parvati and had to be married to Shiv only. Then according to protocol all the persons in marriage party were given lunch etc. and as per custom the ladies shower abuses while the marriage party takes meals. These abuses are taken in correct spirit by the marriage party and such custom is with a view to make otherwise sad atmosphere of the girl leaving parent's house into harmonious and comedial one. Thereafter, Shiv was called to perform the marriage ceremony. A special seat is made for the groom and the groom occupies that seat after wishing all his seniors/superiors and the God for doing all well.

At first the Lord of all gods, Ganesha is worshipped and then others are worshipped; the bride's father hand over the hand of bride to the groom as if to sermonise him that henceforth he was responsible to protect the bride (his wife to be) from all fears and to bring her up in his house. After the marriage ceremony is over, the bride's parents give to the groom's parents lot of wealth, dasis, chariots, horses etc. in dowry as a symbol for helping the groom to bring up and keep the bride in his house. The bride's parents when saying 'bye' to the bride request the groom to keep the bride even as a maid in his house and as all ill doings of maid are excused so all ill doings of the bride in new house be excused. The bride was also told to follow all naridharma (नारि धर्म) and live in a very cordial way in the groom's house respecting all in that house—the groom's parents, brothers, sisters etc. and treating that house as her own, discharge all household duties to the satisfaction of all in that house. After the marriage is over, the parents of the bride and some senior persons accompany the marriage party for some distance in token of respect for them and then return to their houses. Shiv and Parvati came to Kailash and started living as husband and wife. As a result of their union, Satbadan was born who killed Tarkasur as planned.

At that time, there was difference in belief between shaivites and vaishnavites. Tulsidas has tried to effect compromise in the same by writing the line—

शिवपद कमल जिन्हहिं रति नाहीं, रामहिं ते सपनेहु न सुहाई।

In her previous life as Sati, Parvati had been divorced by Shiv as she had dressed herself like Sita. This had been done with a view to test whether the Ram wandering in forests in search of his wife Sita was the incarnation of God. Sati had to give up her life and had a new birth as Parvati. She was again married to Shiv. Shiv and Parvati had been living on Kailash with all love. Parvati, however, still remembered her doubt about the bonafides of Ram as incarnation of God. So, one day when Shiv was sitting on Kailash in peace then Parvati seeing him in good mood went to him. When one have to get some clarification or favour from someone, protocol requires him to first ascertain the mood of the other person otherwise instead of getting favour he may be a loser. So Parvati saw Shiv in good mood —

पारबती भल अवसरु जानी, गई संभु पहिं मातु भवानी।

Shiv also respected her and asked her to sit by his side. She, thereafter, at first offered prayer to him and then after seeking his permission, expressed her doubt of the previous birth as Sati :

जौं नृप तनय ते ब्रह्म किमि नारि बिरह मति भोरि
देखि चरित महिमा सुनत भ्रमति बुद्धि अति मोरि।

At the time Manas was written, ladies were not considered eligible to hear Ram Katha. Tulsidas has annihilated such belief by saying that —

जदपि जोषिता नहिं अधिकारी, दासी मन क्रम बचन तुम्हारी,
गुढ़उ तत्त्व न साधु दुरावहिं आरत अधिकारी जहं पावहिं।

When ladies are actually lost in devotion to God, they become eligible to listen to all pertaining to God. Shiv, when remembered Ram Katha, lost in himself for a couple of hours and subsequently when he came to senses, he started telling Ram Katha to Parvati. He told Parvati that she having full faith in Ram could listen to the katha but her having said whether it is same 'Ram' whom Shiv and even Vedas had been worshipping or some other person, could not be digested by Shiv, who was utter follower of Ram. This will happen to anyone who had blind faith in a particular God. For having said this, Shiv rebuked Parvati a lot. Since Parvati had doubt about a live Ram being Nirgun Brahma, Shiv started at first telling the difference between Sagun and Nirgun. In Tulsidas time, there were Nirgun bhaktas like Kabir and Sagun bhaktas like Tulsidas, Surdas, Nanddas etc. The two, however, did not see eye to eye each other. To eliminate such a difference Tulsidas said—

"सगुनहिं अगुनहिं नहीं कछु भेदा"

अगुन अरूप अलख अज जोई, भगत प्रेमवस सगुन सो होई।

and told Parvati that Raghukulmani Ram was only his God. Then Shiv explained why Ram had come in the universe as incarnation of God and how Ram in his lifetime had annihilated the rakshasas and encouraged the rishis-munis etc. and established the institutions of varan and ashram propounded by Manu and which are the fundamentals of Hindu dharam. After hearing all this, Parvati's doubts about Ram being Brahma vanished but then she requested Shiv to tell her the entire Ram katha. Shiv then explained why Vishnu had come incarnated as Ram. Same katha was retold by Bhusandi to Garud and Yagvalka muni to Bhardwaj muni. The same katha Shiv narrated to Parvati and then Tulsidas tells to his followers. Since this katha had gone from one person to another i.e. from one heart (मन) to another, it has been named as Manas. While telling it Shiv mentioned that it cannot specifically be stated that this is the only reason for Ram's incarnation as there would be so many reasons for any incarnation and all are fulfilled in the lifetime. So after many reasons had come up necessitating the incarnation, the God adopted one as Ram, Krishan, Narsingh, Baman etc. But as per his knowledge and also having known a few reasons for Ram incarnation, Shiv explained the same to Parvati. The reasons are:

(1) When dharam is made to vanish by rakshasas, who exercise their powers and annoy the sadhus, other human beings and other creatures, and do not submit to God's will etc.

और जब जब होई धरम कै हानी तब तब प्रभु धरि विविध सरीरा।

हरहिं कृपानिधि सज्जन पीरा।

then God comes in one incarnation or the other. Ram had come when rakshasas like Ravan etc. had been trying to destroy all religious institutions and killing the sadhus, rishis, munis etc. and annoying all human beings. This precisely was the reason Ram had come. He killed all rakshasas and established dharam raj.

(2) Gods' escorts Jaya and Vijay had been cursed to become rakshasas and could again become Jaya and Vijay after being killed by Ram, the incarnation of Vishnu. Then Jaya and Vijay had come as Ravan and Kumbhkaran and had been killed by Ram after which they became Jaya and Vijay again.

(3) Kashyap and Aditi had performed great tapasya and as a result of the fulfilment of tapasya, Vishnu asked for anything they wanted. Then they prayed for Vishnu becoming their son. So Vishnu had assured that he himself would be their son. Therefore, Dasrath and Kaushalya had Ram as their son.

(4) Narad had passed a curse to Vishnu for not adhering to his request that vanaras will help him when like him, Vishnu will also be in trouble on his wife having been kidnapped. On hearing how Narad, who was Vishnu bhakta, could curse Vishnu himself, Parvati requested for full incident being told. Shiv had then told a thing of policy —

बोले विहंसि महेश तब ज्ञानी मूढ़ न कोई,

जेहि जस रघुपति करहिं जब, सो तस तेहि क्षण होई।

i.e. Nothing is bad or good but it is what God makes one to think about.

Here there is also a mention —

"सुमिरत हरिहि शाप गति बाधी"

By remembering God all evil effects get vanished. Narad had been cursed that he could not sit at one place but this curse got vanished when he remembered God and had attained samadhi. Seeing his samadhi, Inder, the king of Swarga feared that Narad might be doing tapsya to have his throne. He requested Kamdev to disturb the samadhi but Kamdev was unsuccessful. After the samadhi was over,

Narad came to know of "no effect of Kamdev on him" and he became proud of it. He told this to Shiv, Brahma and Vishnu. Vishnu saw some pride in Narad and he finished that by creating a town and the marriage of a beautiful girl. Narad got attracted towards her and requested Vishnu to give him his beauty so that the lady could accept him as her husband. Vishnu had created all this to finish his pride as he did not want his devotee to be proud of any achievement as being proud one loses tapsya. So with a view that Narad did not get married, he made him vanar. Eventually Narad could not be married. Having known this fact, he cursed Vishnu that he would also wander after his wife when she would be kidnapped during his incarnation as Ram. This also shows a protocol between the God and his devotee. God does not allow his devotee to get strayed by one reason or the other and in case he does, God saves him.

राम कीन्ह चाहहिं सोइ होई, करै अन्यथा अस नहिं कोई।

His wish of marriage not having been fulfilled, Narad went to Vishnu and abused him for having granted him vanar vesh. He told him that Vishnu being at the top could not afford to do whatever be wanted to do and that he too could be questioned by someone.

"परम स्वतंत्र न सिर पर कोई, भावइ मनहि करहु तुम्ह सोई"

Here indirectly it has been said that even the person at the top cannot afford to do whatever he wanted to do and ultimately he is also answerable to someone for his doings. Tulsidas's indication here is towards the Muslim kings, who had been doing whatever they wanted to harass the Hindus. Such things could be questioned by someone and dethroned.

Another reason for God to come incarnation is to kill and provide nirvan to Raja Pratap Bhanu, who had become rakshas because of the curse of brahmins, he had earned. Raja Pratap Bhanu was a great conquerer and had defeated almost all rajas existing at that time. He allowed those rajas to rule after taking lot of khazana from them and keeping them as his vassals.

सप्त दीप भुजबल बस कीन्हे, लै लै दंड छाडि नृप दीन्हे।
सकल अवनि मंडप तेहि काला, एक प्रताप भानु महिपाला।

Pratap Bhanu became the king emperor of the entire universe. Taking khazanas from the rajas and keeping them to rule under him is just like the institution of vassalage of the present concept of international relations. All these vassals had been paying their contribution to the king emperor annually and with a view to see that all such rajas continue to obey the king emperor, the king used to hold Aswamedh Yagya from time to time in which all such kings used to offer their obedience to the king emperor and present themselves before the king emperor at the time of such yagya. The praja was all happy in his rule. He had a mantri, named Dharam Ruchi, who was well versed with the diplomacy and the art of rule and had been advising the king emperor from time to time on all political matters.

सचिव धरमरुचि हरिपद प्रीती, नृप हित हेतु सिखव नित नीती।
और
भूप धरम जे वेद बखाने सकल करइ सादर सुख माने।

This shows the king had well versed and religious minded advisers under him who used to advise the king on all matters. The king had been ruling as per canons of the vedas. So our vedas and shastras contained all rules/ laws pertaining to the discharge of duties of the king toward his people, his mantries, with other kings, with rajas under him and pertaining to social and religious matters which a king was required to know. Only a king well aware of such discourses and having good advisers/ mantries could become a successful king. The kings had been keeping in mind the rules of general welfare of the public also. The King Pratap Bhanu had constructed many bapies, wells, gardens, and had made good arrangements at the places of pilgrimage. In the middle ages the kings had forgotten to do these welfare works and had been after filling their treasuries or in leading a lavish life. This gave way to the Mohammedens ruling India and when Mohammeden kings also became lavish, English took over from them. Even the King Pratap Bhanu fell in trap of a raja whom he had defeated and who had since become a sanyasi. The sanyasi after overpowering the raja advised him to arrange a feast of the brahmins so that after getting their blessings he/his successors, could rule till perpetuity. The king without consulting his advisors in the matter fell in trap of the sanyasi, who mixed human beings' flesh in the meals. The brahmins came to know of it and they cursed the king to become a rakshas. This is how a king is advised not to have blind faith in such people and should do all big jobs after consulting his mantri etc., who are the people of his confidence. Here Tulsidas has in the book narrated some laws of rule to be followed by the kings and are applicable to all times. At the same time the Manaskar has also told that the king, due to bad times, had come to the forest and fell in trap of the sanyasi having been isolated by all his guards/escorts etc. Here one is said to be governed by what is in store as per his fortune and all the environs become helpful in that direction.

तुलसी जसि भवतव्यता तैसी मिलइ सहाइ,
आपुन आवइ ताहि पहिं ताहि तहां लै जाइ।

Such things have to be faced by everyone day in and day out but whatever is written in the fortune, has to be faced, where none of the intelligence of the person works. Such an intelligent emperor fell in trap only because of the unfortunate time. The motto 'all is well in love and war' also stands fulfilled here as the sanyasi was actually a raja, who had been in the past defeated by Pratap Bhanu and now was his turn and he decided to destroy the king, who had fallen prey to him—

बैरी पुनि छत्री पुनि राजा, छल बल कीन्ह चहइ निज काजा।

Tulsidas warns that one should not go by the living and dress of the incumbent as the living can prove to be deceitful—

तुलसी देखि सुवेषु भूलहिं मूढ़ न चतुर नर।

King Pratap Bhanu became fully convinced of the bonafides of the sanyasi who told that—

सुत तप तें दुर्लभ कहु नाहीं।

and although had warned the king

सुनु महीस असि नीति जहँ तहँ नाम न कहहिं नृप

but he was so much in for the sanyasi that all these things the king could not follow and he told all about himself to the sanyasi, which is not as per the canons of the kingship. The sanyasi made king agree to arrange the meals of brahmins where he would work as the cook. The cook added brahmins' flesh in the meals. The brahmins came to know of this fact and cursed the king to become rakshas with his family. Accordingly, the king became Ravan, his brother became Kumbhkaran and his mantri Vibheeshan in the next birth. Vishnu as Ram killed Ravan and Kumbhkaran and gave them mukti as designed by the brahmins, who had cursed the king to become rakshas and subsequently on his request made the curse milder so that the rakshasas shall be killed by God and have mukti. So Ravan was born. He did tapsya as a result of which he got desired boons from Shiv and Brahma that he could not be killed by anyone except vanar or human being. He could never think that even a human being could kill him or God can come incarnation as human being. He then established Lanka as his kingdom and as any such king would do, Ravana considering him overall Lord; defeated the gods, who shivered even on thinking of Ravan. Ravan got married and his offspring included Meghnad, Atikaya etc. who too were very brave and warriors like their father. Ravan gave orders to all his sons and other people to kill the rishis, destroy their yagya etc. so that even gods were not able to survive on yagya-avshesh etc. There was lawlessness all around; there was no dharam or respect for any one anywhere. Then having not been able to tolerate all this, the bhoomi went to Brahma to find out some solution of the trouble as the trouble was only his creation. Brahma asked Bhoomi and other gods to go to Vishnu, who only would come incarnation as Ram and then kill Ravan etc. Then the question was where to find the Almighty Vishnu. His devotee Shiv then told that God is everywhere and he would appear when remembered with all devotion;

हरि व्यापक सर्वत्र समाना, प्रेम ते प्रगट होहिं मैं जाना।

One, therefore, has to find the correct person who could be helpful in a particular problem and not just go on searching vaguely or grope in the dark. Here the real bhakta of Vishnu, the Shiv could tell the whereabouts of Vishnu otherwise go on searching the entire universe. Then God appeared and assured to assuage the position on his next incarnation in the house of Awadh's Raghukul Tilak Dasrath and Kaushalya as after tapsya they had sought Vishnu to be their son. Here the poet has tried to show that —

(1) God is present everywhere;

(2) He can be traced by devotion; and

(3) He only could help the gods in the situation and having known the gods to be in trouble, he certainly would help them.

Kashyap and Aditi became Dasrath and Kaushalya in next birth. Dasrath became the king of Awadh. As required by protocol, Dasrath had all the ingradients necessary in a king e.g. intelligence, bravery, religious minded and devotee to God. He had queens, who too were very submissive and God fearing. He was not having any sons. Since protocol required all problems faced by the king to be discussed with the Raj Guru, who would remedy the situation and give some solution to the problem, Dasrath went to Guru Vashishth, who after giving a thought to the problem told the king that he would have four sons. For every purpose there was some modus operandi to be adopted. For the purpose of having sons, the king was advised to hold Putresthi Yagya. All solutions are available in our shastras. The only thing is one has to know where and how the operation is to be conducted. This job was that of gurus. Putreshti Yagya might have been some sort of purification operation or a cure leading to the lady becoming pregnant. Dasrath, therefore, held the required yagya and the ksheer (क्षीर) recovered as prasada from the yagya was distributed amongst the three queens.

On the Navmi of Chaitra Shukal, Ram was born. Now if Kaushalya had just given birth to the child in normal way then how could she know that she had given birth to the God incarnate as promised by God in her previous birth. To make her understand this, Vishnu at first appeared in his usual form with four hands and other garments etc. Kaushalya could remember the things of the previous life and then requested Vishnu to take birth as an ordinary child so that she could bear him up as her son as per her desire. Vishnu then became child and started crying as such. The maid having known the birth of a son immediately went and told the king. According to protocol, one who gives such a good news was profoundly rewarded. The king, therefore, gave her the costly mala worn by him and told the others in the darbar and apprised Guru Vashisth as well. Necessary ceremonies on the birth of the child were conducted and alms given to all as per the requirement. There was all jubilation in entire Awadh. The ladies duly well dressed had arti ceremony and pandits were doing requisite pooja. Gold, clothes, land etc. were given to all. Then Kaikayee queen gave birth to one son and Sumitra to two. They started growing in the rajmahal. After sometime there was a custom of namkaran. As already indicated all these ceremonies were conducted by the Raj Guru. Here again Guru Vashisth was invited. One was named by the sanskar or what he would come out to be as per destiny read out by jyotish.

'धरिअ नाम जो मुनि गुनि राखा'

The eldest was named as 'Ram', who could provide pleasantness and peace to all. The second, who could bring up entire universe was named 'Bharat'. Third, whose remembrance could annihilate the enemies, was named 'Shatrughan' and the fourth on whom entire universe rested was named 'Lakshman'.

The 'namkaran' sanskar was done after great thinking and with great pomp and show. After 'namkaran', the next ceremony was 'churamani' (चूड़ामणि). This was also done by Guru Vashisth. On all of these ceremonies, alms were given to brahmins and poors. In fact such ceremonies after some gap were fixed so that the brahmins and other could collect alms and valuables from the lords frequently. The four brothers by dint of their childhood plays, gave pleasure to all, particularly, those in rajmahal. All the four grew up in that environ. Then came the time of studies. In those days the education was imparted by the Raj Guru. He used to be well-versed in vedas, shastras as also in the use of arms by the kshatriyas. He could teach the administration, management, religion, diplomacy, rajneeti, protocol (political, international, social and spiritual). So all the four brothers were sent to the ashram of Guru Vashisth. During this period of attainment, the pupil had to live in the ashram of the guru and not at home. Even Ram had to leave the rajmahal and live in ashram with all others and like all others. It is during this period that one is taught how to leave all luxuries, had to earn livelihood by bhiksha. In bhiksha one had to forget that he was the son of a king or of a vaish or a brahmin. All were equal here. It is here that theory of equality used to get in their minds. They had one job of attaining education and no diversion. Character building was also taught here. How to respect elders, and relations, raja-praja relation, varan-ashram etc. Varan and ashram institutions were the base of the Hindu religion. It is in this period that one learnt how to go by varan and ashram. It was the first of the ashram i.e. brahmcharya ashram, when one was to live like a brahamchary leaving all ambitions, ill and sensuous feelings, wrong-notions, characterlessness etc. The pupils had to submit to the guru completely and since the gurus had no love for the materialistic world, they taught the pupil selflessly and with a view to make them the worthy Indians. The kshatriyas were taught to become warrior and good kings, the vaishyas were taught as per their professional requirements. The brahmins were taught all vedas, shastras and the requisites of a brahmin etc.

After the education was completed, the four rajkumars came to rajmahal and started helping the king in the dicharge of his duties.

Vishwamitra was an kshatriya turned rishi. By dint of tapsya, he became Brahmrishi from a king. He was disturbed by the rakshasas in doing yagya etc. As already indicated Ravan had directed all his followers not to allow the rishi-munis to do yagya etc. so that the gods did not get their share of ahutis and die of hunger. Vishwamitra had been a great warrior and kshatriya king and could fight out all the rakshasas but he had now become a rishi and according to protocol it was not for a rishi to fight with rakshasas. It was the job of the kshatriya to help the rishis in the discharge of their yagya etc. without any fear from anyone and fight with rakshasas to bring peace and law and order in the kingdom. Vishwamitra, therefore, went to Awadh to bring Ram and Lakshman for killing the rakshasas so that he could conduct the yagya without any disturbance. When Vishwamitra went to Awadh and the king Dasrath came to know of the arrival of the rishi, he went to receive him as per protocol after taking some mantris, brahmins with him. He paid all respects to the muni and brought him to the mahal and made him sit on 'singhasan' as a mark of respect for the muni. He worshipped the muni, served good meals to the satisfaction of the muni, brought all four sons and they also after touching muni's feet sat there. Then only the king asked muni of the purpose which brought him to Awadh. The muni told that rakshasas had been annoying him in holding yagya. Therefore, he had come to seek the king's assistance in the shape of lending his two sons, Ram and Lakshman, with a view to annihilate the demons. Dasrath was put in deep thought as he did not want to separate himself from the sons and secondly thinking that the sons still being in their childhood, how could they face the rakshasas. But Guru Vashisth made the king agree to the proposal. The king as a matter of protocol could not disagree with what the guru said as the guru was in for all well being of the king only and could never advise anything not in the interest of the king — socially, religiously or politically. The king, therefore, agreed to send his two sons. King taught them how to behave on the assignment. The two took permission from the mothers and followed the muni. Having learnt that Guru Vashisth and the king had agreed for the two—Ram and Lakshman going with the muni, the mothers could not disagree. The muni left Awadh with the two rajkumars. He was happy that the rajkumars had left even their parents for the sake of helping the muni. On the way they saw Tadka. Vishwamitra told Ram about the demon and Ram with one arrow killed her. Having satisfied that the rajkumars would be able to do the assigned job, Vishwamitra also taught them the art of fighting. After all he had been a warrior and a king and now turned a rishi. The trio came to muni's ashram. The rajkumars were settled. Next day the kumars told rishi to conduct his yagya fearlessly. When the muni started yagya, the rakshasas came to disturb the yagya but they all including Subahu and others were killed by Ram and Lakshman. Marich was not killed but thrown away to a distance near Lanka.

After the yagya was completed, Vishwamitra told Ram and Lakshman that Raja Janak had to hold a swayambar in which his daughter Sita shall select a groom for herself through 'Dhanush Yagya' and if they agreed, they could witness the function. Ram and Lakshman readily agreed seeing the dhanush yagya which all kshatriyas liked. On the way they found an ashram where Ahilya was lying as a stone due to the curse earned from Gautam Muni. Vishwamitra told Ram the story and by touching Ram's feet she came in her realself and got mukti. It is here for the first time that Ram had shown that he was an incarnation of God Vishnu and Tulsidas was forced to say—

अस प्रभु दीनबंधु हरि कारन रहित दयाल,

तुलसीदास सठ तेहि भजु छांडि कपट जंजाल।

Ram and Lakshman, with Vishwamitra, reached Janakpuri. As usual all kings had been arranging wells, bavaris, parks, gardens, roads, water tanks and ghats on rivers as the jobs of the well being for their people. So was in Janakpuri. In the town, there were bazars, where the stores were full of materials. The people were all very respectful for others and were quite content, gentle, God fearing and religious minded. The rajmahal had a fencing wall for protection, which showed the strategies existing at that time. In the rajmahal, there were mantries, brave warriors, commanders, and the town was on the bank of the river. Vishwamitra and the rajkumars decided to settle under a mango tree. Till they were formally received by the king, the guests had to settle themselves outside the town.

When the King Janak came to know of the arrival of Vishwamitra, he came to formally receive him as per protocol. The king was accompanied by his mantris, escorts, brahmins etc. He paid respects to Vishwamitra and the rishi in turn gave him his blessings. All king's followers also paid their respects. Then Vishwamitra after asking king's well being asked him to sit. Then came the rajkumars, who had gone to see the garden. When they came, all stood up to pay their respects and Vishwamitra asked them to sit closeby. Janak became very happy to see them and then asked the rishi about their whereabouts. Rishi told him that they were king Dasrath's sons and had come to protect his yagya from rakshasas. After the yagya was over, they accompanied him to witness the dhanush yagya arranged by Janak. Since the rishi was accompanied by rajkumars, Janak took them to rajmahal and allotted one very comfortable suite for them to live in according to their position. Thereafter seeking muni's blessing, the king went to his house.

After the muni was settled, Ram and Lakshman desired to see the town but were having some hesitation in asking for the same. Ultimately Ram asked the muni, if he permitted, he could take Lakshman to show the town as he desired to see but was not able to express his desire. This is again fulfilment of protocol, Lakshman being younger had to seek permission of the muni through Ram only. The muni too in turn could understand the entire thinking and allowed them not for seeing the town but to show themselves to the people so that they could feel happy seeing them. In other words the muni was also preparing Ram and Lakshman to become the point of attraction and love for all the residents of Janakpuri so that all may wish Sita's marriage to take place with Ram only. Even Ram did not straight-away ask the muni to permit them to see the town. He at first asked for muni's permission to speak and then only asked his permission to go and see the town.

परम बिनीत सकुचि मुसुकाई, बोले गुरु अनुसासन पाई।

Nowhere can we find so much protocol amongst the muni and his disciples. All residents came to know of the two rajkumars having come to see the town. All left their engagements and came to see them. Everyone felt happy and pleasant after seeing them. The ladies as per custom could not come on road to see them. They, therefore, saw them from the windows of their houses. They all started comparing them even with gods but thought none equalled them in beauty. While going there Lakshman being younger followed Ram, his elder brother. As per protocol he could not walk side by side with Ram and could only follow him.

गौर किसोर वेषु बर काछें, धर सर चाप राम के पाछें।

Everyone wished Ram to marry Sita but since the dhanush was rather heavy the rajkumar may not be able to fulfil the condition and for his sake they wished the king should give up the condition. Some also thought that they were quite brave as they had already killed rakshasas and protected muni's yagya. So they were capable even of fulfilling the condition. Ram and Lakshman saw entire arrangement made for the dhanush yagya too. It was like a battlefield and an kshatriya had to see it before commencement of battle as per requirement. It took some extra time and they had fear the muni may not mind their having been late. This again is the fear a disciple had for the guru. They came, paid their respects to guru and sat after having guru's permission. In the night it is the duty of the pupils to sleep after the guru had slept. Ram served the guru till he slept and Lakshman served the guru and then his elder brother till he slept and after that only he went to sleep. In the morning again Lakshman got up first and then Ram also got up before the guru. They completed their daily jobs before reporting to guru. Then with guru's permission went to take flowers for the pooja. In the garden, Ram and Lakshman sought gardener's permission to take flowers. All above actions were as per protocol.

At the same time Sita had come to the garden, where there was also Parvati temple, for Parvati pooja. This is necessary for the bride to seek an able groom from the God/Goddess. One of the followers of Sita had in the meantime seen Ram and Lakshman in the garden. She told the news to others and took Sita also where Ram and

Lakshman had been as they were the talk of the town those days. Ram saw Sita and was very happy to see her beauty. He told Lakshman that it was the bride for whom the dhanush yagya had been fixed. He also told that after seeing her, he got attracted towards her. Sita also saw Ram and got lost. They both fell in love with each other — may be being gods, they knew what is going to happen otherwise Ram, as a matter of protocol, never allowed such thinking to come to his mind at all after seeing a girl being a man of character as all in Raghukul dynasty had been. Same thing Ram mentioned to Lakshman also —

जासु बिलोकि अलौकिक सोभा सहज पुनीत मोर मनु छोभा,
और
रघुबंसिन्ह कर सहज सुभाऊ, मनु कुपंथ पग धरइ न काऊ।
मोहि अतिशय प्रतीति मन केरी, जेहिं सपनेहु पर नारी न हेरी।

Such was the character of the rajkumars at that time that they never looked with evil eye towards any girl. Same was with Sita. She had been a girl, who had never thought of any rajkumar at all, had got attracted towards Ram but the marriage depended upon fulfilment of the condition of swayambar which was rather tough and the father stuck to the same. Sita with the followers then went to the temple of Gauri and asked for a boon to get Ram as husband. Gauri had granted fulfilment of the desire. Similarly the two brothers went to guru and explained what had happened in the garden, as nothing could be kept secret from the guru. The guru also blessed for the desire of Ram being fulfilled. In this way Ram and Sita, both got the blessings of the respective Goddess and the guru.

सुफल मनोरथ होहु तुम्हारे, राम लखन सुनि भए सुखारे।
और
सुनु सिय सत्य असीस हमारी, पूजिहि मन कामना तुम्हारी

Next day was the day of swayambar. The rajas had collected at the place of swayambar. As per protocol Janak called Satanand, the administrator of the show to escort Muni Vishwamitra to the place of swayambar. The muni called the two rajkumars, who sat close to the muni after paying respects to Satanand. Vishwamitra told them to accompany him as Janak had called them. They reached the yagyashala. All residents of the town came to know of the rajkumars having come to the place and all came to that place leaving all their assignments. Raja Janak having seen that big crowd had come to witness the swayambar, ordered to see that each person got proper place to sit. The managers of the show went to all persons and requested them to sit at appropriate places.

कहि मृदु बचन विनीत तिन्ह बैठारे नर नारि,
उत्तम मध्यम नीच लघु निज निज थल अनुहारि।

Here the poet has shown full protocol and respect for others, existing at that time, which is only partially available these days.

'मृदु बचन और विनीत' words show that the managers requested each person to take his seat comfortably. There was no show of strictness or strength on the part of the persons policing the place. Then each person was provided with seat according to his position. 'उत्तम, मध्य, नीच, लघु' show the distribution of the people in these four categories which indicates that like the 'order of precedence' existing in modern times for making seating arrangements at formal occasions, there must have been some such system in those days. Further, here the Manaskar has not made the people sit according to their 'varan' i.e. brahmin, kshatriya, vaish and shudra but according to their position at that time otherwise Vishwamitra, who was by birth a kshatriya, could sit only in kshatriyas and not at the top most place reserved for the person of his level as 'Brahmrishi'. So the persons were recognised broadly by their varan but particularly by their capability and worth. In the swayambar, the persons were made to sit "निज निज थल अनुहारि" according to their worth and the position then existing and not according to what they were as per birth. When Vishwamitra came to the place with two rajkumars, the attendance there saw Ram according to what their faculties were e.g. the rishis and bhaktas saw in Ram, the almighty God, the kshatriya; a very learned and brave rajkumar, the demons as their enemy, Awadh residents as their son (as he was considered to be the son-in-law of the town). This is spiritual protocol which is bestowed by God that he is seen by everyone according to what in the inner sense he was!

जिन्ह कें रही भावना जैसी, प्रभु मूरति तिन्ह देखी तैसी।

Vishwamitra seem to have been the chief guest of the show. Raja Janak as per protocol took him and showed the entire arrangement at that place. When the muni approved and appreciated the arrangement made, the raja felt satisfied. Thus Vishwamitra and the rajkumars were allotted and made to sit at the supreme stage, being the chief guests, again as per protocol.

At the appropriate time, Sita was called. She came duly escorted by the followers with jayamala in her hands. Tulsidas had to remain within limits and could not explain the beauty of Sita when she reached the pandal and could not find any equivalent to her to give a simile.

Then Raja Janak called the announcers to announce amidst the audience, all about the family of Janak and the conditions of the swayambar. This is the protocol to announce all conditions as also what the family is like modern procedure of any election in which the conditions of eligibility to fight the election and the voter are indicated. So nothing was left in confusion.

सोइ पुरारि कोदंडु कठोरा, राज समाज आजु जोइ तोरा।

त्रिभुवन जय समेत वैदेही, बिनहिं विचार बरइ हठि तेही॥

The conditions of swayambar, which were quite unambiguous were—

(1) There is the Shiv dhanush.

(2) In that gathering the dhanush had to be broken.

(3) Whosoever broke the dhanush shall have respect in the entire universe and shall also have Sita in marriage.

(4) Whosoever broke the dhanush shall without any further questioning become the husband of Sita.

(5) The word 'जोइ तोरा' gives an indication that anyone who broke the dhanush could marry Sita, not by group of persons.

One by one the rajas tried to pick up the dhanush but nobody could even move it. Then all having failed,

भूप सहस दस एकहि बारा लगे उठावन टरइ न टारा।

Suddenly (सहसा) ten rajas got up and tried to pick up the dhanush but they together too could not move it. Here some people interpret literally as "भूप सहस दस", ten thousand rajas but this would be against the protocol as

(1) there won't be ten thousand rajas at that time in entire India and in its neighbourhood;

(2) how could ten thousand rajas even touch the dhanush, not to speak of trying to pick it up;

(3) if ten thousand rajas had been able to get up and tried to pick up the dhanush, how could they be allowed by the authorities responsible for proper conduct of the swayambar; and

(4) in case they had been able to pick up the dhanush and break it, whom of the ten thousand could Sita accept as her husband.

The correct and logical interpretation, therefore, can be that suddenly (सहसा) ten rajas would have got up and before they could be checked for trying to pick up the dhanush, they had already tried and failed to move it. So there was no problem from protocol point of view.

The rajas from various countries, who had come to try their luck

"दीप दीप के भूपति नाना"

failed even to move the dhanush. This annoyed Raja Janak, who got enraged and told the gathering that the universe was without brave persons. Raja Janak at the same time could not give up his condition of marrying Sita to the one who broke the dhanush as it would malign his image. So there was no alternative except to keep Sita unmarried. This infuriated Lakshman and breaking all protocol of seeking permission of Guru Vishwamitra or elder brother Ram, stood up in rage and after payig respects to Ram challenged Janak for saying such words that the universe was without brave persons, when persons of Raghukul dynasty, having brave persons, had been witnessing the show. Then he also mentioned that but for the fear of breach of protocol and subject to permission of Ram, he could pick up not only the dhanush but the entire universe and throw it like a pitcher—

कहि न सकत रघुबीर डर लगे बचन जनु बान,
नाइ राम पद कमल सिरु बोले गिरा प्रमान।

और

कही जनक जसि अनुचित बानी, विद्यमान रघुकलमनि जानी।

Guru Vishwamitra and Ram were in core of heart happy that Janak had said some unpalatable words for which he got appropriate reply but signalled Lakshman to take his seat. Then Vishwamitra having seen appropriate time asked Ram to get up and redress Janak's grievance by breaking the dhanush. Ram paid respects to guru and got up. He was neither happy nor sad "हरष विषादु न कछु उर आवा". This is how, the great men see all problems to be solved. Ram sought muni's permission/blessings and went to break the dhanush. Everyone present prayed for Ram's success. The queen, Sita, and all others had been cursing Janak for putting such harsh condition which could not be fulfilled by anyone then how Ram, a rajkumar could do it. They had their doubts. Sita prayed for Ram's success as such because Janak was not going to relax the condition of swayambar. The breaking of Shiv dhanush could cause upheaval on earth. Lakshman, who was the incarnation of Shesh, therefore, ordered all responsible to hold the universe, to be alert. This shows that apart from what the arrangements for yagya had been made, this aspect, perhaps, was not thought of by Raja Janak as to what will happen after dhanush was broken. This could be foreseen by Lakshman, who warned in time. Ram again paid respects to guru in his heart and with his blessings picked up the dhanush and broke it in a second. With the dhanush having been broken, there was great upheaval on earth as envisaged by Lakshman but things could be kept under control as per Lakshman's orders to all responsible. On Ram's success, what to speak of human beings, who were happy, even gods expressed their happiness. There was all pleasant. Sita too was happy on Ram's success and had been awaiting for the orders of Satanand, who was the overall incharge of the show.

सतानंद तब आयसु दीन्हा, सीता गमन राम पहिं कीन्हा

Then on Satanand's orders, Sita went to Ram and garlanded him in acceptance as her husband. Here special attention has been paid to protocol. On Ram's breaking the dhanush, Sita did not herself go and garland Ram but awaited Satanand's, who was the incharge of the show, orders as in the present day election, a returning officer is appointed and unless he puts his hand on who stands elected, one is not considered to have been successful even though the counting of votes had indicated the successful person. After garlanding Ram and touching his feet in respect as per protocol, Sita went to her mother.

At that time having known that Shiv-dhanush had been broken, Shiv-bhakta Parushuram muni came there in rage. As per protocol all kings paid their respects to the muni indicating their full introduction e.g. name, father's name and the name of the kingdom so that the person, to whom respects are paid, could know him fully.

पितु समेत कहि कहि निज नामा, लगे करन सब दंड प्रनामा

Raja Janak also came as he was the host there. He brought Sita along and asked her to pay respects to the muni. In return the muni gave her blessings. Once Sita was given blessings by Parushuram muni, everyone heaved a sigh of relief as the muni having wished her well, will not do any harm to the matrimony now. Then came Vishwamitra with Ram and Lakshman. Ram and Lakshman, who were introduced to the muni, also paid respects and the muni in turn gave them also ashirwad. This was the way how the heart of the opposite party in rage could be won. Having once given the ashirwad, the munis struck to the same. Janak then narrated the purpose of the rajas having gathered there. Muni then saw the broken Shiv dhanush and desired to know as to who had broken the dhanush. Out of fear nobody replied. Then Ram only came and accepted that he only i.e. one of his sewaks had broken the dhanush. Lakshman, however, took the querry very lightly and said in childhood they had broken many such dhanushas but nobody checked up, then why this rage for this particular dhanush. Although it was for Vishwamitra or Janak or Ram to tackle the matter with the muni, but Lakshman could not digest the querry and, therefore, gave the reply. Parushuram then introduced himself to Lakshman that he had killed all kshatriyas in the universe several times and he should have been afraid of him. Lakshman still took the matter lightly as he, being a brave rajkumar, did not have any fear of muni's fury but as muni he had all respects for him as per protocol because the brave kshatriyas did not show their bravery on gods, brahmins, bhaktas and cows, they being considered as sacred. Rather than tackling the matter with Lakshman, thinking him a young boy, Parushuram requested Vishwamitra to forbid him from quarrelling with him. Vishwamitra then requested Parushuram to excuse Lakshman being a child. Parushuram told Vishwamitra that he was leaving Lakshman from being killed only because of his being a child otherwise he would have been killed. All this was according to the prescribed channel. Lakshman and Parushuram still continued rebuking each other. Then Ram came in and requested Parushuram to be cool and punish him only as he had broken the dhanush for which Lakshman was not responsible. Although Lakshman was speaking against protocol as Vishwamitra, Ram and Janak were there to deal with the muni but as accepted by Parushuram also, Lakshman was intentionally not checked by Ram and others as they wanted the muni to atleast take cognisance of the particular rajkumars and not to treat them as ordinary kings whom Parushuram had killed.

बंधु कहइ कटु संमत तोरे, तू छल विनय करसि कर जोरे।

Parushuram still went on rebuking Ram, who had been respecting him being a muni otherwise he would not have even once requested him as a kshatriya to cool down.

जौ हम निदरहिं विप्र बदि सत्य सुनहु भृगुनाथ,
तो अस को जग सुभटु जेहि भय वस नावहिं माथ।

Then Parushuram handed over another dhanush of Vishnu and if Ram was able to break that too, he would feel satisfied. The Vishnu dhanush automatically operated after being touched by Ram. Parushuram recognised him as almighty and after paying his respects and requesting for being excused, went to forests.

After Parushuram left, all rajas also went to their kingdoms. Then, as per protocol, Raja Janak requested Vishwamitra to tell as to how to proceed further. Vishwamitra advised Janak to send the news to Awadh and also request Raja Dasrath to come with marriage party so that the marriage could be solemnised as per traditional protocol and as ordained in vedas and shastras. Accordingly Janak sent his messenger to Awadh with the requisite request. Meantime Janak called his managers to decorate the town befitting the occasion. All obeying the raja's orders started preparing to receive the marriage party. The entire town was decorated immensely as per tradition of the time. The same traditions even continue today in a Hindu marriage. The bride's father invites the groom's father with marriage party and the marriage party is appropriately entertained by the bride's father. All this is done with a view to—

(1) Solemnise the marriage in a big way as it is a great occasion in one's life;

(2) This becomes a proof amongst all present from the bride's side and the groom's side that the marriage had taken place;

(3) The bride and groom also considered the marriage with all the sanctity attached as it is witnessed by so many; and

(4) It being celebrated according to vedic traditions, attaches spiritual importance also to the occasion and imbibes the spiritual sanctity in the minds of the groom and the bride and their respective families.

When the messengers reached Awadh, they sent in their introductory cards to King Dasrath, who immediately called them in darbar. The messengers after paying respects to the king as per protocol, handed over Janak's letter to him. The king was very happy as he had heard about Ram and Lakshman after a long period and that too with such an achievement. After reading the letter, Raja Dasrath according to protocol first went to Guru Vashisth to break the news and then only went to the queens to tell them what was written in the letter. All were very happy.

जा दिन तें मुनि गए लिवाई, तब तें आज साँच सुधि पाई।

Since the messengers from Janak had brought very happy news, the king as per tradition, ordered for lot of wealth being given to them but as per social protocol the people from bride's side donot accept any gift etc. from the groom's side, so the messengers respectfully declined to accept anything saying it was against the tradition—

"कहि अनीति ते मूंदहि काना"

However, the king then made proper arrangements for their stay. Lot of alms were given to the brahmins and others, who deserved. Entire Awadh was happy and they rejoiced on the great news of Ram-Sita marriage. The entire town was decorated and all invitees prepared themselves to join the marriage party. The entire arrangement of the marriage party was entrusted to Bharat and Shatrughan as according to the canons of proper management, one or two persons have to be made overall incharge of any project. Here the two rajkumars were made incharge. They made all arrangements necesary for the occasion. The barat got ready with chariots, horses, elephants etc. There were all good omens when the barat departed. The barat was accompanied with eatables for the journey and all kinds of weaponary. The ladies, according to the tradition at that time (or as per the tradition when Manas was written in 16th century), did not accompany the marriage party nor did they come near the place of departure of the barat and only saw the departure of the barat from their housetops. On one chariot the royal belongings were loaded, on another Raja Dasrath boarded and still on the third Guru Vashisth boarded. Guru, as per protocol, was given the top stage and then after the guru gave permission (assessing the correct time of departure astrologically), the barat started.

On the journey, proper arrangements for serving eatables to the barat had been made; on rivers and rivulets, bridges had been provided to enable the barat to cross them. When the barat reached close to Janakpuri, the seniors of the bride's side came to receive the barat as a matter of protocol. They served the barat with drinks and eatables and handed over costly clothes, jewellery, horses, elephants etc. in dowry. This shows that the institution of dowry by the bride's side to the groom's side existed during the Ram kal but it was given out of the sweet will and not in consideration of the marriage. The barat was received by the Janak's people with warm welcome. The king of Awadh accepted the gifts sent by the king of Janakpuri, and distributed amongst the needies. The barat went to the lodge which had been properly decorated to suit the occasion.

Ram and Lakshman came to know of their father's and barat's arrival but did not go to meet them without Vishwamitra's permission and they felt hesitation in asking for permission. Vishwamitra, however, could know their feelings and took them to the place of stay of Dasrath. King, having seen Vishwamitra coming with the two sons, became very happy and advanced to receive them. He paid respects to the muni and the muni gave him blessings. The rajkumars paid respects to their father, who embraced them. Then the rajkumars paid respects to Vashisth, who again embraced and gave them ashirwad. Then Ram and Lakshman met Bharat and Shatrughan. Bharat and Shatrughan paid respects to Ram being their elder brother, who embraced them and then Lakshman met Bharat and Shatrughan. Then Ram and Lakshman met all, who had come in the marriage party as per requisite protocol laid for each. Satanand, other brahmins and seniors from Janak's side paid their respects to Dasrath and others in barat and then after seeking permission went to Janak's house. All in Janakpuri were very happy to witness the barat. They lived happily for some days, when the auspicious day came for the marriage. The day of marriage was assessed by the pandits. Satanand, who was the incharge of the show from Janak's side called in the mantri to bring all necessary material pertaining to marriage ceremony. The seniors, with ladies singing songs, went to the place of stay of the marriage party. They told of the proper day and time of marriáge. Raja Dasrath too consulted the guru and accompanied the barat. All gods, Shiv and Brahma too had come incognito to witness and enjoy the marriage.

Having known the arrival of barat, the ladies, as per protocol, prepared themselves to receive them by singing songs, arranging aarti etc. At this occasion ladies in their best come to receive the groom and welcome him to the house. The ladies might have been fixed to receive the groom so that they may see from women's eye the suitability of the groom for the bride. Sita's mother was very happy to welcome Ram and seeing him in groom's dress. Dasrath, Ram and others were then taken to the site of marriage. There, Dasrath and Janak met formally with great pleasure. Both were equal in image, greatness etc. —

सकल भांति सम साजु समाजु, सम समधी देखें हम आजू।

In other words the poet tells that both the bride's and groom's sides should be on equal footing. Then the marriage is considered to be successful. Janak brought Dasrath to the mandap with all respects. Since Janak was host, he had to welcome the groom's father. Even otherwise as per protocol in Hindu dharam, groom's father occupies higher place than the bride's father. Raja Janak paid respects to all others. He made sitting arrangements for the rishis, pandits, seniors and ladies and gents from both sides. Janak then honoured Dasrath, other baratis and those, who were present at that place by giving them appropriate gifts etc. At appropriate time Guru Vashisth invited Satanand for performing the ceremony from bride's side as he was the incharge of the show appointed by Raja Janak for this purpose.

On the other side all elder ladies had been invited, who started singing the songs of the occasion as per tradition. Even the wives of gods had joined this group of elder ladies incognito. Then Sita was brought to the mandap. All present paid respect to her and the rishi paid their blessings. As per religious protocol, at first Gauri and Ganesh were worshipped; then other gods/goddesses had been worshipped before Sita could sit at the appropriate place. Sunaina (Janak's wife) was sitting on left of Janak. Golden pitchers and utensils full of jewels were presented to Ram by Janak and his wife, who subsequently washed Ram's feet, as per custom, in token of accepting him as their son-in-law. The marriage ceremony was performed. Janak handed over Sita to Ram and as per Guru Vashisth's orders, Ram and Sita, after marriage, sat together. With Guru's permission Mandvi, Urmila and Shrutkirti were brought in brides' dress and were married to Bharat, Lakshman and Shatrughan respectively as per customs adopted in the case of Ram and Sita's marriage. Lot of dowry was given in marriage of all the four brothers and Raja Dasrath accepted happily and further gave away to beggars, brahmins and other deserving persons as per their wishes. Janak then paid respects to all baratis and worshipped all gods. He then requested Dasrath to accept the girls thinking them as his maids and requested for being excused for any short-coming. This is customary for bride's father to put such submission before the groom's father.

Raja Dasrath and others then left for the place where barat had been staying. All in barat were served meals amongst abuses by the bride's side. All took the abuses in light vein to make the environ lively as it is generally marred by the marriage on the bride's side. Dasrath entrusted the job of distributing alms to all brahmins and others as per their wishes to Raja Janak. They in turn gave blessings to Raja Dasrath. Afterwards many days passed staying in Janakpuri. Then Dasrath begged Janak of his leave. Vishwamitra, Satanand etc. all made Janak agree for the departure back of the barat. Lot of dowry and eatables for the journey were given. The queens taught Sita and others how to conduct themselves in sasural and offered their blessings. They should respect father-in-law and mothers-in-law and behave in accordance with the wishes of their respective husbands. Ram and other brothers came to rajmahal for permission to leave for Awadh. Ram's asking for leave is full of affection :

राउ अवधपुर चहत सिधाए, विदा होन हम इहां पठाए।
मातु मुदित मन आयसु देहु, बालक जानि करब नित नेहु।

There can't be any better presentation than what Ram said as above. The queens handed over Sita and others to Ram and other brothers and requested them to accept the wives as their maids. After obtaining permission to leave, Ram with his brothers and their wives departed. Then Raja Janak came to see the daughters off. Janak's feelings have been aptly narrated by the poet saying —

सीय विलोकि धीरता भागी, रहे कहावत परम विरागी।

Janak was known for not having any attachment with the universe but at the time of departure of his daughter Sita, he too was rather sad. After attaining some courage, he told Sita of the wife's job and dynastic rituals involved after marriage. With these words Sita was departed. The marriage party set for Awadh with requisite pomp and show and after giving lots of alms to the deserving ones. As a matter of protocol, Raja Janak accompanied the barat and was not able to compromise to coming back. Dasrath then persuaded him to return after performing all rituals. He begged return from Ram as a father-in-law and more as a bhakta.

सादर पुनि भेंटे जामाता, रूप सील गुन निधि सब भ्राता।
और
बार बार मागउँ कर जोरें, मनु परिहरै चरन जनि भोरें।
सुनि बर बचन प्रेम जनु पोषे, पूरन काम रामु परितोषे।

On the other side arrangements had been made in Awadh to receive the bride and others. It was all pleasantry. The town was fully decorated. Groups of people went to receive the people returning from Janakpuri; alms were distributed amongst poors, brahmins and others. Special rituals have been prescribed to suit each occasion. To receive the daughter-in-law in house special customs are performed.

विविध विधान बाजने बाजे, मंगल मुदित सुमित्रा सांजे।

Sumitra was considered to be well versed with such traditions.

कनक थार भरि मंगलन्हि कमल करन्हि लिएं मात,

चली मुदित परिछनि करन पुलक पल्लवित गात।

The marriage party entered Awadh after the guru permitted assessing proper time for the occasion. According to Hindu customs, the assessment of time is made as favourable or otherwise and all actions are done on most favourable timings.

समउ जानि गुर आयसु दीन्हा। पुर प्रवेषु रघुकुलमनि कीन्हा।

All the four sons with their wives were made to sit at appropriate setties and some rituals completed.

लोक रीति जननीं करहिं बर दुलहिनि सकुचाहिं,

मोद विनोद बिलोकि बड़ रामु मनहिं मुसुकाहिं।

Customs are specially designed to make the bride at home. All baratis were duly supplied with clothes, ornaments etc. and alms were again given to all as per their wishes. Guru and Dasrath then entered the rajmahal and all customs were performed as ordered by the guru. Dasrath paid respects to all munis — Vashisth, Vishwamitra etc. and expressed his obligation to all and the munis gave their blessings in turn. The king placed before them everything he had but the guru and munis were so content that they took only what they wished/deserved to have at the occasion. This shows the submission of the rajas for the munis and the contentment amongst the gurus/munis, etc.

विनय कीन्हि उर अति अनुरागें, सुत संपदा राखि सब आगें।

नेग भागि मुनिनायक लीन्हा, आसिरवाद बहुत विधि दीन्हा।

Manas mentions in detail the alms given to all and the customs/rituals for the occasion as done and laid in shastras. The king then called in all the queens and told them that the daughters-in-law are rather young and have come to their house leaving their parents' house. They, therefore, had to be kept with great attention so that they get adjusted to the new environ.

बधु लरिकनी पर घर आईं, राखेहु नयन पलक की नाईं।

After staying for some days, Vishwamitra departed. He was paid respects by all sons, Dasrath, all queens and others. The muni in turn gave ashirwad.

Bal Kand of the Manas narrates the protocolic relations and respects/affection for each other amongst father and son, among brothers, mother and son, raja and raj guru, raja–praja, raja and rishis, munis, brides' father and groom's father (groom's father is better placed compared to bride's father), the rituals at marriage parties, giving of alms etc. At places, the Manaskar has shown the superhuman jobs done by Ram, which Kaushalya has summed up — killing of the rakshasas (Subahu, Marich, Tadka etc.), in the young age, grant of mukti to Ahilya, Gautam's wife, breaking of dhanush, which could not even be moved by any, teaching a lesson to Parushuram, who became Ram's devotee etc. were super human jobs done by Ram.

2

Ayodhaya Kand

Here again Tulsidas starts the chapter at first worshipping Shiv-Parvati, then Ram, Sita, guru, etc. After the marriage, Ram and other brothers started taking part in governance of the kingdom. Since the entire performance was as per religious canons, there was all pleasant in the kingdom. The poet has tried to prove that in case the kingdom is managed with dharam, there cannot be anything wrong with the people in the kingdom.

सब विधि सब पुर लोग सुखारी, रामचंद्र मुख चंदु निहारी।

Everyone started feeling that it was appropriate time when king should coronate Ram as the yuvraj (successor). There may be some reasons for it also. One, the public at large were very fond of Ram and he being eldest also public wanted king Dasrath itself designating Ram as the yuvraj so that there was no dispute among the other brothers afterwards. Secondly, the public had become so much fond of Ram that they wanted him to be king even preferring over King Dasrath. That is why Manu had introduced the institution of ashrams so that the king in old age leaves the kingdom and becomes sanyasi in a cordial atmosphere.

सब कें उर अभिलाषु अस कहहि मनाइ महेसु,

आप अछत युवराज पद रामहिं देउ नरेश।

At the same time once King Dasrath saw his face in mirror and seeing some grey hair thought, he had become old to renounce the universe and become sanyasi after handing over the rule to Ram. He immediately went to guru's ashram as all major jobs were done in consultation with the rajguru only. While deciding this the king had taken his view, the views of all his ministers, the friends and others into consideration. This shows the element of democracy working at that time indirectly in the monarchy—

कहइ भुआल, सुनिअ मुनिनायक, भए राम सब विधि सब लायक,
सेवक सचिव सकल पुरवासी, जे हमारे अरि मित्र उदासी।
सबहि राम प्रिय जेहि विधि मोही, प्रभु असीस जनु तनु धरि सोही

Raja submitted his proposal to the guru. The guru agreed to the proposal but knowing what is in store for the future, although muni accepted the proposal yet without assessing the proper day for this job as was done always by the rajguru, he only said —

सुदिन सुमगंलु तवहि जब रामु होहिं जुबराजु।

Whenever Ram becomes yuvraj that is the only day with good omens. In other words Ram's becoming yuvraj now was doubtful. The raja did not, however, catch the language and started preparing for Ram to become yuvraj. He obtained the approval of all his ministers, sewaks, secretaries, advisers and others and asked if all approved he proposed to coronate Ram —

जौं पांचहि मत लागै नीका, करहु हरषि हियं रामहि टीका।

All unanimously accepted the proposal. The king then ordered to check up from the rajguru and made arrangements as desired by him. All arrangements were made as asked for by the guru. King had been praying all gods to make his proposal successful. Everyone was happy. Guru also told all that was indicated in vedas —

वेद विदित कहि सकल विधाना, कहेउ रचहु पुर विविध बिताना।

It means that all modus-operandi had already been prescribed in the vedas and accordingly as advised by guru every job was done —

जो मुनीस जेहि आयसु दीन्हा, सो तेहिं काजु प्रथम जनु कीन्हा।

This shows how anxious everyone was to get Ram coronated. As per protocol, the guru was invited to rajmahal to teach Ram the rajniti. Having heard of guru's arrival at rajmahal, Ram alongwith Sita paid respects to guru and worshipped him in 16 ways. It shows the entire procedure of how a guru is to be honoured must have been given in shastras indicating 16 types of puja. After marriage the respect is not only by Ram but by both Ram and Sita. He requested the guru that on his indication he himself would have come to guru's ashram rather than the guru coming all the way to rajmahal. Then guru told Ram that raja Dasrath wanted Ram's coronation and for that certain precautions had to be taken which should be started immediately. It indicates that Ram was not so far aware of his being coronated and it was the guru, who brought the news to him. Guru, after telling Ram of the precautions to be adopted, went to Dasrath. Ram was, however, surprised on knowing the news of his coronation as he felt that all the four brothers were born together, were educated together, even married together but he alone was being coronated now, particularly when Bharat and Shatrughan were not there. As it came to Ram's mind so would have come to so many others' mind too. Whatever may be Dasrath's strategy in coronating Ram at that point of time when Bharat and Shatrughan were not there, it does not appear palatable and proved to be wrong too as in case Bharat and Shatrughan were there, as they should have been on this very important occasion, things would have been different; Ram would not have gone to forests for 14 years. Ram was also not happy over the custom of coronating only the eldest.

विमल वंश यहु अनुचित एकू बंधु विहाई बड़ेहि अभिषेकू।

Lakshman also came to know then only of Ram's coronation. He was happy but he too thought it better if Bharat too was there. The town was decorated in entirety and everyone was happy. The gods were, however, not happy as they wanted Ram not to sit on singhasan but move out and kill the rakshasas. They, therefore, went to Goddess Sharada for help. She, with hesitation, agreed to help the gods. She came to Awadh and manipulated Kaikayee's maid's mind to cause disturbance in entire affair.

नामु मथंरा मंद मति चेरी कैकइ केरि,
अजस पेटारी ताहि करि गई गिरा मति फेरि।

She came out of the rajmahal and seeing a lot of hustle and bustle came to know of Ram's coronation. She immediately sensed some wrong being done in the absence of Bharat. She, therefore, immediately went to Rani Kaikayee and narrated the entire matter. Kaikayee was happy to know it as she knew according to tradition it was the right of the eldest of the sons to succeed the raja and also Ram was equally sincere to all the queens and was also capable of becoming the raja. She, therefore, abused Manthra of the bad feelings in her mind but after some discussion succumbed to her thinking. She told that Kaikayee would be rendered as a maid when Ram's mother Kaushalya became rajmata. Afterall being a step mother for Ram and a co-wife of Dasrath such things naturally come to mind. That is why in shastras there is the concept of one wife only. Multi-wife system, therefore, goes against the dharam generally but rajas seem to have been given exception otherwise Dasrath would not have done anything not approved by religion. At the time of Sarupnakha's meeting Ram and Lakshman and requesting for marriage, Lakshman had told her that Ram being the raja of Awadh, could have more than one wife and, therefore, she should insist on marrying Ram only. But such things at one point of time or the other causes some hardship to the person having more than one wife. According to custom, which Kaikayee knew

जेठ स्वामि सेवक लघु भाई, यह दिनकर कुल रीति सुहाई।
और कौसल्या सम सब महतारी, रामहि सहज सुभायँ पिआरी।
मो पर करहिं सनेह बिसेषी, मैं करि प्रीति परीक्षा देखी।

Kaikayee had tested and was convinced that Ram loved all the queens equally rather he loved Kaikayee more than the others. But Manthra went on insisting on her point that this was all till Ram was coronated and things would change after Ram became raja and their purpose was served. Then all will consider Kaikayee as second-rated as all this been timed by Kaushalya when Bharat was not there. She narrated many stories of co-wives' behaviour with others till Kaikayee gave in. She even said that in case Ram became raja, then Lakshman will be his lieutenant and Bharat will be put behind the bars. Any mother has weakness for the son. When something bad is narrated for the son, the mother becomes intolerant and tries not only to do away with the evil but also tries to do good to him. Manthra after seeing that Kaikayee was completely under her thumb, reminded her of the two promises raja had made to her and now was the time to avail of the same; asking Ram to go to forests for 14 years and Bharat in turn to become raja instead of Ram. Kaikayee put off all her ornaments and went in rage when Dasrath came to her in the night. Seeing her in that condition, Dasrath enquired about the reason. Then after making the raja pucca to agree to give what she demanded, she told him of the two promises being fulfilled — one for Bharat's coronation and the other for sending Ram to forests for 14 years. The raja cannot do justice to the public and to himself if he had several queens. Plato in his theory of State has even forbidden king having a married life as being involved in his own family's interests, he would not look after the welfare of the public at large. It is for such occasions that Plato had foreseen and indicated his State being governed by a king without family. The entire praja was now waiting for Ram's coronation but the raja being in hands of the queen, was not able to fulfil the public's desire. To please the queen, the raja promised to do anything on earth. There was a policy in Raghukul that whatever they said was done also at any cost —

रघुकुल रीति सदा चलि आई प्राण जाहुँ बरु वचनु न जाई।

She demanded Bharat's coronation and Ram being sent to forests for 14 years. Dasrath was prepared, though against the tradition, to coronate Bharat as the theory of primogenitor was in vogue at that time according to which the eldest could ascend the throne unless incapable. Ram being eldest and capable could not be divorced from this right. Yet the raja was prepared to coronate Bharat but could not stand Ram going to forests. Ram going to forests was very cleverly designed by the queen as in case Ram continued to live in Awadh, he might snatch raj from Bharat with the help of the public at large, who were very fond of Ram. Therefore, she wanted Ram to go to forests and live like a tapasvi so that he does not dream of becoming raja and within this period of 14 years, Bharat would gain popularity in public, who would forget Ram. So Bharat would be raja till end. Here Kaikayee had first asked for Bharat being coronated and if raja had given a little thought, he could have agreed to implement the first commandment first and the second later. He could have called Bharat and arranged for his coronation. King would have known Bharat's affection for Ram by now. So Bharat would not have accepted coronation and would have rather insisted on Ram being coronated. In that case the matter could have been solved for the better. So in the entire episode, king was wrong—

(1) In having more than one wife.

(2) In having arranged for the coronation of Ram in absence of Bharat — both politically as well as socially.

(3) In having succumbed to the tactical pressure by Kaikayee in giving two boons.

(4) In not having implemented the two boons in order as the same had been sought for i.e. first being implemented first — calling Bharat and coronating him and the second of sending Ram to forests later on after Bharat's coronation.

In this way the king could have saved the situation from going out of hand. King might have lost his balance but guru Vashisth etc. also did not think in these terms is a tragedy of the environ.

Next morning all the people came to rajmahal to see Ram's coronation but when raja did not come out of the mahal, all were surprised as raja used to awake quite early in the morning. After having waited for raja's arrival in vain, all requested Sumant, the raja's minister for mahal to go into mahal and check up the position. According to the protocol, everyone was not allowed to go into the mahal and only the minister in charge of the job could enter the mahal. Even now the subordinates are entrusted with various functions and each could do his own only and not interfere in others' functions. There was, therefore, an appropriate division of jobs amongst all ministers, who did fulfil their own jobs only. Out of the gathering in front of the mahal, only Sumant could enter the mahal. Sumant then went in and was shocked to see raja's condition. He was not able to speak but then gathered courage and requested Kaikayee to tell the position. Kaikayee too did not consider it proper to tell the position to him and only asked him to send for Ram, who only could check up the position from the raja. Sumant could sense something wrong done by the queen but silently left to inform Ram. After seeing Sumant, who was a minister, Ram paid his respects as an elderly man and accompanied him to where the raja was lying. Ram was shocked to see the raja in that bad condition. He gathered courage and asked Kaikayee about what had happened. Kaikayee narrated the entire proceedings. Ram readily accepted going to forests and for the coronation of Bharat. As per protocol, the son had to accept what parents wanted him to do :

सुनु जननी सोइ सुत बड़भागी, जो पितु मातु वचन अनुरागी।
तनय मातु पितु तोषनिहारा, दुलर्भ जननि सकल संसारा।

Ram was, happy to go to forests in compliance with the desire of parents as in forests he would be able to see many rishis etc. and at the same time shall fulfil parents desire (Ram going to forest was Kaikaye's desire duly approved by the raja), as also see Bharat his favourite brother, as the raja of Awadh. When raja came in senses, he saw Ram ready to go to forests. According to Hindu religion one resorts to a favour from God when all other methods do not work. Raja Dasrath prayed his God to change Ram's mind so that he somehow does not go to forest. But it was not to be. Everyone who came to know of the incident abused Kaikayee and said—

सत्य कहहिं कवि नारि सुभाऊ, सब विधि अगहु अगाध दुराऊ।
निज प्रतिबिम्बु बरुकु गहि जाई, जानि न जाइ नारि गति भाई।

What is there which a woman cannot get done—

काह न पावकु जारि सक, का न समुद्र समाइ,
का न करै अबला प्रबल केहि जग कालु न खाइ।

All ladies and guru mata told Kaikayee not to insist on Ram going to forests as in his absence raja will not survive and Sita and Lakshman will not stay back in Awadh and will accompany Ram to forest. Even Bharat, who is very fond of Ram, may not accept raj. Then whatever she gained was of no avail.

लगीं देन सिख सीलु सराही, बचन बान सम लागहिं ताहीं।

It is here that God's maya works. One does not make out what is good or bad for him and only insists on what is in store for him.

Ram left for Kaushalya's mahal. Kaushalya did not so far know about the latest position in rajmahal. Ram paid his respects and mother gave him ashirwad and asked him to get ready for the coronation. Ram, however, told the mother that he had got the kingdom of forests and not of Awadh. He narrated the whole proceedings and begged for mother's permission to proceed for forests. The mother, who had happily permitted Ram to go with Vishwamitra, was very sad now although both times Ram was to go to forests only. She was not so much worried for Ram going to forests as for Bharat and the praja of Awadh. She knew Bharat will not live to rule without Ram. But then she compromised and said—

जौं केवल पितु आयसु ताता, तौ जनि जाहु जानि बड़ि माता,
जौं पितु-मातु कहेउ बन जाना, तौ कानन सत अवध समाना।

According to Hindu legends, mother has been given overruling power over the father so far as the governance of the ward was concerned. Narrating the same power, Kausalya said that in case the orders for going to forests were those of the father then she over-ruled the same being in a superior position but if the orders were those of father and mother then Ram had to carry out the order taking forests as better than Awadh. Then the brave mother coached Ram how he should live in the forests and told that according to the institution of Ashrams in Hindus, the raja had ultimately to go to forests but it was the tender age at present which was coming in the way of sending him there. She was feeling difficulty in living without Ram in Awadh but at the same time did not want to stand in the way of Ram carrying out the order of the parents. She ultimately agreed in Ram going to forests.

Sita came to know of the happenings. She came and paid respects to mother-in-law, who inturn gave blessings. She was thinking as to how she could accompany Ram to forests as she felt it difficult to live without Ram in Awadh. Kaushalya told Ram that Sita was very tender and she would keep her in all comforts in the absence of Ram going to forests. But Sita expressed her desire to accompany Ram in forests. Kaushalya told all fears of living in forests but Sita said she would not have any difficulty in living in forests with Ram but it would be difficult to live in Awadh without Ram. Kaushalya then left it to Ram to decide whether Sita should stay in Awadh or accompany him to forests. This shows that after the marriage all decisions about the daughter-in-law have to be taken by the husband and the parents should not enforce their will on them. Kaushalya accordingly asked Ram's reaction so that she could coach her for living in Awadh or in forests.

सोइ सिय चलन चहहि बन साथा, आयसु काह होइ रघुनाथा।
और
अस विचारि जस आयसु होइ मैं सिख देऊँ जानकिहि सोई।

Ram also persuaded Sita to stay back in Awadh but she was hesitant and said—

राखिअ अवध जो अवधि लगि, रहत न जनि अहिं प्राण,
दीन बंधु सुंदर सुखद, सील सनेह निधान।

Then,

देखि दसा रघुपति जियँ जाना, हठि राखें नहि राखिहि प्राना।

This shows, how submissive the wife had been to husband in Hindus as depicted by manaskar. Even on date while settling the matrimonial alliance, parents look into the sanskar of the other party and agree for marriage in a house with acceptable sanskar.

Meantime Lakshman also came to know of the developments. He came running to Ram and requested that he too be allowed to accompany him to forests. Ram persuaded him to remain in Awadh as Bharat and Shatrughan were not there and it would be difficult for the father and mother to live without all. Above all the praja would feel it much. Here Ram made policy statement of raja and the praja relations.

जासु राज प्रिय प्रजा दुखारी, सो नृप अवसि नरक अधिकारी।

As per Hindu shastras, whereas the praja used to pay to the exchequer, they were entitled to proper protection. The king too was obliged to see that the public at large was not put to any discomfort. Where the king had been ruling as per dharam, all peace and pleasantry was seen in the kingdom. This is what is found in Ram rajya or Keshav raj in Awadh or Dwarka respectively. Ram was aware that on his going to forest the praja would be put to discomfort which could be consoled to some extent if Lakshman remained there to look after them. But then Ram had to go to forests in obeyance of the desire of parents and Lakshman considered it his dharam to accompany his elder brother in forest because,

मन क्रम बचन चरन रत होई, कृपासिंधु परिहरिअ कि सोई।

Then only Ram agreed to take him along and as per requirement asked him to beg leave of mother.

माँगहु बिदा मातु सन जाई, आवहु बेगि चलहु बन भाई।

Ram had asked him only to take leave from mother to accompany him to forests as it would have been wrong to take him without his mother's approval. Ram did not ask Lakshman to take leave from Urmila too as already indicated the elder did not interfere in the husband-wife affair of the youngers. So it was for Lakshman to make out whether he considered it necessary to meet Urmila too. Perhaps Ram did not want Lakshman to meet Urmila too as—

(1) It would have taken more time and Ram was in a hurry to leave,

(2) Urmila might have also insisted on accompanying them to forests like Sita and since Sita had already been allowed to accompany, it would have been difficult to dissuade Urmila from going to forests.

(3) If Sumitra gave permission to Lakshman to enable him to accompany Ram, she would have taken it to herself to console Urmila staying back in the rajmahal.

(4) Since Bharat and Shatrughan had already gone to Raja Kaikaye, probably with their wives, atleast one lady should have been left behind to look after the mothers.

It would have been better if Lakshman had gone to Urmila and she out of her dharam had permitted Lakshman to go with Ram and she would somehow live in Awadh for the sake of her husband.

Lakshman went to his mother and told the entire happening. The mother was shocked and Lakshman doubted whether mother would permit him going with Ram or not but Sumitra knew Ram and Sita's mentality and Lakshman's devotion for them. She readily agreed to the request and said :

जौं पै सीय रामु बन जाही, अवध तुम्हार काजु कछु नाहीं।
अस जियं जानि संग बन जाहू लेहु तात जग जीवन लाहू।

This was the protocol where in the interest of the son's future, the mother sacrificed herself and her affection. The mother has shown even great spiritual protocol in saying :

पुत्रवती जुवती जग सोई, रघुपति भगतु जासु सुतु होई।
नतरु बांझ भलि वादि बिआनी, राम विमुख सुत तें हित जानी।

She coached Lakshman to serve Ram and Sita as (1) his father and mother, (2) as a swami by sewak; and (3) as a God by the bhakta. These jobs could be done after leaving love, rage, jealousy, pride and affection (रागु, रोष, ईर्ष्या, मद ओर मोह)। The mother then gave him his blessings and departed him. Lakshman immediately left her and reported to Ram and Sita. They all then went to meet the raja. Everyone in the mahal was sad. Seeing Ram, Lakshman and Sita going to forests, the raja was very upset. Ram then begged his leave and requested for his permission to go to forests and blessings for completing the period successfully. Raja got hold of Ram and asked him that rishis and munis told Ram as being God, he should tell him how this all had happened. When the Karma theory prescribes that one lives on his deeds then how one could suffer because of the deeds of others. Here the boons had been given to Kaikayee by Raja Dasrath and as a result of those boons, Ram and others had to go to forests —

औरु करै अपराधु कोउ और पाव फल भोगु,
अति विचित्र भगवंत गति को जग जानै जोगु।

Dasrath tried his level best to retain Ram etc. in mahal but seeing that Ram will not buzz, he told Sita about the difficulties one had to face in forests and so she should stay back. Meantime Kaikayee brought the tapsvi clothes for all the three and asked them to leave lest there should be any change. The raja became unconscious. Ram Lakshman and Sita left as if they were the residents of forests.

सजि बन साज समाजु सबु बनिता बन्धु समेत,
बंदि विप्र गुरु चरन प्रभु चले करि सबहि अचेत।

Ram requested all to take care of the raja with queens and rajmahal. He distributed alms and foodgrains sufficient for an year to brahmins and then with their approval left for the forests. When Ram left, entire Awadh was under shock; there were bad omens for Lanka and the gods were happy on tneir going to forests as then Ram would kill all rakshasas and were also sad to see the shocked Awadh residents. When raja came in senses, he asked Sumant to take the chariot and after wandering about in forest for a few days with Ram, Lakshman and Sita, bring them back or to bring back Sita, if the two brothers did not return as within a few days Sita would have been frightened after seeing the forests. Sumant requested Ram etc. to board the chariot which they did. All the Awadh residents accompanied Ram's chariot. Ram requested the residents to return but they did not. Then during the night, when all were asleep, Ram requested Sumant to leave. Next morning not seeing Ram as also not finding where the chariot had gone, the residents returnd to Awadh. Every one was so much attached to Ram that he preferred to die rather than living without Ram. This was the protocol under which the raja should become favourite of the praja that the praja are prepared to even die for his sake. This can be possible wherever the raja became so much caring for the public at large. Even after returing to Awadh they continued to lead a life of tapsavi as Ram had been put to during the period Ram lived in the forests—

राम दरस हित नेम ब्रत लगे करन नर नारि,
मनहुँ कोक कोकी कमल दीन विहीन तमारि।

Ram Lakshman etc. reached at the bank of Ganga. They paid their respects to Ganga as Ganga was considered to be capable of giving all comforts of life and eliminate all difficulties. Ram was the creator of Ganga but still he worshipped it as he was living like an ordinary human being.

शुद्ध सच्चिदानदमय कंद भानुकल केतु,
चरित करत नर अनुहरत संसृति सागर सेतु।

When Nishadraj, the raja of Sringverpur, came to know of Ram's arrival, he called for some of his ministers etc. and with a lot of presents went to meet Ram. This area was under Awadh kingdom and Nishad was like a vassal of Awadh. So when he came to know that Ram, the rajkumar of Awadh had come then he had to pay all respects as his vassal. He, therefore, paid respects and presents as per protocol for the occasion. Ram after asking about his well being asked him to sit by his side. Here Ram has accepted the hospitability of Nishad thereby proving that for a king or the God all were equal and Nishad being a shudra, Ram met him like an equal. It shows that the division of society into varans was for proper management and administration purposes and were not to be strictly followed. Anyone of the lower caste, if he had full devotion, he could rise above his caste and would then be honoured by the people of upper castes accordingly. This has to be seen in the background of the historical environ of the time when Manas was written. At that time there was Mohammedan rule in the country and the Hindus had been awfully divided into castes. This was in fact the reason why the Mohammedans were successful as invaders to India and then in establishing their kingdom. Due to division in castes, fighting in battlefields was left for the kshatriyas and all others had sealed their fate with whosoever ruled them. Subsequently same thing happened in Mohammedans and with division within themselves, Europeans took advantage and became overall lords of India. Through this assimilation, Tulsidas has tried to eliminate the strict division in the Hindus and alerted them to be one in facing the troubles.

Ram narrated how he had been to forest as a result of the father's orders. Knowing this, Nishadraj was quite upset. The residents abused the parents who sent out such rajkumars and rajkumari to forest. Then arrangements were made under a tree for their rest duing the night. Here starts the day to day living of the three in forests. In the night Lakshman served Ram till he slept and then sat at a distance to protect Ram and Sita in the forest from animals etc. This was the protocol amongst brothers. Nishad was very upset to see Ram and Sita sleeping on earth leaving all the comforts of the rajmahal. Seeing all this he was forced to accept that one has to live according to what is in fate.

सिय रघुवीर कि कानन जोगू, करम प्रधान सत्य कह लोगू।

Lakshman then consoled Nishadraj and also told the karma theory to him. The poet was not satisfied in mentioning karma through Nishad but wanted to further confirm it through Lakshman—

काहु न कोउ सुख दुख कर दाता, निज कृत करम भोग सब भ्राता।

Lakshman knew that Ram was almighty God and had been suffering like human beings as he did not want others to know it. He told Nishadraj also accordingly—

भगत भूमि भूसुर सुरभि सुरहित लागि कृपाल,
करत चरित धरि मनुज तनु सुनत मिटहिं जग जाल।

Next day Ram requested Nishad and Sumant to return to their respective places. Sumant told Ram as Dasrath had said i.e. to bring them back after showing forest for a few days. Ram, however, told him that it was not possible as per dharam and that he would now return obeying the raja and the father as per canons of dharam and at the same time it was the tanet of protocol too. The protocol in that period was all as per dharam and in fact dharam and protocol were synonyms. Same dharam was explained by Ram to Sumant to which Sumant yielded. Ram requested Sumant to tell the raja not to worry further and that he would return as soon as the period of 14 years was over. Lakshman, out of rage for having sent Ram to forest, had said some unpalatable words but thinking the same as against protocol, Ram forbade Lakshman from uttering such words and also requested Sumant not to convey those words to Raja Dasrath. Sumant then conveyed raja's message for bringing back Sita if Ram did not turn up. Ram again persuaded Sita to return but Sita after asking to be excused (as protocol did not allow a daughter-in-law to speak before the elders) for speaking to him directly and told that she could not live without her husband and requested Sumant to tell raja that she was happy in forests. Sumant, after paying respects to Ram, Lakshman, and Sita, returned for Awadh. Even the horses of the chariot felt the return in separation of Ram.

Ram set forward. On the way there was Ganga. Ram asked the boatman to carry them to the other side. The boatman, however, knew Ram and the incident of Ahailya having appeared out of the stone with Ram's foot touching. He was devotee of Ram and under the excuse of the boat flying away with the touch of Ram's feet, requested for his feet being washed to save his boat from flying away. He actually out of devotion wanted to wash Ram's feet as a matter of spiritual protocol. Ram agreed. The boatman with washing Ram's feet, attained Ram's bhakti. He then took Ram etc. accross the river. Reaching the other side, Ram had to pay the boatman's fee but he did not have any money with him. He looked towards Sita, who immediately took out her ring and gave. The boatman, who had already attained Ram's bhakti, did not accept anything towards labour charges for taking Ram accross the Ganga inspite of repeated requests of Ram.

पिय हिय की सिय जाननिहारी, मनि मुंदरी मन मुदित उतारी

This was the protocol between husband and wife. Ram only thought that something should he paid to the boatman and Sita could read her husband's mind and handed over the ring without any hesitation.

According to Hindu dharam, when one goes to a tirath, he asks for any boon. Sita requested Ganga for a boon that she along with Ram and Lakshman should return back to Awadh peacefully. Such was the only wish and none else. This is complete samarpan for the husband and his family. Subsequently they reached Prayagraj. Then again they took bath and worshipped the Triveni. From there Ram went to Muni Bharadwaj. He paid respects to muni and muni embraced him and gave ashirwad, asked for the well-being and requested for sitting and served meals comprising of roots, fruits etc. (कंद मूल फल)। Muni was very happy. He worshipped Ram as God and his Ishwar and prayed for showering his bhakti on him. Here is Ishwar-Bhakta protocol on one side under which Bharadwaj worshipped Ram and prayed for being showered with his bhakti. On the other side, Ram as kshatriya paid respects to muni and muni in turn gave him ashirwad and served meals as a guest. Although Ram was living like an ordinary human being yet muni knew, as he had already heard in Ram katha, that he was incarnate of Vishnu. That is why there was complete submission for him —

करम बचन मन छाड़ि छलु जब लगि जनु न तुम्हार,
तब लगि सुख सपनेहुँ नहिं किएँ कोटि उपचार।

Ram stayed there for the night and departed next morning after paying respects to the muni and obtaining muni's permission to depart.

On the way whosoever saw them paid their respects and appreciated their fortune that they had been able to have Ram's darshan. They all did appropriate hospitability—

एक कलस भरि आनहिं पानी, अँचइअ नाथ कहहिं मृदु बानी।
सुनि प्रिय बचन प्रीति अति देखी, राम कृपाल सुसील विसेषी।

Seeing two rajkumars and one rajkumari, the ladies with some anxiety asked Sita to tell who Ram was to her. They would guess the other one but the way in which they asked and the way Sita gave reply shows the traditional Indian shyness and hesitation. The ladies asked—

कोटि मनोज लजावनिहारे, सुमुखि कहहु को आहिं तुम्हारे।

and Sita replied :

तिन्हहि बिलोकि विलोकति धरनी, हुहुँ सकोच सकुचति बरबरनी।
सहज सुभाय सुभग तन गोरे, नामु लषनु लघु देवर मोरे,
बहुरि बदनु बिधुअचंल ढांकी पिय तन चितइ भौंह करि बांकी।
खजंन मंजु तिरीछे नयननि, निज पति कहेउ तिन्हहि सियं सयननि।

1. It shows the shyness and natural reaction to the same; looking towards them and then looking towards the earth.
2. Then tells that the person with fair complexion was Lakshman and her brother-in-law. She told Lakshman by name.
3. She, as per Indian tradition, did not name the husband and by her movements only indicated Ram as her husband.

In this way, Ram with Lakshman and Sita had been going giving all on way the pleasure of their darshan. On the way Ram, Lakshman and Sita had been going in a particular system; Ram in front; followed by Sita and then Lakshman.

आगे रामु लखन बने पाछें, तापस वेष विराजत काछें।
उभय बीच सिय सोहति कैसे, बह्म जीव बिच माया जैसे।

This system shows :

1. From security angle, Sita had to be given proper protection and this system gave her full protection from all sides. If they had gone all together then someone from behind could attack.
2. Socially the eldest has to be followed by the youngers. Ram being the eldest was, therefore, in the forefront,

followed by Sita the next younger (may be she was younger to Lakshman also but she got the position superior to Lakshman by virture of being Ram's wife) and then the youngest Lakshman was third.

3. Politically, the leader is followed by others. So Ram being the leader was followed by Sita and Lakshman.
4. As swami-sewak, Ram (swami) was to be followed by Lakshman and Sita. Then Sita being sewak for Ram had to follow him and Lakshman being sewak to Ram and Sita, had to follow them both.
5. Sita was the awtar of Lakshmi and Lakshmi being very chanchal (चंचल) had to be properly protected from all sides as also to see that Lakshmi does not go away herself. So Lakshmi had to be protected from not leaving Ram and Lakshman and also from all sides so that she is not taken away by others.
6. From spiritual point of view Ram was the incarnate of Brahma, Sita of maya and Lakshman as jeeva. For jeeva to reach Brahma, he has to cross maya. Therefore, Lakshman had to cross/overpower maya (Sita) to reach Brahma (Ram) so Lakshman was at the end and Ram in forefront and Sita in-between.
7. Further Ram was vairagya (वैराग्य), Sita was bhakti (भक्ति) and Lakshman was gyan (ज्ञान). For gyan to reach varaigya, he had to pass through bhakti. Sita was, therefore, in between Ram and Lakshman.
8. Sita as a pativrat (पतिव्रत) had to walk in the footsteps of Ram. If Lakshman had come in between or they were walking together, how could it be possible. Sita, therefore, had to follow Ram only and Lakshman was to follow them both. At the same time Lakshman could not afford to spoil the footstep sign of Ram and Sita from the universe. He, therefore, was putting his footsteps avoiding those of Ram and Sita.

प्रभु पद रेख बीच बिच सीता, धरति चरण मग चलति सभीता।
सीय राम पद अंक बराएं, लखन चलहिं मगु दाहिन बाएँ।

9. Manaskar has also given the simile of basant followed by Rati and Kamdev. The kam has to over-power Rati to reach basant (ultimate goal).

In this way the manaskar has kept fully the protocol in his mind even in the minutest action of Ram, Sita and Lakshman going to forest.

Then next day Ram reached Guru Valmiki's ashram. When Valmiki came to know of Ram's arrival, he went to receive them as a matter of protocol because Valmiki having written Ramayan in advance knew that Ram was the incarnate of Vishnu. He, therefore, as the Vishnu bhakta had gone to receive his God. Otherwise ordinarily Ram as a human being would have himself gone to the ashram.

'सुनि रघुबर आगमनु मुनि आगें आयउ लेन'

Then Ram paid respects to muni as a rajkumar and muni gave him ashirwad.

मुनि कहु राम दंडवत कीन्हा, आसिरवाद विप्रवर दीन्हा।

Here, therefore, the poet has shown the mutual protocol of God (Ram) and bhakta (Valmiki) and muni and rajkumar. Muni brought Ram etc. to his ashram with all respects due to a raja as a guest and his God, served him meals and asked him to take rest. Ram then said that although as a muni he knew all but he narrated how they had been sent to the forest. Ram had never felt his having been sent to the forest. He was rather happy and this happiness he had expressed time and again. This is Hindu culture. If parent's words have to be carried out, it should be with all pleasure and without keeping anything in mind.

तात बचन पुनि मातु हित भाइ भरत अस राउ
मो कहु दरस तुम्हार प्रभु सब मम पुन्य प्रभाउ।

Ram told that by coming to forest he had been able to fulfil his father's word and had done it in the interest of mother Kaikayee, who wanted Bharat to become raja. Ram had no grudge in Bharat becoming raja as he knew Bharat was a deserving person. At the same time he could have darshan of many munis in the forests. One of the tasks for Vishnu to come incarnate was also to meet all munis and give them pleasure of his darshan. So in this way Ram was fulfilling his job. The second job was to kill the rakshasas.

That job would also be possible in having come to forests, which would not have been possible sitting as raja of Awadh.

मुनि तापस जिन्ह तें दुख लहहीं, ते नरेस बिनु पावक दहहीं।

Having told the purpose of his visit to forests, Ram asked muni to advise him the place where he should stay so that his jobs, meeting the munis and killing the rakshasas could be fulfilled. Muni appreciated the way in which Ram requested muni to tell the place for his stay and said,

सोइ जानइ जेहि देहु जनाई, जानत तुम्हहिं तुम्हइ होइ जाई।

The muni could not have also given a better reply to Ram in telling the place for his stay than saying that there is no place where Ram was not there. Then where is the question of finding a palce to stay.

पूछेहु मोहि कि रहौं कहँ मैं पूछंत सकुचाऊं,
जहं न होहु तहँ देहु कहि तुम्हहिं देखावौं ठाऊँ।

Entering the sphere of spiritualism, the muni narrated the places where the God should live as a matter of spiritual protocol. In other words it was for the muni to even tell Ram, how he had to deal with his bhaktas in the universe :

(1) He should stay in the hearts of those, who have always been listening to Ramkatha.

(2) He should stay in the hearts of those, who have always been eager to have the darshan of the almighty.

(3) He should stay in the hearts of those, who always speak of his bhakti only.

(4) He should stay in the hearts of those, who take their meals after presenting the same to the almighty and after they have had the smell of the prasad in the shape of meals presented to almighty.

(5) He should stay in the hearts of those, who always pay respects to gods, guru and brahmins.

(6) He should live in the hearts of those, who always perform Ram pooja.

(7) He should stay in the hearts of those, who have all the

dependence on Ram only and have no confidence in any one else.

(8) He should stay in the hearts of those, who use their legs in going to the tirathas.

(9) He should live in the hearts of those, who always remember Ram mantra only.

(10) He should live in the hearts of those, who perform proper yagya etc. and serve meals to brahmins, pay respect to guru even treating him greater than the almighty.

(11) He should stay in the hearts of those, who for all they do, have only one ambition of having almighty's bhakti.

सब करि माँगहिं एक फल, राम चरन रति होउ,
तिन्ह कें मन मंदिर बसहु सिय रघुनंदन दोउ।

(12) He should live in the hearts of those, who are above passion, rage, pride, love, image, cheating and assumption (काम, क्रोध, मद, मोह, मान, कपट और दम्भ)।

(13) He should stay in the hearts of those, who consider other ladies as their mothers and others' wealth as poison.

(14) He should live in the hearts of those, who feel happiness seeing others happy and feel sorry on the sorrows of others.

(15) He should stay in the hearts of those for whom he is only the father, mother, master, friend, guru etc.

(16) He should stay in the hearts of those, who adopt all virtues and leave vices and face difficulties in the interest of brahmin and cow.

(17) He should stay in the hearts of those, who love the Rambhaktas.

(18) He should live in the hearts of those, who have no attachment to his caste, wealth, dharam, praise, house and his family and always think of Ram only and serve Ram only.

Having had all this spiritual dialogue, muni told Ram to live in Chitrakut, where he would be able to discharge his duty of meeting the munis and killing the rakshasas. Ram, with Lakshman and Sita went to the place told by the muni keeping in view the availability of water and fruits from trees. These are the things necessary for one to live in forest, and made their ashram there. There were two rooms in the ashram— one small and one big. Here also the ashram has been made as per protocol, the big room was for Ram and Sita and smaller one for Lakshman to stay and rest.

Having known of Ram's arrival in Chitrakut, all munis came there for Ram's darshan. Ram paid his respects and the munis gave ashirwad. Ram also told all munis to perform their tapsya without any fear of rakshasas. Ram, Lakshman and Sita, had been living in the ashram pleasantly. As per protocol, Lakshman had been serving Ram and Sita and Ram and Sita made all endeavour to keep Lakshman amused so that he did not worry for the mother, father, and those in rajmahal. Whenever Ram worried about the rajmahal, mother and father, he forgot the same seeing Sita and Lakshman and thinking that they would worry more if they saw Ram worried. Ram would keep them amused telling pauranic stories. This way all the three lived pleasantly with the mutual help. Ram and Sita had been keeping Lakshman like their son and Lakshman respected them as his father and mother; Ram taking care of both Sita and Lakshman.

On the other side Sumant on his return back after leaving Ram and others, was very worried as to how he would reach and tell raja that Ram etc. did not come back. He had all the fear of raja not living without Ram etc. On the way even the horses would not agree to go without Ram to Awadh. This only shows how difficult it is to live without Ram.

पूंछिहि जबहिं राउ दुख दीना, जिवन जासु रघुनाथ अधीना।
देहऊँ उतरु कौन मुहु लाई, आयउँ कुसल कुअंर पहुँचाई।

The normal duty of the sarthi is to take the rajkumar to the destination but this time he was afraid how he would tell about his job of Ram etc. having been left in forest, and how raja would be able to survive without Ram. Sumant, therefore, entered Awadh at night so that none was able to see him and ask him about Ram. When Sumant reached rajmahal, he as usual paid his respects and then raja got up and asked Sumant where Ram was and embraced him as if he would have brought him back. Dasrath was so sad without Ram etc. that he asked Sumant either to make him reach where Ram was otherwise he would not be able to live. Sumant told raja to have courage to face the difficult time as according to religious tanets courageous people are same in good and bad days.

सुख हरषहि जड़ दुख बिलखाही', दोउ सम धीर धरहिं मन माहीं।

Sumant told raja that Ram had directed him to make environ in Awadh such that the raja could pass the time peacefully and to tell Bharat, when he comes, not to forget the tradition or law and his duty towards parents after getting raj. Here Ram indicates about the normal behaviour of a person after attaining high position :

कहब सन्देसु, भरत के आएँ, नीति न तजिअ राजपदु पाएँ
पालेहु प्रजहि करम मन बानी, सेएहु मातु सकल सम जानी,
ओर निबाहेहु भायप भाई, करि पितु मात सुजन सेवकाई।

In the above message Ram through Sumant has conveyed an important policy of protocol—social and political. He conveyed—

(1) Message to be given when Bharat comes. Ram knew his message could be conveyed by Sumant only as he would be the only senior mantri then available.
(2) After attaining raj, Bharat should not absolve himself of the relevant canons—social and political—and should not be proud of getting raj as ordinarily people do become. In pride, man forgets all his duties and gets absorbed in lavish life, which Ram wanted Bharat should not do.
(3) He should rule and serve the praja with his action, from heart and speech (मन, कर्म और बचन) as is the duty of a raja.
(4) He should serve all mothers equally, as Ram had been doing, without an iota of partiality to one against the

other. This had two meanings—one if he gets absorbed in raj then he should not betray Kaushalya accepting what Kaikayee said and if he continues to be Rambhakta as he always had been, then he should not have affection for Kaushalya and rebuke Kaikayee for having sent Ram to forests. Either way he should serve all mothers with equal affection.

(5) He should not forget that he is Ram's younger brother. This also conveyed that Ram was the actual successor to throne, being the eldest of all and that Bharat had got it only during Ram's absence to forests. Bharat should, therefore, remember this fact and return raj after he returns back after 14 years from forests. Secondly, he should continue to have same respect for all the brothers as he has before he becomes raja of Awadh.

(6) As a resident of rajmahal in the absence of Ram, he should serve all, the father, the mothers and seniors (mantris, advisors etc.) with same degree of devotion as each deserved. Ram had sent the above message to Bharat as an elder brother. It also shows that the tenets of rule would have been taught by the guru to Ram, thinking him as successor to throne being eldest, but since it did not come through, it was his duty to tell all this to Bharat, who was succeeding the throne. Sumant told the raja that it had been difficult for him to return to Awadh leaving Ram behind but as a matter of protocol, it was his duty to convey the message of Ram to raja and Bharat and others, that Ram continued to have affection for all and also requisite interest in the rule of Awadh and that he was in the forests for a short period of 14 years and environ pre his departure to forests would get restored.

After hearing Sumant, the raja became very sad leaving all hopes of Ram returning. So was the condition of mothers. It was only Kaushalya, who took courage and advised raja also to have courage to pass the period of separation. Ram's separation had made it difficult for raja to live. It is not raja but anyone who loves Ram cannot live without him.

भयउ विकल बरनत इतिहासा, राम रहित धिग जीवन आसा।

and ultimately he left the universe in absence of Ram—

राम राम कहि राम कहि राम राम कहि राम,
तनु परिहरी रघुबर बिरहँ राउ गयउ सुरधाम।

Entire Awadh was lost in sadness. Raja Dasrath had died in absence of Ram. He had also faced such separation when Vishwamitra had taken Ram and Lakshman to forest and was able to live for a long time without them because at that time—

(1) Ram had gone with raja's permission only;

(2) Ram was going for a good cause which was relevant in dharam for the raja to do, i.e. killing rakshasas and serving the munis in enabling them to perform pooja etc. without any fear;

(3) Shiv as an astrologist had come to Awadh and told Kaushalya that Ram would come duly married after the muni took him to forest; and

(4) Raja thought Ram would come as soon as the job was over, but now—

   (1) The period of 14 years—a long period to be passed was known.

   (2) With Ram, Sita had also gone and he was not able to reconcile to the situation in which Sita would have to live in forests, whereas he had told Janak that he would keep Sita etc. with all affection in rajmahal.

   (3) Now Dasrath was not able to compromise how he would face the mantris, the seniors, guru and praja after having sent Ram etc. to forest. In other words he was dying of his own guilt.

   (4) He was not able to see how he would face the universe that he was in the hands of a queen and because of his weakness for her, he sent Ram etc. to forest, and gave rajya to a younger son Bharat which was not according to the rule of primogenittor.

In a situation in which everyone was very sad it was for the guru only to have courage and make others also to be courageous to face the situation.

तब वरिष्ठ मुनि समय सम कहि अनेक इतिहास
सोक नेवारेउ सबहि कर निज विज्ञान प्रकास।

In Hindus, jobs have been entrusted to everyone according to his capacity and capability to rise to the occasion and handle the situation. When everyone was doomed with the sadness of Ram's separation and on raja's death, it could have been possible only for a guru, who was above all the worldly comforts and sadnesses to console others. Raja's dead body was put in oil. This shows the science existing at that time. There were chemicals under which the dead body could be kept without getting spoiled for long periods. Also in the situation, the guru sent a message to Kaikayee's father's house to bring back Bharat. He told the messengers to tell Bharat only that guru had remembered him and not to tell all that had happened in Awadh as guru knew what type of a person Bharat was and it was likely that he would not return to Awadh knowing what had happened in his absence because of him and a situation which he did not approve of.

धावहु वेगि भरत पहिं जाहू, नृप सुधि कतहुँ कहहु जनि काहू।
एतनेउ कहेहु भरत सन जाई, गुरु बोलाइ पठयउ दोउ भाई।

Guru knew that the two brothers would definitely come back on the order of the guru.

When the messengers reached, Bharat immediately started for Awadh with Shatrughan. When Bharat reached Awadh, he found all in sadness. The people there would not respond to his paying them respects and none acutally welcomed Bharat then as everyone thought Bharat was a party to all that had happened. It was only his mother, who came out of the mahal to welcome Bharat in a traditional way as a raja is received on return to rajmahal with aarti etc. She asked Bharat about the well being in her father's house as she thought Bharat could be sad because of something wrong in his father's house and in Awadh he would be rather pleased to know that he had become the raja of Awadh. Kakaiyee told that everything had gone on smoothly except that in the process raja died. Hearing of father's death, he became very sad and asked where Ram was. When the entire story was told, Bharat being completely devoted to Ram, forgot his father's death and became shocked over the fact that because of him Ram had to go to forests with Lakshman and Sita. This was rather unbearable for him and he divested her right of being his mother and divorced himself from her.

भरत हि बिसरेउ पितु मरन सुनत राम बन गौनु,
हेतु अपनपउ जानि जियं थकित रहे धरि मौन्।

He abused the mother and when Manthra came in the hope of getting reward for making Bharat, the raja, she was beaten by Shatrughan. The two brothers immediately left to see Kaushalya. They found her very sad. Seeing Bharat, Kaushalya came forward to receive him as per protocol but became unconscious and fell. Bharat too fell in her feet and started crying. He cursed mother Kaikayee and himself for being son of such a mother. After hearing Bharat, Kaushalya got up and embraced Bharat having known that he at least was not a party to the entire episode. She encouraged Bharat to act as per the time and environ. Even telling that Ram was neither happy nor sad on the raja's decision to coronate him as also on his being sent to forests. They made all efforts to retain Sita and Lakshman but they wished to accompany Ram. There was sadness all around. In such environ, it was for mother Kaushalya only to ask Bharat to have patience. To clear himself from the doubt of his being a party to the proceedings, Bharat said that all sins on earth may be bestowed on him if he were a party to his ascending the throne and Ram going to forests.

जे परिहरि हरि हर चरण भजहिं भूतगन घोर,
तेहि कइ गति मोहि देउ विधि जौ जननी मत मोर।

Hearing Bharat, Kaushalya told him that she already knew the sincerity of Bharat for Ram but the entire happening is the creation of misfortune and even said—

मत तुम्हार यहु जो जग कहहीं, सो सपनेहु सुख सुगति न लहहीं।

Then Guru Vashisth and Bamdev came and told Bharat to have patience.

तात हृदय धीरज धरहु करहु जो अवसर आजु,
उठे भरत गुरु बचन सुनि करन कहेउ सबु साजु।

Whereas the guru had all good wishes for the raja and rajkumar, they too had all the respects for the guru. On guru's askance Bharat immediately got up and started the jobs required to be done by him i.e. the cremation of the raja and subsequently to handle the rule of Awadh. The dead body of the raja was cremated with all rites. The mothers had expressed desire to burn themselves alive with the raja e.g. to perform the rite of sati but Bharat with great difficulty persuaded them not to resort to that and await for Ram to return to Awadn. Bharat gave alms to brahmins and others.

After the cremation of raja, meeting was called in rajmahal at the instance of the guru. According to protocol, ministers, secretaries and advisers had been called. This shows that for any important decision, all these persons were invited and a decision was taken with the concensus.

सुदिन सोधि मुनिवर तब आए, सचिव महाजन सकल बुलाए।

This also shows that there was an element of democracy in India and the raja did not do everything according to his will. The house of seniors comprised of guru, mantris, secretaries, advisers and other respectable persons (महाजन) of the kingdom. Muni told that whatever had happened was bad but now in the situation in which raja had died and Ram had gone to forests, there was no alternative but to coronate Bharat as raja of Awadh as the singhasan could not be left unoccupied. He told Bharat the goodness of raja, Ram, Sita and Lakshman and said although it was all attributed to Kaikayee, but in fact it was all ordained to take place.

सुनहु भरत भावी प्रबल बिलखि कहेउ मुनिनाथ,
हानि लाभु जीवनु मरनु जसु अपजसु विधि हाथ।

This statement of religious tanet was made by Muni Vashisth as he only was competent to make such discourse and Tulsidas had selected the competent person only to say anything according to occasion. Here this job could be done by Vashisth only to make it authoritative and credible. Such a discourse is even today accepted not only in Hindus but also in all religions of the world and will continue to be honoured by mankind always. It is resort to destiny that can give courage to a person in time of trouble and to reconcile to the situation otherwise one would continue to remain sad all his remaining life. Here the muni had by the way told the duties and priviledges attached to the persons of all varans, ashrams, professions etc. and any departure from that duty was considered to be against the tanets of protocol or religion. The muni told that Raja Dasrath was not to be worried for as throughout his life he had performed the duties of a raja and ultimately gave up his life on separation from Ram. He was, therefore, not to be worried for at all. One has to worry for a brahmin, if he had no knowledge of vedas and on the contrary leaving his dharam indulges in vices; a king has to be worried for if he does not know the canons of governance and who does not love his people and live for his ownself. One should worry for a vaish, if he is wealthy and at the same time miser too, who does not respect the guests and the gods; a shudra is to be worried if he insults the brahmins and indulges in his own praise only. A woman is to be worried for if she cheats the husband and acts according to her desire; one should worry for a brahmchari if he does not fulfil his duties and does not obey the guru. A household is to be worried if he does not perform his duties as laid down and remains too much involved in the family. A sanyasi is to be worried for if he leaves the sanyas and indulges in vices. Similarly a vanprasth is to be worried for if he leaves the bhakti and indulges in worldly comforts; one should worry for a backbiter and for one, who does not pay respects to his guru, parents and other brothers. Then one should worry for a person who cares for himself only and is cruel to others. Raja Dasrath did not fall in the above categories and is, therefore, not to be worried for at all. Now without worrying for the death of the raja, he should do as desired by the raja i.e. accept the coronation as the raja had entrusted the rajya to him only and it is the privilege of the raja to make anyone of the sons as his successor. For the sake of fulfilling his word, the raja accepted death and Ram accepted to go to forests. The order of the same raja for him to accept throne, should be fulfilled.

अवसि नरेस बचन फुर करहु पालहु प्रजा सोक परिहरहू।

This will give peace to the soul of raja and he would be doing his duty to rule and keep the praja comfortable and troublefree. The muni even said that the father had been allowed by vedas to entrust throne to anyone of his sons—

वेद विदित समंत सब ही का, जेहि पितु देइ सो पावइ टीका।

Therefore,

करहू राजु परिहरहु गलानी, मानहु मोर बचन हित जानी।

This will also give satisfaction to Ram and Sita in forests. Guru Vashistha also told Bharat to hand over raj to Ram when he returned thereby telling that actual successor to the throne is Ram and for Bharat it was a stopgap arrangement.

सौंपेहु राजु राम के आएं, सेवा करेहु सनेह सुहाएँ।

The ministers and others present also endorsed the views of the guru but they only told him to do as per situation when Ram returned. Whereas guru had said he should hand over raj to Ram when he returned, the mantris only said he might do as situation warranted when Ram returned because they could not think of the situation fourteen years hence which muni could. Also the mantries thought that the affection Bharat had for Ram today may not continue for 14 years as no one having tasted raj wanted to leave it. Mother Kaushalya also told Bharat to do as the guru had said. She had also desired the raj to be handed over to Ram when he returned. She too knew Ram was God and he would come back.

गुरु के बचन सचिव अभिनन्दन सुने भरत हिय हित जनु चंदन।

Bharat had heard guru's order as endorsed by secretaries and mother Kaushalya and said that guru's orders as endorsed by others should be accepted by him as according to protocol the orders of guru, father, mother, master and well-wishers should be carried out thinking them as correct and in his interest.

गुरु पितु मातु स्वामी हित बानी, सुनि मन मुदित करिअ भलि जानी।

But he was not satisfied and begged to be excused for saying that—

पितु सुरपुर सिय रामु बन करन कहहु मोहि राजु,
एहि तें जानहु मोर हित कै आपन बड़ काजु।

All wanted him to accept raj saying that it was in his interest but he thought they said so in their own interest as Bharat's interest lied in serving Ram only which he had been deprived of by his mother. All the raj and its luxuries were of no avail for him without once meeting Ram and Sita. He, therefore, desired to go to forests to see Ram once as all wanted him to accept raj out of the requirement of the situation only as someone should accede to throne without which the entire governance was being ignored. He appreciated Lakshman, who had been lucky enough to serve Ram. This in other words was the protocol then existed between brothers. They had no greed for raj but for serving the elder brother and accepting him as the successor to the throne according of the institution of primogenitor. He, therefore, decided to proceed next day to see Ram and Sita and being benevolent to him Ram would welcome him.

एकहिं आंक इहइ मन माहीं, प्रातकाल चलिहऊँ प्रभु पाहीं।
और
आपन जानि न त्यागिहहिं मोहि रघुबीर भरोस।

All approved what Bharat had said and many of them including the mothers got prepared to proceed to see Ram. In fact every one wanted to go to Ram but Bharat thought that the kingdom and its wealth all belonged to Ram and he could not afford to take all to forest without making proper arrangements in Awadh for their protection. This was a political necessity as in the absence of all, some one could have invaded Awadh and looted it. Then Bharat would have been responsible for not doing his duty properly.

संपति सब रघुपति कै आही जौ बिनु जतन चलौं तजि ताही,
तौ परिनाम न मोर भलाई, पाप सिरोमनि सांई दोहाई।

Then करि सबु जतनु राखि रखवारे, राम मातु पहिं भरतु सिधारे।

Accordingly Bharat made adequate arrangements for the protection of Awadh in his absence. He also took the mothers to forests as he thought Ram had gone to forests on the order of mother and now mothers could help in his efforts to meet Ram and also endorse that he was not a party to the entire happenings. Bharat went to forests with all material required for coronation.

कहेउ लेहु सबु तिलक समाजू, वनहि देव मुनि रामहि राजू।

Bharat had prepared to go to forest to meet Ram and put him on throne but at the same time he knew that Ram, being obedient to father, would not return without fulfilling the desire of the father of remaining in forests for 14 years because of which father had already sacrificed his life. Bharat, therefore, arranged to take all material required for coronation of Ram in forest itself and make Ram agree to accept the kinghood and in that case Bharat could come back and rule on his behalf as his lieutenant. That is why he had also desired to take along with him the guru, mothers, secretaries, ministers and others, who could be considered essential for this purpose. Infact whatever Bharat had thought came out to be true. Entrusting the kingdom to his confidants, the two brothers left to see Ram in forest.

सौपि नगर सुचि सेवकनि सादर सकल चलाइ,
सुमिरि राम सिय चरन तब चले भरत दोउ भाइ।

This indicates—

(1) While proceeding to see Ram and Sita, proper arrangements were made for protection of Awadh and the governance was handed over to the confidant secretaries;
(2) All, who were required to accompany him had been taken with all respects;

(3) Since all jobs are started in Hindus after remembering the almighty, Bharat also remembered Ram and Sita as they were the almighty for him; and

(4) After doing all this, both brothers proceeded to see Ram meaning thereby that both were of the same view to coronate Ram.

Since Ram and Sita had gone on foot to forests, Bharat and Shatrughan also started on foot as a matter of protocol amongst the brothers but then the other protocol of all who accompanied could also not ride on chariots, horses, etc., Bharat and Shatrughan were persuaded by mothers to ride on the chariot, otherwise all had got down from their respective means of transport.

बन सिय रामु समुझि मन माहीं सानुज भरत पयादेहिं जाहीं।
देखि सनेहु लोग अनुरागे, उतरि चले हय गय रथ त्यागे।

Then Kaushalya told Bharat that on their proceeding on foot, others had also got down and in separation of Ram, people were not having strength enough to proceed on foot for such a long distance. Then Bharat and Shatrughan accepting mother's saying boarded the chariot. All had set on a project and in Hindus people observe a day's fast and not indulge in any vice on the starting day.

करत राम हित नेम ब्रत परिहरि भूषण भोग।

This was the thinking of the people towards their raja at that time.

All reached near Sringberpur, the kingdom of Nishadraj. Nishadraj could not make out why Bharat was proceeding to the forest where Ram had gone as he thought Bharat was a party to the entire happening and he should have been busy in enjoying the raj and if he only had proceeded out of affection then why he took along with him so many people. Nishadraj thought Bharat was going with a view to wipe off Ram for good and enjoy undisturbed raj.

This is what anyone would think and since Nishadraj was a devotee of Ram, he called all his people and alerted them to be ready to give Bharat a good fight and not to provide him any boat to cross Ganga.

जानहि सानुज रामहि मारी, करउँ अकंटक राजु सुखारी।
भरत न राजनीति उर आनी, तब कलंक अब जीवन हानी।

Nishad thought Bharat was not going according to the protocol or ethics of governance. All were prepared to sacrifice their lives for the sake of Ram. In the meantime some old person told that possibly Bharat had been going to make Ram agree to return. It was, therefore, better to meet Bharat before starting fighting with him. Nishadraj agreed to the proposal. He told all that he would meet Bharat and know what he wanted to do and then he shall advise to act accordingly. Then as per protocol, Nishad prepared presents to be offerred. After all Nishad was a small vassal of Awadh raja and a vassal when meets the raja, he offers some presents. According to tradition Nishad cited his name, his father's name and his identity from a distant place in introducing himself to muni. Nishad being a small raja under Awadh and belonging to shudra community, could not go very close to muni. So he introduced himself from a distance.

देखि दूरि ते कहि निज नामू कीन्ह मुनीसहि दंड प्रनामू।

Taking him as a devotee of Ram, the muni gave him ashirwad. Bharat left the chariot and came forward to meet him knowing that he was a friend of Ram. Nishad introduced himself to Bharat also. Bharat embraced him. Everyone appreciated that Bharat met Nishad, a person belonging to shudra community, with great affection only because he was a friend of Ram. This shows that although the institution of varans, was very much in existence in those days, this, however, could be relaxed in deserving cases. Nishad having been a devotee of Ram, had attained his closeness which led Bharat to embrace him. It was all because of Ram having his bhakti bestowed on Nishadraj.

लोक वेद सब भांतिहिं नीचा, जासु छाहं छुइ लेइअ सींचा,
तेहि भरि अंक राम लघु भ्राता, मिलत पुलक परिपूरित गाता।

Bharat asked his well being as per tradition and Nishad narrated all that happened on arrival of Ram at that place. Nishad then met Shatrughan and Ram's mothers. They all blessed him with ashirwad. Nishad then gave favourable signal to all and made arrangements for their stay all around and arranged for their meals etc. All took bath in Ganga and Bharat also took bath after obtaining guru's permission. Mothers took bath and then after checking up all, they proceeded further.

Wherever they stopped on the way, Bharat checked up each other's difficulty and checked that all had been accompanying him. Bharat entrusted the service of mothers to Shatrughan and himself called in Nishad and asked more and more about Ram, etc. What they talked, where they slept, what they ate etc. Nishad took Bharat to the place where Ram had slept—

जहं सिंसुपा पुनीत तर रघुबर किय बिश्रामु, अति सनेहँ सादर भरत कीन्हेउ दंड प्रनामु।

This was the protocol and devotion of a younger brother for the elder one. Bharat paid respects to the place and the earth of that place. Bharat wept having come to know that the queen Sita had to sleep on earth along with Ram, particularly since this all happened because Kaikayee wanted Bharat to become raja. So Bharat held himself responsible for all the sufferings of Ram and Sita but then he had to console himself knowing it all written in fate for him. Resorting to fortune gives consolation in Hindus—

सुख स्वरूप रघुबंशमणि मंगल मोद निधान,
ते सोवत कुस डासि महि बिधि गति अति बलवान।

All the persons accompanying Bharat also saw the place and paid their respects. Next day all crossed river Ganga. On the other side of Ganga, Bharat checked up all accompanying him and started further. Bharat again started walking on foot with Nishad inspite of all asking him to board the chariot or the horse. He said—

सिर भर जाउँ उचित अस मोरा, सबतें सेवक धर्म कठोरा।

This shows the master-servant relation and mutual protocol. The duty of the servant is very tough to discharge, if discharged in real sense of the term. They went to Prayag where again all took bath and Bharat after checking all proceeded further. Bharat was so much devoted to Ram that he had no desire for anything except the devotion to him.

अरथ न धरम न काम रुचि गति न चहउँ निरवान,
जनम जनम रति राम पद यह बरदानु न आन।

This is the climax of devotion for a bhakta for his God. For Bharat, Ram was his elder brother, a master and above all a God. After taking bath in Prayag, they all came and met rishi Bharadwaj. Bharat paid respects to the rishi, who embraced him and gave asheesh. The rishi offered him seat and Bharat sat feeling obliged. Rishi told Bharat that he had known all that had happened in Awadh but it was all in store in fortune for them—

विधि करतव पर किछु न बिसाई।

Rishi told Bharat that neither he should feel it nor hold mother Kaikayee responsible for it as it was all the creation of Saraswati, who spoiled the mind of Manthra and that of Kaikayee in turn. Bhardwaj also persuaded Bharat to accept the raj as—

लोक वेद समंत सबु कहई, जेहि पितु देइ राजु सो लहई।

Bharadwaj actually repeated the same principle as was enunciated by Vashisth in Awadh. But he appreciated Bharat's action in proceeding to see Ram before accepting coronation as per ethics of religion. He consoled Bharat by saying that he might feel this incidence as bad but the muni thought it was the start of good future.

तुम्ह कहं भरत कलंक यह हम सब कहँ उपदेसु,
राम भगति रस सिद्धि हित भा यह समउ गनेस।

This is how the rishi interpreted it and rightly so. The Rishi was fully devoted to Ram and in turn to Rambhakta Bharat. Bharat was rishi's guest and a respectable person too. He, therefore, offered hospitability to Bharat for the day. Bharat could not decline the offer and said—

सिर धरि आयसु करिअ तुम्हारा, परम धरम यहु नाथ हमारा।

Bharat explained to rishi that he was not interested in the raj. He was not worried for his father's death too as he died in separation of Ram after having passed his life peacefully and having got Ram etc. as his sons. He was also not worried about his mother's wrong doing but what worried him was Lakshman and Sita had to wander about in forests, eat roots, flowers, friuts etc.; sleep on earth; and all these because of him.

The rishi called all his disciples and Ridhi and Sidhi to arrange for the meals and stay and all comforts to Bharat and his companions. It was all organised and arranged very well. Rishi also wanted to check up Bharat's devotion for Ram—

राम विरह व्याकुल भरतु सानुज सहित समाज,
पहुनाई करि हरहु श्रम कहा मुदित मुनिराज।

The Ridhi and Sidhi made all arrangements of comforts and leisures. All were happy but kept themselves aloof from all leisures and pleasures. They only took as was necessary to live. They left to proceed further next day. All in forests appreciated Bharat's devotion for Ram but the gods on their part had fear that Ram might not give in on Bharat's request for returning to Awadh as Ram could not disappoint his devotees. They all went to Guru Brihaspati. Brihaspati advised gods not to interfere in Ram-Bharat's devotion othrwise it may prove bad for them as Ram cannot tolerate anything wrong done to Bharat.

जो अपराध भरत कर करई, राम रोष पावक सो जरई।
भरत सरिस को राम सनेही, जग जप राम राम जप जेही।
सुनु सुरेस उपदेसु हमारा, रामहिं सेवकु परम पिआरा।

Then all started praising Bharat's nature and his devotion for Ram.

Bharat reached Yamuna and after taking bath crossed it next day. On the way Bharat and Shatrughan paid respects to places where Ram had stayed during the night. They proceeded further enquiring from all on the way about the place where Ram had been living. From some distance, Nishad showed the place of Ram's ashram. All paid respects to the place and became very eager to meet Ram and others.

On the other side, Ram, Lakshman and Sita got up in the morning. Sita told that during the night in her dream she saw Bharat going to forests with all his close people. He appeared very sad in absence of Ram. Ram told the dream was indication of some bad news. All saints come to know of what was going to happen in future through dream or good or bad omens. At that time some locals came and told about Bharat's arrival with many people with him. Ram was happy but then thought why was Bharat coming with many people including army. Lakshman seeing Ram in an anxious mood, said, after begging to be pardoned for speaking without prior permission as per protocol, that Ram was very benevolent to all and had confidence in all but after attaining raj, one could have bad mentality. Bharat after attaining raj might be thinking that he might annihilate Ram and then rule without any fear from that side but he had forgotten that he would not be successful in his ambition till Lakshman was there.

विषई जीव पाई प्रभुताई, मूढ़ मोह बस होहि जनाई।
तेऊ आज राम पद पाई, चले धरम मरजाद मेटाई।
भरतहिं दोष देइ को जाएँ, जग बौराइ राज पद पाएँ।

Everyone becomes mad after attaining raj. So Bharat after having occupied raj which actually belonged to Ram now wanted to have it perpetually and was not content in having it for 14 years only and for this purpose he wanted to fight out Ram and have raj without any future claimants. Bharat could not be blamed for it as it is common human weakness that one becomes mad after raj after once having tasted it. Bharat knew the policy that debt and enemy should he wiped out as soon as possible and now Ram being alone in the forest and he being in command of all Awadh force could get rid of Ram easily but he has not taken into account that Lakshman too was there and he would fight till end so that he got tit for tat. Lakshman actually was already in rage against Kaikayee and Bharat eversince Ram had been sent to forests and Bharat was to become raja. Now was the chance to show his entire anger against him. He asked for Ram's permission to get ready for giving Bharat a good fight—

आज राम सेवक जसु लेऊं, भरतहि समर सिखावन देऊं।

All this Lakshman was thinking of doing for the sake of Ram as his sewak and nothing for himself. Therefore, he wanted Ram's permission for doing all this.

आइ बना भल सकल समाजू प्रगट करऊ रिस पाछिल आजू

This was a good chance for Lakshman to show his previous anger also. Seeing Lakshman in so much rage, all the persons present there became very fearful and wanted to run away from there. At that time there was akashwani to say that Lakshman was actually very brave and no one could stand before him in battle but the ethics is that any action—good or bad—should be done after adequate thinking otherwise one has to repent for having done any action in haste.

अनुचित उचित काजु किछु होऊ, समुझि करिअ भल कह सब कोऊ।

After hearing this, Lakshman was down in shame. Then Ram and Sita consoled him. They told him that he was correct in principle as anyone could lose senses after attaining greatness.

कही तात तुम्ह नीति सुहाई, सब ते कठिन राजमद भाई।

It is very difficult to contain it but this did not apply to Bharat. There cannot be an equal to Bharat in this universe.

भरतहिं होइ न राजमद, विधि हरि हर पद पाइ,
कबहू कि काजी सीकरनि छीर सिंधु बिनसाई।

Raj is two small a thing to pollute Bharat. He cannot be polluted even if he gets the raj of all the three lokas. Ram even lost in himself in praising Bharat. Ram even said—

जौ न होत जग जनम भरत को, सकल धरम धुर धरनि धरत को।

If Bharat were not there, there would not have been any dharam in this universe. After hearing the akashwani, everyone had a sigh of relief and all were happy to get a chance to see Bharat.

On the other side Bharat saw from a distant place Ram and Sita's ashram. He, leaving behind all others, came forward to go himself first after taking guru's permission. This was necessary as per protocol first to find out Ram's reaction to Bharat's arrival there. If Ram was in rage, Bharat could bear it and console him rather than making a show before all Awadhwasis. Secondly, as Nishad had thought so Ram/Lakshman should not also think that Bharat had come to give them a fight and something untoward may not take place. Thirdly, it was the custom that Bharat should go first and tell Ram about the arrival of the guru and then Ram should come forward to receive and escort guru to his ashram. Fourthly, with Bharat there was Kaikayee too and Bharat feared that things may not be as peaceful after Ram, Lakshman and Sita saw Kaikayee there. Fifthly, after seeing the mothers as widows, Ram etc. may not get a shock and that the news of raja's death could be told to them when all settled there first. Then Bharat wanted to first meet Ram and express his innocence in the entire happenings and then only Ram should face others. If all had gone simultaneously then Bharat would not have got an opportunity to express himself to Ram. Bharat, therefore, went along with Nishad and Shatrughan first. He also had a fear in his mind that seeing the army of people Ram may not flee from the place rather than face them.

राम लखनु सिय सुनि मम नाऊँ, उठि जनि अनत जाहिं तजि ठाऊँ।

And if Ram accepted him as his sewak and forgave him then it would be easy to call all others too. Even Bharat, while going was not firm in his mind as to whether Ram would excuse him or not for the treatment meted out to him. As already indicated, when an action is done in good faith; the omens, good or bad, tell the result of the things as they would happen. Here too the omens showed that Ram would meet Bharat in a cordial way and there would be all pleasant but there would be worry in the end as Nishad knew that Bharat had come to take Ram back to Awadh but Ram being firm in his mind, would not agree to such a proposal. This will make Bharat sad. Bharat agreed with Nishad but presently the anxiety was to meet

Ram and Ram to forgive him. Bharat was happy to see the surroundings of Ram's ashram. It is well known strategy to see the person, whom one is going to meet with anxiety, from a distant place and if possible to know the situation by seeing the environ. Here there was a hillock. Nishad climbed up and showed to Bharat and Shatrughan, Ram's ashram and vedi prepared by Sita where Ram and Sita could sit and hear discourses from the rishis. As already said, Ram had come incarnation with a view to please the rishis and to eliminate the fear of rakshasas from the universe. This purpose was being served by meeting all rishis there and killing rakshasas as dared to disturb the living of the rishis at that place. After all Bharadwaj and Valmiki had spotted the place to best suit the interest of Ram. Bharat could sense the environ as favourable. He paid respects to Ram and proceeded to meet him with all pleasure. Even the inanimates praised the affection Bharat had for Ram then what to speak of other living creatures.

होत न भूतल भाउ भरत को, अचर सचर चर अचर करत को।

If Bharat were not there, the inanimates would not have sensed the feelings of the animates and vice-versa

देखे भरत लखन प्रभु आगे, पूँछे बचन कहत अनुरागे।

Bharat saw Lakshman standing before Ram and had been telling Ram something he had asked for. This was the natural posture for Lakshman to stand before Ram as—

(1) it was necessary from the point of providing security to Ram and others present there as there was constant fear of rakshasas coming up that place;

(2) as a sewak to Ram, it was necessary for Lakshman to be attentive and ready for any job on askance.

(3) anybody wanting to see Ram had to come through proper channel after getting clearance from Lakshman. This is the procedure of normal protocol even existing today.

(4) any small jobs/difficulties arising in staying there could be tackled by Lakshman without Ram even knowing the same what to speak of bothering him for the same.

Seeing Ram, Bharat lost in himself. He laid himself down on earth before Ram could see him and begged to be pardoned for whatever had happened. Lakshman recognised the voice of Bharat and felt he was paying respects to Ram. As Lakshman was faced towards Ram, he could not immediately see Bharat coming. On one side there was Bharat's affection and on the other the service to Ram. Lakshman could not afford leaving Ram's sewa. After recognising Bharat's voice, Lakshman intimated Ram that Bharat had been paying his respects to him. Hearing Bharat's arrival, Ram immediately got up, without even thinking of all his belongings such as dupatta, bow and arrow, which he already had on his body. He picked up Bharat and embraced him.

बरबस लिए उठाए उर लाए कृपानिधान।
भरत राम की मिलनि लखि बिसरे सबहि अपान॥

Seeing Bharat and Ram meeting each other, everyone lost his senses and got absorbed in them. Then Ram met Shatrughan and Nishad with all affection. Then Lakshman paid respects to Bharat and then met his younger brother and Nishad. The entire meeting was according to protocol.

(1) Bharat meeting Ram and paying his respects by lying on earth;
(2) Ram picking him up and embracing him.
(3) Shatrughan paying respects to Ram and Ram embracing him.
(4) Nishadraj paying respects to Ram and Ram embracing him.
(5) Lakshman paying respects to Bharat and Bharat embracing him.
(6) Shatrughan paying respects to Lakshman and Lakshman embracing him.
(7) Nishad paying respects to Lakshman and Lakshman embracing him.
(8) Bharat and Shatrughan paying respects to all the rishi and munis present there and they in turn giving their ashirwad.

(9) Then Bharat and Shatrughan paid respects to Sita by lying in her feet. Sita picked them up and gave ashirwad in her heart as she after meeting them got lost.

Bharat had fear from Sita's side as she had been made to suffer so much because of him. Now seeing Sita cordial, Bharat became fearless. Nobody was saying any thing and none asked anything. Everyone was having the feeling of each other only. But then somebody had to tell that Muni Vashisth, mothers and other people of Awadh had come too. They were all in very bad shape (due to separation of Ram). Hearing of guru having come, Ram immediately got up and leaving Shatrughan in attendance with Sita (such an arrangement was necessary for the requisite protection of Sita as the forest was quite infested with rakshasas, who could attack any time). In the situation to receive and welcome guru and mothers, it was necessary to take Lakshman along and Bharat in any case had to accompany them. So the fittest thing was to leave Shatrughan to look after Sita as according to protocol it was not necessary to take Sita along with them by Ram and Lakshman. After seeing guru, Ram and Lakshman, paid respects to guru. Guru held them and embraced. Nishad also paid respects to the muni from a distance as being from a shudra community, he could not touch guru Vashisth but guru Vashisth taking him as Rambhakta and Ram's friend, embraced him perforce. This is where the poet has shown that although the institution of varan and ashram existed in those days, anyone could rise above those by dint of his achievements and then he became entitled to same respects and recognition. This has been amply shown by a person not less than the stature of Guru Vashisth. The poet had intelligently put forward such things through the most competent person.

प्रेम पुलकि केवट कहि नामू, कीन्ह दूरि ते दंड प्रनामू।
राम सखा रिषि बरबस भेंटां, जनु महि लुठत सनेह समेटा।
एहि सम निपट नीच कोउ नाहीं, बड़ वशिष्ट सम को जग माहीं।

Similar recognition had been given by the poet at the time of Sita's swayambar, where arrangements had been made for each other's sitting according to his capability and not according to varan ashram i.e. brahmin, kshatriya, vaish and shudra. The poet has shown that these were not strictly applied and could be relaxed according to situation.

When Ram met the people, who had come with Bharat, everyone wanted to meet Ram but it was not possible for Ram to meet each one. Therefore Ram made his as many resemblings and met each one according to his wish.

जो जेहि भायँ रहा अभिलाषी, तेहि तेहि कै तसि तसि रुख राखी।
सानुज मिलि पल महुँ सब काहू, कीन्ह दूरि दुख दारुन दाहू।

Everyone was Ram's guest there. As a matter of protocol, therefore, it was necessary for Ram to meet each one so that he felt contented. There was, therefore, no other way possible. All met Nishadraj too. Then Ram met the mothers. At first he met Kaikayee because he saw her very guilty and hesitant in meeting Ram. To do away with that hesitation, Ram met her first; then his mother Kaushalya and then Sumitra. Here the poet has mentioned that after meeting Kaikayee, Ram met all other mothers and consoled them all.

भेटीं रघुबर मातु सब करि प्रबोधु परितोषु,
अब ईश आधीन जगु काहु न देइअ दोषु।

After Kaikayee only two mothers Kaushalya and Sumitra remained but the poet's saying that Ram met all the other mothers indicates there were more than two. In those days the rajas could have many wives. From that angle there is nothing wrong in it but no where is there the mention of Dasrath's queens other than the three. Might be either the poet is referring to the two only or alternatively there might be more than three queens in all. From protocol point of view, it hardly matters. Ram met them all and consoled possibly for the death of Raja Dasrath as after seeing them in widows' dress, Ram would have already known this fact. Again as already indicated, the greatest consoling factor in Hindus is to leave everything shocking to the will of the almighty. The two brothers then met guru's wife, who gave them ashirwad. Then they met Sumitra and Kaushalya. Here again there appears some duplication as already it is mentioned that Ram met all mothers after meeting Kaikayee and then again meeting Sumitra and Kaushalya brings some confusion in it. Might be that at first they had brief meetings and now they sat in their laps. Anyway after meeting the mothers, Ram invited guru Vashisth and others to his ashram. As per protocol the host has to put forth a formal invitation. Even now when some minister etc. wants to visit a particular country, the Govt. of that country is obliged to send a formal invitation to the minister. Then after obtaining permission of the guru all Awadhwasis got down and settled at appropriate places. Guru, mothers and some selected persons were taken by Ram to his ashram. Sita, in the ashram paid respects to the muni, who gave ashirwad. Then she paid respects to guru's wife and other wives of rishis and obtained ashirwad from all. When Sita saw the mothers, she got shocked and closed her eyes. She may have closed the eyes seeing the mothers as widows which she could not stand or it can be that she had already adjusted to the living in the forests and now again falling in their affection, it would again be difficult to reconcile to the living in forests or it might be that she felt guilty that because of her they had to come to the forests after suffering all the difficulties or she did not want her mothers to see her in the jungle dress and feel annoyed. She then fell on their feet and cursed the fortune. They also were sad seeing sita in forests in that dress but said all that God bestowed had to be withstood. Sita then had courage; met all mothers and; got their ashirwad. It was then the guru, who saw Sita and mothers very sad and asked them all to take their seats. When guru told about the death of Dasrath, though all had already known it, Ram became very sad. He was particularly sad after knowing that he died because he could not withstand Ram's separation. Then Lakshman, all queens and Sita also started crying in sadness. The entire environ was full of sadness. Muni then asked Ram to have patience. He asked all to take bath and all observed fast on that day in view of Dasrath's death. Next day Ram performed the last rites of his father as told by muni and became sudh. According to Hindus on death and birth of anyone in the family, there is impurity (अशुद्धि) and everyone has to take bath and perform havan etc. to purify (शुद्ध) the environ. Next day Ram told guru that they all had been facing discomfort staying in forest; eating flowers, fruits, roots etc. So all should return particularly when Raja Dasrath too was not there, but guru appreciating Ram's gesture asked him to let all live there for a few more days. All stayed there and enjoyed the nature and living in that environ. The bheels (भील) and tribals of the area used to bring fruits, honey and other eatables for all and gave without any charges. If anyone tried to give, they would return in the name of Ram. They praised their fate that they could have their darshan and a chance for hospitability because of Ram otherwise they used to steal whatever anyone had in that area. All had in this way been living in forest. Sita had made herself in as many resemblings as the mothers were and had been serving them all day and night. No one except Ram could know it. All the mothers were satisfied with her service and blessed her. Kaikayee, seeing Ram, Lakshman and Sita in forests was very much repentant on her action in sending them in exile to forests. This is normal psychology of a person as any person being against the faith in Ram has to face such a situation.

Bharat was sad and very upset thinking how Ram would accept coronation and without that it would be difficult for him to return to Awadh. If he requested the guru for help he was likely to speak as Ram wanted; the mothers too may not be of any help and being a sewak, he could not with any force ask Ram to accept his coronation as it would amount to insubordination. He had all through been thinking but could not find a solution. After a few days a meeting of all present was held and the Muni, being in the chair (being respectable to all) told all that Bharat was entirely a Rambhakt and Ram had come incarnate of God to bless the rishis and kill rakshasas. On his father's orders, he had come to forests. Now they all had to decide keeping in view what Ram wanted and what they desired. Ram's coronation would be the best that all wanted but how shall Ram accept this should be thought over by all and a solution found out. No one could think of a solution and all became dumb. Then it was for Bharat only to speak as he had come there for a purpose so he could not afford to remain silent when guru asked. He said that there had been so many rajas in Awadh and it was the guru only who had been taking all important decisions but why now without taking any decision he asked Bharat to find out a solution. It was only his misfortune that even the guru was not helpful to him and asked him only to find a solution—

बुझिअ मोहि उपाउ अब सो सब मोर अभागु,
सुनि सनेहमय बचन गुर उर उमगा अनुरागु।

In a way Bharat blamed guru that everything had happened in his presence in Awadh and he knew the temperaments of Ram and others and he had been helping all the rajas in the past in all bad and good times but why in his turn he had not been helpful and in case he so desired, he might have been able to avoid the situation of Ram coming to forests and the raja dying, being the most competent and respectable of all. Guru agreed but only said that whatever had happened it was so desired by Ram but one solution could be that Bharat and Shatrughan go to forests and Ram, Lakshman and Sita return to Awadh. Bharat and Shatrughan were happy on this decision but there did not seem to be any logic in it as Ram was in forest because of the orders of Dasrath and after his death these orders could not be amended. All were happy on this proposal except the mothers for whom it was same sadness whether Ram and Lakshman had gone to forests or Bharat and Shatrughan. Bharat agreed to live in forests for life and not only for 14 years for the sake of Ram. He then asked guru that he being very learned, knew of Ram and Sita's mind and in the situation, he should, get his proposal fulfilled as it must have been duly thought over. Seeing Bharats' devotion for Ram, the guru lost in himself and was in all praise for Bharat's affection for Ram. Vashisth then came to Ram. Ram paid respects to guru and offered seat. Ram asked that the guru knew what was in each one's mind and what was in the best interest of all, including mothers and Bharat. He might, therefore, tell and whatever he ordered would be carried out. It was, therefore, for him to give a solution. First should be what Ram should do and then whatever could be ordained for others would be carried out. Guru then said Ram was correct but he was misled by the Bharat's affection for him. Let, therefore, Bharat tell the solution first what he felt. Ram agreed with the proposal seeing that guru had equally lot of affection for Bharat as Ram had. Guru then asked Bharat to say whatever he wanted. Bharat then said that Ram had always been very kind to him. Even in childhood, he would accept defeat with a view to see that Bharat had won. This was the protocol amongst the brothers—mutual respects for each other—right from the childhood itself. Bharat then told his guilt of having born from a mother, who worked against the interest of all and above all sent Ram to forests and got singhasan for him. Ram then asked him not to feel guilty as it was all ordained by God only and told Bharat that for his sake he would do whatever was desired by Bharat. Everyone was happy to hear this from Ram but the gods were upset as their interest was in Ram continuing in forests. They went to Guru Brihaspati. As per protocol in case of difficulty it was the guru only who could suggest the correct path to be followed. On one side, Ram etc. were dependant on Guru Vashisth to show them the path and on the other the gods were requesting Guru Brishaspati to tell what should be done. Guru Brihaspati only told the gods to request Bharat in their mind to do whatever was in their interest. Bharat had known all this and having been confused left it for Ram to take a decision in the interest of all.

सुनि सुरगुर सुर समंत सोचू, अंतरजामी प्रभुहि सँकोचू।
निज सिर भारू भरत जिय जाना, करत कोटि विधि उर अनुमाना।

It is observed that even gods had interaction in the affairs with Ram and Bharat and had been requesting to serve their interest. If one was so much devoted to Ram as Bharat was then even gods were helpless in their own affairs too and had to come to Ram's bhakta for help. Even Ram is helpless before his bhakta Bharat. In the situation, Bharat thought it best to leave it to Ram to suggest a way out in the interest of all after listening to his wish of sending him and Shatrughan or even all the three including Lakshman, to forests and himself accepting the coronation and going back to Awadh along with Sita. He had brought all requisites for the coronation. Now Ram was free to take any decision keeping everybody's interest in view. While Ram was still pondering over what Bharat had said, a messenger came to tell that Raja Janak's messenger had come there and wanted to meet the guru. Guru immediately called in the messenger. By sending the messenger first, Raja Janak was acting strictly according to protocol to see that —

(1) Since it was a meeting of the people of Awadh whether his having come there was welcome by them or not.

(2) This could be known if after hearing of Janak's arrival, Ram would be interested in escorting him to his ashram.

(3) As Raja Janak was coming without prior intimation, it was a matter of protocol to enter the estate of another raja only with his permission and if he had been welcome there.

The messenger paid respects to the guru and guru Vashisth as usual asked about the well being of Raja Janak. The messenger was sad on knowing Dasrath's death and so was entire Janakpuri. On this, all became upset for some time. Raja Janak had not so far gone to Awadh after the entire happening as :

(1) It was an internal affair of a family and a raja and it was not proper for him to interfere in others' affairs. Even today a country is not welcome to interfere in others' internal matters.

(2) Raja Dasrath would feel awkward in facing Raja Janak as he considered himself guilty of having sent Ram and

Sita to forests although he had full affection for Ram and wanted him to succeed to the throne.

(3) Raja Janak was not in a position either to plead for Ram's case for succession or that of Bharat.

(4) Janak consulted all his advisers but could not reach any conclusion whether to go or not to go to Awadh. Janak had been awaiting for Bharat's reaction to the entire episode as it had happened in his absence. If Bharat on arrival to Awadh accepted the throne then the matter ended and he would have dealt with him accordingly and if he did not accept then only to take part in finding a solution to the problem.

(5) In fact Raja Janak was closely watching whatever had been happening in Awadh and when he came to know that on arrival to Awadh, Bharat was not found interested in succeeding to throne and had gone to forest to bring Ram back that he had got courage for himself proceeding to forest to meet them all there only after consulting his advisers.

(6) At each stage Janak had been consulting his advisers in the matter. The above deliberations had taken place in Mithila when Janak had consulted his ministers as to what was proper for him to do as he was in a fix whether or not to go to Awadh. Raja Janak had acted strictly according to the protocol of international relations in checking the position and then only going to forests to meet all.

नृप बूझे बुध सचिव समाजू, कहहु विचारि उचित का आजू।
समुझि अवध असमजंस दोऊ, चलिअ कि रहिअ न कह कछु कोऊ।
नृपहि धीर धरि हृदय विचारी, पठए अवध चतुर चर चारी।
बूझि भरत सति भाउ कुभाऊ, आएहु वेगि न होइ लखाऊ।
दूतन्ह आइ भरत कइ करनी, जनक समाज जथामति बरनी,
घर पुर देस राखि रखवारे, हय गय रथ बहु जान संवारे।
दुघरी साधि चले ततकाला, किए विश्राम न मग महिपाला।

Guru Vashisth sent back the messenger giving them a few of the tribals present in Ram's service in token of having welcomed the arrival of Janak there. All from Awadh were happy to hear of Janak's arrival as they expected some favourable decision taking place now. Ram fell in confusion and the gods were again anxious about the decision to follow. Kaikayee was down with guilt. The people were happy as it gave them a chance to live there for a few more days. As demanded by protocol, Ram alongwith guru, brothers, ministers and other seniors started to receive Raja Janak. When a raja comes to another state, the raja of that state has to receive him even as per present day protocol. In Awadh there was no raja. Therefore, Ram being eldest had to go to receive Raja Janak. Even otherwise Raja Janak had come to the ashram of Ram. Ram, therefore was the host and had to go to receive Raja Janak. On the other side Raja Janak left the chariot and started on foot deeply involved in affection of Ram and Sita. The two met at some distance. In order of priority—

(1) Janak paid respects to munis (Vashisth etc. on Ram's side),

(2) Ram paid respects to the rishis with Raja Janak,

(3) All brothers met and paid respects to Raja Janak and then escorted them to the ashram along with all those who accompanied Raja Janak.

They reached the ashram. Both sides were very sad because of Raja Dasrath's death. All cursed the misfortune for bringing such a day. Although there was Raja Janak (Videh विदेह) and rishis, and munis, who were all above such worldly anxieties but at that time everyone was sad and no vairagya to be seen anywhere. Then only the Muni Vashisth requested all to have courage. All passed that day without taking anything. As already indicated, according to Hindu dharam, on death one does not take anything for atleasth one day. All sat under a tree and the munis told many pauranic stories to console the gathering. Next day Ram invited everyone for meals but as per tradition, even existing today, the father of the girl does not take anything in the house of in-laws of the daughter. So Janak politely told that it would not be proper for them to take meals at Ram's ashram. Everyone readily agreed to this and Janak went to the place where his people were staying.

रिषि रुख लखि कह तेरहुतिराजू, इहां उचित नहिं असन अनाजू।
कहा भूप भल सबहि सोहाना, पाइ रजायसु चले नहाना।

Tribals brought lot of eatables for the people of both sides. All took meals and as directed by Ram, Janak and the munis settled here and there. In this way four days passed. Everyone was happy even to stay in forest with Ram. Rightly so. One who has dedicated himself to Ram, feels having attained everything if he gets a chance to live with Ram. Everyone wished Ram and Sita to return to Awadh. At that time the maid servant of Sita's mother came to meet mother Kaushalya to seek her permission for the queen of Janak to come to see her if she was free. Having got concurrence the queen came to meet Kaushalya and others. Here again political as well as social protocol requirements had been fulfilled.

(1) The meeting between the queens of Awadh and Janakpuri had to be sought by the mother of the girl's side as she is considered lower in position to that of the mother of boy's side.

(2) Sita's mother, therefore, sent her maid to seek approval from Ram's mother for their meeting if she was free.

(3) After getting such approval, Sita's mother came to Ram's mothers.

(4) On arrival Ram's mothers honoured Sita's mother being the guest and gave proper seat to her.

(5) Even otherwise at this time Kaushalya was down with sadness because of the death of Raja Dasrath. It was, therefore, for the queen of Janakpuri to come and condole the death of the raja.

All were very sad. In the situation Sita's mother broke the ice and said the God had been very unkind as he had been giving one shock after the other—the first was Ram's going to forests and then the death of Raja Dasrath. On Ram's side it was Sumitra, who said that it was all in fortune and none could be blamed. It was very strange, she said, that the same God, who at first creates the human beings; then brings them up and ultimately annihilates them from the universe. Kaushalya also said that no one could be blamed as it was in store as per each one's fortune. She even said that they were sad because of raja's death by looking into their selfish interest. If one delinked oneself from one's gains out of the deceased, there would be no sadness.

भूपति जिअब मरब उर आनी,
सोचिअ सखि लखि निज हित हानी।

This was quite deep and enough to console others at the death of any close person. This was readily agreed to by Sita's mother too and said that such deep thinking could be brought about by Kaushalya only; being Ram's mother. Being more practical, Kaushalya also said that she was not worried about Ram, Lakshman and Sita living in forests but was worried for Bharat as to how he would live in absence of Ram living in forests. This was a very meanigful statement by Kaushalya. By saying so —

(1) Kaushalya expressed that she was not at all minding Ram, Lakshman and Sita going to forests and this removed the anxiety in the mind of Kaikayee, who had been feeling guilty of having been responsible for sending Ram etc. to forests.

(2) Indirectly told Kaikayee that she considered Bharat and Ram equally and so did Kaikayee but it is some super power which prevailed upon Kaikayee being responsible for all that had happened.

(3) This indicated the mind of Kaushalya that she was not worried for his son Ram and Sita living in forests and so the mother of Sita should also not mind it.

(4) It showed to the queen of Janakpuri that there was full cordiality still in the minds of all the queens of Awadh inspite of all that had happened and that they had already reconciled to the situation and all the queens loved all the four sons equally.

(5) She expressed and recommended to Sita's mother that she should brief Raja Janak who would be a party to any decision in the matter of Ram etc. continuing in forests or going back to Awadh keeping Bharat's position in view.

(6) She expressed upon the queen of Janakpuri that although the entire happening had taken place because of raj, in fact none of the four brothers is after the raj and this could happen only in the absence of Bharat not being in Awadh at the time of Ram's proposed coronation.

लखनु राम सिय जाहुं बन भल परिनाम न पोचु,
गहबरि हियँ कह कौसिला मोहि भरत कर सोचु।

Kaushalya then praised all the four sons and all the four daughters-in-law. Any girl's mother would like to know how her daughter had behaved and put her image in the mind of the in-laws and it could be best told by the mother-in-law of the daughter only. Kaushalya, therefore, hastily swore by this statement so that Sita's mother could believe this statement without any hesitation. She then praised Bharat. Thereafter she told Sita's mother that she being the queen of Raja Janak knew it all and no one was capable of sermonising her at all. She even recommended to Sita's mothers to tell Raja Janak to ask Bharat to go to forests with Ram and ask Lakshman to return to Awadh as the condition of Bharat was more tense compared to that of Lakshman. Even being the mother of Ram and having come there to take Ram back, Kaushalya did not even once recommend to Sita's mother to brief Raja Janak to persuade Ram to return to Awadh as she knew her son was firm on fulfilling the desire of the father and mother Kaikayee as she had already tried it before permitting Ram to proceed to the forests. There was talk and talk. Then someone had to call it a day. It was mother Sumitra only to interfere and say that almost the entire night had passed and now they should take rest in their respective places. Kaushalya bade farewell to Sita's mother and told her that now they had dependence on God, whatever he does or on Raja Janak as he too had a say in the matter being the eldest of all and respected by all. Sita's mother praised Kaushalya for having so much confidence in Raja Janak. She even told that Rishi Yagbalika had already told in anticipation (भविष्यवाणी) of Ram's birth that Ram would proceed to forests; kill all rakshasas and then have eternal chakravarti raj. She then paid respects to Kaushalya and sought permission for taking Sita along with her for sometime. Sita having been married, her mother had no right on her and all her movements depended upon as desired by the in-laws. Sita's mother, therefore, out of social protocol, sought Kaushalya's permission to take Sita with her.

सिय समेत सिय मातु तब चली सुआयसु पाइ।

Having gone with the mother, Sita met everyone from Janakpuri according to each one's wish and position—

प्रिय परिजनहिं मिली वैदेही, जो जेहि जोग भांति तेहि तेही।

This again was as per laid down protocol that Sita met her people in the way each deserved. All were, however, sad to see Sita in tapasvi's dress. They had seen her as a princess only and seeing in this young age as a tapasvi, one really gets upset. Raja Janak was with Ram and Vashisth. Having known that Sita had come to his dera, he after seeking guru's permission left for his dera. He embraced Sita and lost himself in affection of Sita which was actually against the temperament of Janak as he had renunciated the worldly attachments but even he lost his senses in Sita's affection. Similar was the position of Sita's mother too. In the situation someone had to break the ice and put the ball into rolling. So here it could be done by Sita only. Raja Janak was in all praise for Sita, who by coming to forests with Ram had raised the two 'dynasties' image. There can be nothing more of pride for a father than to see his daughter being praised by all for the sacrifice done by her. The parents then embraced Sita, gave their ashirwad and appropriate coaching.

Sita had been brought by her mother with Kaushalya's permission to her dera with a view that she may meet all those, who had come from Janakpuri. Now that purpose was over and Sita thought, as per protocol, it was proper for her to stay with her mother-in-law, in her service, during the night and not with the mother as after the marriage the girl has more of her duty towards her in-laws. Sita, therefore, wanted to go to mother Kaushalya during the night :

कहति न सीय सकुचि मन माही, इहां बसव रजनीं भल नाहीं।
लखि रुख रानि जनायउ राऊ, हृदय सराहत सीलु सुभाऊ।

Sita, as usual, had been hesitating in asking her mother's permission to return to Kaushalya. Sita's mother could, however, sense the thinking and told Raja Janak too about it. They appreciated her thinking and permitted with all affection. Then Sita's mother made mention about Bharat to Raja Janak as told by Kaushalya. Knowing Bharat's devotion to Ram, Raja Janak lost in himself for sometime and they both praised what Bharat had done. Having added all adjectives in Bharat's praise, Raja Janak ultimately said there was no equal of Bharat in the universe. He was unique—

निरवधि गुण निरुपम पुरुषु, भरतु भरत सम जानि,
कहिअ सुमेरु कि सेर सम कवि कुल मति सकुचानि।

They both also were in favour of Bharat and Lakshman going to forests and Ram and Sita returning to Awadh. This would have everyone's approval. But no one could even imagine the mutual affection amongst Bharat and Ram and Bharat could renunciate everything for the sake of Ram provided Ram agreed to such a proposal and since Ram would not agree to such a proposal and Bharat could not go against Ram's wishes, this proposal of Bharat and Lakshman going to forests and Ram and Sita returning to Awadh could not be carried through. The entire night passed in this dialogue. Next morning all woke up; took bath; and worshipped the respective deities. Ram went to guru and told him that Bharat, all mothers and others from Awadh had already lived for so many days in forest and may be feeling inconvenient to stay any more. Also Raja Janak had been staying with his people for the last so many days. Therefore, something, as may be considered proper, might be done by him as now the decision rested on him only. Since it was difficult for Ram to say so to the muni, he could say all this with great hesitation, such being the protocol amongst the guru and the pupil. The hesitation on the part of Ram was :

(1) Because all were Ram's guests and Ram being the host, it was not proper for him to have sought their going back.

(2) Everyone was happy in staying with Ram for the maximum period but Ram thought that they might be feeling uncomfortable in staying in forest and eating whatever was available there.

(3) Ram could not think of anyone being uncomfortable because of him. He, therefore, requested muni to do something in the interest of all so that all could return to Awadh or Janakpuri, as the case might be. Muni appreciated Ram's gesture but at the same time removing his anxiety told Ram, that no one would be happy without Ram even in Awadh/Janakpuri. Any way, he asked Ram to return to his ashram and he would do whatever was possible. Now the decision was not in the hands of guru only as Raja Janak had also come and he had a greater say in the matter. He told Raja Janak what Ram had desired and requested him to do something in the interest of all as he only was the person capable of finding a solution to the problem. Since the question was as to who should be coronated and Raja Janak was an experienced raja, he could give a better solution. Hence the request was made to him.

ज्ञान निधान सुजान सुचि धरम धीर नरपाल,
तुम्ह बिनु असमजंस समन को समरथ एहि काल।

He told that the situation was such that a decision could be taken only by a person, who was very intelligent, puritan, selfless, knowing the tanets of religion and diplomacy and an experienced king and all such merits were available in Raja Janak only. Raja Janak was perplexed after hearing the guru as the guru even being all capable of taking a decision which had to be respected by all, did not want to take a decision and had thrown the ball in his yard. At one time he even thought that he had not done a good thing in having come to that place. From protocol point of view, yes. He should not have come there and should have paid a visit to Ayodhya only as a raja. At the same time he was the father-in-law of both Ram and Bharat and therefore, it was proper for him to have come there and contributed to the decision making based on his intelligence and experience.

सिथिल सनेहं गुनत मन माही, आए इहां कीन्ह भल नाहीं।

As a matter of fact, he has shown that the father of the girl should not interfere in the domestic problems of the in-laws of the daughter. Whenever such interference has taken place it has worked awkwardly as Raja Janak was not in a position either to ask Bharat to go to forests and Ram to return to Awadh as it was against the Ram's purpose of incarnation nor he could tell Bharat to return to Awadh and accept coronation as Bharat would never agree to it. Then Ram had come to forests as per orders of Raja Dasrath then how could Raja Janak ask Ram not to fulfil Dasrath's last desire. On the other hand, he was himself not able to return to Janakpuri leaving Ram and Sita in forests psychologically. Then keeping in mind the time and environ, Raja Janak went to Bharat with all seniors. Bharat welcomed them and offered seats as available. Then he told Bharat that Ram was utter religious and knew everyone's difficulty. He was already feeling it that because of him all were living in forests in an uncomfortable situation. Bharat, in all benevolence told him that he was like his father and then there were Guru Vashisth, Rishi Vishwamitra and other seniors, who just could order him to do anything which he would happily carryout, then why ask him what should be done. In presence of all, Raja Janak was asking him and he was confused and if he did not respond then he would be considered tarnished and if he spoke it would be against protocol. Still he might be excused in saying that he would accept whatever is decided here keeping in view his devotion for Ram, including that Ram should not feel awkward in carrying out any decision because of him, (this was the real devotion) and what may be in the interest of all and religiously sound. Hearing Bharat everyone appreciated how Raja Janak had handled the situation and all praised Bharat for having such a thinking for Ram. Then they all went where Ram was staying. Everyone was entirely absorbed in Ram's devotion. The gods feared that things might not come out against their interest and requested Saraswati to help them by managing Bharat's mind. Saraswati, however, told that nobody could change Bharat's mind, and went away.

Raja Janak went to Ram. Ram conveyed his respects. Bharat then said after remembering Ram and Sita that Ram was for him a father, mother, guru, swami and friend and he could not afford doing anything which he did not approve of. Already he had done something against the protocol in having come all the way to the forests inspite of clean direction from the father for him to rule. But still he was glad that Ram had forgotten everything and recognised his devotion for Ram. There was, therefore, no equal to Shri Ram as a swami. This was the complete faith in the swami, which one could have.

When Janak etc. went to Ram, he welcomed them all. There it was for Guru Vashisth to speak. He at first narrated the dialogue between Janak and Bharat and asked Ram to tell what should be done in the situation as may be acceptable to all and be in the interest of all. Ram, however, as a matter of protocol, could not give any decision when Raja Janak, Vishwamitra and Vashisth were there. He only said whatever was decided by all would, he swore, be acceptable to him. Hearing Ram's sapath, everyone fell in dilemma. The gods were again having anxiety in the ultimate decision to be arrived at. They created a lot of irritation amongst the people to go back.

सो गोसाईं नहिं दूसर कोपी, भुजा उठाइ कहउँ पन रोपी।
राखा मोर दुलार गोसाईं, अपने सील सुभायँ भलाई।

Bharat after saying all this requested Ram to take any decision and it would be carried out :

आयसु देइअ देव अब सबइ सुधारी मोरि।
आज्ञा सम न सुसाहिबु सेवा, सो प्रसाद जन पावै देवा।
अस कहि प्रेम बिबस भए भारी, पुलक सरीर बिलोचन बारी
प्रभु पद कमल गहे अकुलाई, समय सनेहु न सो कहि जाई।

For such a sewak, Ram was equally a good swami. He respected Bharat's feelings and made him sit close by him.

कृपासिन्धु सनमानि सुबानी, बैठाए समीप गहि पानी।

Everyone was in full praise for the devotion Bharat had for Ram and the affection Ram had for Bharat. On the other side, Devraj Inder had all the fear of Ram accepting Bharat's request for returning to Awadh as Ram was always in for fulfilling the wishes of his sewaks. Inder had always thought of himself only even at the cost of others. He had no confidence in anyone. For the sake of his benefit, Inder has been shown in Hindus as a character, who is the ruler of Swarag and had a fear in his mind always that anyone by virtue of his tapsya or cruelty would snatch Swarag from him. This the poet has depicted, would be the condition of anyone, who was in possession of a lot of wealth and anyone coming close by would give him a sort of feeling that he was after his wealth only. Such a temperament is common in the universe. A man with pure soul like Bharat could not, however, be effected by any ill designs. Inder, though tried to make the minds of all favourable to him, could not succeed in winning over Bharat.

कपट कुचालि सीवं सुरराजू, पर अकाज प्रिय आपन काजू।
सुरमाया सब लोग विमोहे, राम प्रेम अतिसय न बिछोहे।
भय उचाट बस मन थिर नाहीं, छन बन रुचि छन सदन सोहाहीं।

Everybody was in utter confusion. At one time he felt like leaving for Awadh but in Ram's affection again wanted to stay in forests. Although everyone's mind was alike but no one was telling it to others. This 'maya' did not, however, affect the munis, Bharat, Janak, ministers, sadhus and alert people.

भरतु जनकु मुनिजन सचिव साधु सचेत बिहाइ,
लागि देवमाया सबहि जथाजोगु, जनु पाइ।

Here the poet wants to warn everyone that a human being was always subject to a lot of harassment and ill designs by others but if one was alert enough and had his full faith in himself and the God, no ill-designs could do any harm to such a person.

Everyone was now waiting for the final decision by Ram and was lost in having seen Bharat's devotion for Ram. Ram then said that in devotion no one could equal Bharat. It was, however, not apt to praise Bharat when guru and other seniors were sitting.

करम बचन मानस बिमल तुम्ह समान तुम्ह तात,
गुर समाज लघु बंधु गुन कुसमयँ किमि कहि जात।

Here Ram had acted according to the social protocol, namely :

(1) He had, in response to what Bharat had said in praise of Ram and his bhakti for him, said that there was none equal to Bharat in bhakti and devotion and thus recognised his devotion for Ram.

(2) In the meeting where guru and other seniors were sitting it did not behove well to praise a younger brother.

(3) The time was such where every one was deeply sad, that the mutual praise of Ram and Bharat would be taken otherwise by all present there.

(4) Ram, therefore, in a way had said all in praise of Bharat and at the same time observed protocol as well.

(5) Ram also paid tributes to guru, who was in the chair saying that after the death of Raja Dasrath, he had managed the affairs of Awadh and encouraged everyone, not himself losing courage; making everyone submit before fate; and preparing everyone for further course of action, otherwise all, including the kingdom, family and the praja, would have gone to dogs.

(6) Ram also praised Janak, who had been feeling that it was not good for him to have come there at a time when domestic matter was to be decided, that his blessings

had saved them from being annihilated. This shows that after the death of Raja Dasrath, Janak was keeping a close watch on the affairs of Awadh, in the absence of the brothers, in conjunction with the guru, who only was present in Awadh and saved Awadh from any untoward happening like someone invading Awadh, or doing some mischief in the management of the affairs of Awadh.

(7) Henceforth too the entire affairs, Ram had told Bharat, would be handled under the guidance of guru only so that the raj, management, image, religion, land, wealth and habitation remained well protected. Guru, therefore, had all the say in the affairs of the state. That exactly is the Chanakya Niti too.

(8) Ram even admitted that not to speak of Awadh, where guru lived, which would be well protected even they in forests also lived peacefully because of the guru's kind blessings.

(9) Ram, therefore, asked Bharat to do and permit him to do as directed by guru.

(10) Ram said that in the troubled time, everyone had been sharing the bad time viz Lakshman and Sita had been facing difficulty in living in forests; the mothers had left behind their affection permitting Ram and others to go to forests; the guru had to share extra responsibility in handling the affairs of the state but in case of Bharat, the responsibility of his share of facing trouble was more as he would have to pass the long period of 14 years in his absence and in keeping the praja and the household protected.

(11) All this trouble would not have been there if Ram was allowed to rule as he had been groomed by the guru and Raja Dasrath to succeed the throne and would have handled the affairs himself.

सो विचारि सहि सकंट भारी, करहु प्रजा परिवार सुखारी
बांटी विपति सबहिं मोहि भाई, तुम्हहि अवधि भरि बड़ि कठिनाई।

After hearing what Ram had said, everyone was lipbound and Bharat was happy as he had seen that Ram was on his right side and requested to direct him as he desired and he would carry out the direction but may be given something to bank upon for the entire period.

सो अवलम्ब देव मोहि देई। अवधि पारु पावौं जेहि सेई।

In other words Bharat had accepted to remain under submission to Ram for this period but then actual successor to the kingdom was Ram and, therefore, he should give him some authority recognisable by all to manage the affairs of the state on his behalf.

He also told Ram that with guru's permission, he had brought the water of all the tiraths and other things required for coronation and desired to have Ram's orders for the disposal of that material and added that if Ram permitted he might use that material in Chitrakut itself. Ram agreed for the material being used in Chitrakut itself. This in other words gives the impression that Ram had agreed to formalise the succession to Awadh throne himself and ceremony to be performed in Chitrakut. That was the only possible use of the raj-tilak samagri in Chitrakut. By now everything was clear that Ram would officially be the Raja of Awadh during the period and Bharat would act as defacto ruler under the authority of Ram, obviously as his lieutenant. This is all as per the ethics of political protocol. This solution of the problem made Bharat happy; Ram to continue in forests; Bharat to manage the affairs of Awadh as lieutenant of Ram; the gods were happy that their purpose was well served; the guru was happy that a solution to the problem had been found without his involving himself much; Janak felt satisfied that it would have been difficult to give a proposal to sort out the matter as any proposal would have been designated 'partial'. It also indicates that domestic problems should better be solved by the persons concerned without involving the outsiders as, if the will is there, then a solution could automatically be found long lasting keeping each other's interest in view. The mothers were neither happy nor sad as ultimately two of their sons had to live in forests, whether they were Ram and Lakshman or Bharat and Shatrughan or Ram and Bharat; the mantris and other elders were happy that at last one of Ram and Bharat had accepted to manage the affairs of Awadh—they considered both equally acceptable.

The rajtilak samagri had been put at a proper place as a symbol of Ram's rajtilak in Chitrakut as Ram could not be coronated formally with all pomp and show as it would have been against the order of his father, who desired Ram to live in the forests like a tapasvi and Bharat to rule Awadh during those 14 years. Then after putting the samagri at designated place, Rishi Atri apprised Ram of the fait accompli that though not with all formalities but his raj tilak ceremony had been symbolically performed. Ram, therefore, became the raja and after having become so, he gave Bharat the necessary authority or letter of credence in the name of his shoes (पादुका). Bharat took that authority and ruled Awadh under the coverage of that authority for 14 years. Bharat then asked for Ram's permission to leave for Awadh and manage the affairs for the period.

अब गोसाईं मोहि देउ रजाई, सेवौं अवध अवधि भरि जाई।

He also requested Ram to coach him how to rule during this period. This confirms the idea that Ram being the rightful successor to throne, had been specially coached by the guru and groomed by raja to be the ruler. Such a coaching had not been given to the other brothers and since Bharat had to discharge that duty, he requested Ram to tell him all canons of raj.

सो सिख देइअ अवधि लगि कोसल पाल कृपाल।

By using the words Bharat has also indicated here again that it was Ram only, who had to manage 'कोसलपाल' the affairs of both the sides during this period. The affairs of ruling Awadh through Bharat and his own jobs of satisfying the rishis, munis etc. by his darshan and protecting them to enable discharge their yagya, hawan, tapsya etc. by killing all rakshasas, who had been causing disturbance and killing the tapasvis.

प्रनतपालु पालिहि सब काहू, देउ दुहू दिसि ओर निबाहू।

Ram again, for the purpose of coaching Bharat as to how to manage the affairs of Awadh, told him that when guru and

Raja Janak were there what was left for him to state. In other words he had got the requisite coaching only from guru and Raja Dasrath. Guru was still there and in the absence of Raja Dasrath, Raja Janak was available. He indirectly requested them to help Bharat in the management—

तात तुम्हारि मोरि परिजन की, चिंता गुरहिं नृपहि घर बन की,
माथे पर गुर मुनि मिथिलेषु, हमहि तुम्हहिं सपनेहुँ न कलेसू।

Bharat had requested Ram to manage the affairs of Awadh and forests but Ram sought the blessing of the guru and Raja Janak to mind the management of both the places—by their presence for Awadh affairs and by dint of their blessings the job in forests. He also indicated that one have to have a viswas (pucca faith) in someone—guru, father, or God and then it is easy to manage the affairs with his blessing. Saying this, Ram asked Bharat to go and manage the affairs of Awadh for the period.

पालहु अवध अवधि भरि जाई।

Ram also told Bharat to act with the guidance of guru and raja and with the advise of mantris and advisers. This indicated that the raja in those days was not an autocrat ruler but he ruled keeping the advice of the guru, mantris and other advisers like one acts in a democratic set up.

तुम्ह मुनि मातु सचिव सिख मानी, पालेह पुहुमि प्रजा रजधानी।

Ram coached Bharat in all respects but the entire job was complete after he gave the authority to Bharat to rule for the period on his behalf.

प्रभु धरि कृपा पावंरी दीन्हीं, सादर भरत सीस धरि लीन्हीं।

Ram gave the authority to rule (पावंरी or shoes is symbolic of the letter of authority) and Bharat also accepted the conditions of ruling as Ram's lieutenant under the authority given to him with all humility and respect. 'पावंरी' word is also symbolic to indicate that Ram considered the raj like his shoes only and had no importance for him as could be one's shoes, which could be thrown away without any hesitation. Bharat accepting Ram as overall raja of Awadh undertook to look after the management on Ram's authority for the period

Ram had to stay in forests. Bharat then asked for permission to return to Awadh. The separation by Bharat, Janak, etc. from Ram was a scene within itself as everyone was out of himself in affection for Ram. A day was fixed for return. At the time of separation all met each other as per protocol. At first Bharat met Ram, who embraced him. Then Ram embraced Shatrughan. All secretaries and workers started preparing for the return as per jobs entrusted to them by Bharat. Here again all workers obeyed Bharat as now he was their raja. Bharat met Lakshman, then paid respects to Sita. Ram and Lakshman paid respects to Raja Janak, who was all out in praise for them. Ram also told Raja Janak that he suffered a lot in having come to forests with his people, as per tradition. Ram then met the mothers with Lakshman and paid respects. Munis gave them ashirwad. Then Ram and Lakshman respected all appropriately and bade good bye to all.

नारि पुरुष लघु मध्य बडेरे, सब सनमानि कृपा निधि फेरे।

Ram had special consideration for Rani Kaikayee as she had all through been feeling guilty of being responsible for the entire episode and in which she did not gain anything. Therefore, Ram bade her good bye after removing her guilt.

भरत मातु पद बंदि प्रभु सुचि सनेहँ मिलि भेंटि,
बिदा कीन्ह सजि पालकी, सकुच सोच सब मेटि।

Sita met her mother, father and others and paid respects. Then she met her mothers-in-law and paid respects. They also in turn gave ashirwad. Ram called for the chariots of the mothers and got them boarded with respect as per protocol. Ram, Lakshman and Sita paid respects to guru and guru's wife and rturned to their ashram. Whereas on arrival Ram etc. paid respect to guru first on return they met guru at the end as per tradition. After return, Ram, Lakshman and Sita had been remembering Bharat etc and repeating all that had happened, as usual. Ram, Lakshman and Sita had been in the ashram as if vairagya, gyan and bhakti were living in those persons.

Bharat etc. returned to Awadh in four days. For a few days, Raja Janak stayed there to guide Bharat in handling the affairs of the state and then returned to Janakpuri after entrusting the raj to guru, Bharat and mantris.

जनक रहे पुर बासर चारी, राज काज सब साज सँभारी।
सौंपि सचिव गुरु भरतहिं राजू, तेरहुति चले साजि सब साजू।

Bharat started ruling the kingdom. All praja settled in Awadh and all started living in absence of Ram leaving all pleasures and leisures. All ministers and advisers started doing their jobs as directed by Bharat. Bharat entrusted the job of looking after the mothers and rajmahal to Shatrughan. He called all seniors and brahmins and requested them to continue telling him wherever he was wrong without any hesitation. It is here that the rajas were subject to be checked by others in their wrong doings. This shows there was no autocracy.

भूसुर बोलि भरत कर जोरे, करि प्रनाम बय विनय निहोरे,
ऊँच नीच कारज भल पोंचू, आयसु देव न करव सँकोचू।

Bharat then called on the guru and sought his permission to live as a tapasvi like Ram had to live and to live in Nandigram away from Awadh leaving behind all pleasures of the rajmahal. He put Ram's shoes or letter of authority on the singhasan and started doing the work as per letter of authority. This was the renunciation (त्याग) for the sake of brother at that time which is never and nowhere else heard of.

नित पूजत प्रभु पावंरी प्रीति न हृदय समाति,
मांगि मांगि आयसु करत राज काज बहु भांति।

3

Aranya Kand

The poet starts this chapter with two slokas. Since in this chapter. Sita is kidnapped after which Ram and Lakshman only two would remain, the poet has given only two slokas. The first is in praise of Shiv and the second in praise of Ram. This is with a view to again emphasise that Shiv was Ram's bhakta and the place of bhakta is above that of Bhagwan himself. So the poet here also complies with spiritual protocol although in worldly protocol Ram, the Lord, should find place before the bhakta. The poet through the medium of Shiv says that Ram have many deep rooted good things, which can be known by pandits and munis, who have fully devoted themselves to Ram. The others would get lost and would rather than reaching the reality involve themselves in worldly life. This Shiv had said keeping in view how Ram had tackled the very ticklish problem on Bharat's arrival in Chitrakut to take Ram back and Ram could not go back firstly because he had come as per his father's orders which could not be betrayed after his death and secondly the purpose of Ram's incarnation was to kill all rakshasas, which would not have been possible in ruling Awadh and getting lost in the kingdom's affairs. At the same time, Ram could not disappoint his very close bhakta Bharat also straightaway as he had devoted himself fully to Ram and had come to Chitrakut in the hope of coronating Ram as raja of Awadh. By dint of assigning Bharat to work as his lieutenant in his absence, Ram solved all the problems to the satisfaction of all.

Although almighty, but is sometimes taken otherwise if one lives in a mild way. One, therefore, should appear to be living as per his capability and capacity otherwise people taking him as rather weak and meak try to overpower him. This is what happened with Ram. Although incarnation of Vishnu Bhagwan, he had been living in the forests in a small ashram and his might could not be judged by someone who did not know Ram as such. This was Inder's son, who once having seen Ram decorating Sita with flowers in the forest tried to do mischief with Sita. He came as crow and bite Sita at her leg. Ram seeing blood oozing out from the leg and with a view to teach the crow a lesson, threw an arrow behind him. The crow went to his father but Inder refused to give him refuge against Ram. He went to Brahma etc. but all refused. Ultimately Narad told him to go back to Ram and to seek his pardon. He did accordingly and Ram, although should have killed him keeping his crime in view, allowed the arrow to spoil his one eye. So Ram left him one-eyed. Here the poet wants to impress—

(1) In worldly life one should behave with others as per their might and not underestimate anyone ;

(2) Should behave with ladies in a benign way and not try to do any mischief towards them.

(3) Even with the greatest fault having been committed by someone, the great persons try to excuse him when he realised having committed the fault.

Apart from above worldly lesson, which the poet desires to impart, he wants to emphasise the spiritual value of the incident in telling that anyone who annoys Ram, has no place to live in the universe, and it is only Ram, who could help in such a situation and keeping in view the realisation of fault, Ram does award a penalty milder than the guilt caused. Similar is the position of anti-grahas. The effect of the grahas gets reduced on the person putting himself to vrat, (व्रत) worship etc. but the effect is not fully annihilated as after all this is what has to be faced according to the theory of karma. Inder's son sought refuge everywhere but no one even dared ask him to sit with him—

काहूँ बैठन कहा न ओही, राखि को सकइ राम कर द्रोही।

and on submission, Ram forgives the person inspite of the great sin having been committed by him :

कीन्ह मोह बस द्रोह, जद्यपि तेहि कर वध उचित,
प्रभु छाड़ेउ करि छोह, को कृपाल रघुवीर सम।

Ram then having realised that many people had known his reality, thought he should go further deep in forests to meet the rishis, who lived there and also to get them also relieved from the cruelty caused to them by the rakshasas—the jobs for which Ram had come in the universe. After leaving Chitrakut ashram, Ram first went to Rishi Atri's ashram. Ram and Lakshman paid respects and the rishi embraced them and brought them to his ashram. He worshipped Ram and gave something to eat. Here a rishi worshipping Ram seems against protocol but

(1) Rishi knew that Ram was almighty God and, therefore, he had to worship him not as Ram but as God incarnate; and

(2) the word 'पूजा' may be for the purpose of अतिथि पूजा, (respect for the guest). In view of above,the rishi after giving Ram appropriate seat, praised him as God incarnate and requested not to forget him ever. Sita paid respects to rishi's wife Anusuya, who gave her blessings and took her to the ashram. She gave Sita very costly ornaments and taught her the dharam of a wife. She told her and the poet through her wants to impress upon all women what they should do in the universe. She told that father, mother and brothers are all well wishers but they can help to some extent only whereas the husband is always in for the help of the wife. Therefore, wife should also be fully devoted to him in all times and particularly in rainy days because a person's courage, religion, dharam, friendship and the wife can be tested only in bad days.

धीरज धर्म मित्र अरु नारी, आपद काल परखिअहिं चारी।

Anusuya then goes on to tell that there are four kinds of women, who claim to be devoted to their husbands, in the world :

(1) In the first category are those, who never think of any other man even in dreams; (उत्तम)

(2) In the second place are those (मध्यम), who treat the other persons as their brothers (of the same age); as father (being older in age); and sons (being younger in age).

(3) In the third category (निकृष्ट) are those, who though have liking for other persons but save themselves because of the fear of religion and the dynastic image.

(4) The fourth category (अधम) of women are those, who pretend to be devoted to the husband because of fear from him or because they could not get a chance to serve others.

And the woman, who deceives the husband and love other persons deserves all kind of punishment. Sita was happy to hear all this. Ram then asked for rishi's permission to go to some other forests to carry on his job elsewhere too. He requested the rishi to continue to be kind towards him. This Ram had sought as a human being but then the rishi taking him as almighty requested him to be kind towards him as none of gods was his equal in being kind to the poors and meaks. As usual the rishi could not say 'yes' to Ram on his request for going from that place. Ram then paid respects to rishi and left.

While going again Ram, Lakshman and Sita were in the same order—Ram in forefront followed by Sita and then Lakshman as if the trio representing Brahma, Maya and Jeeva were going. On the way Viradh Rakshas appeared, who was killed by Ram and awarded paramgati (परमगति).

Ram accompanied by Sita and Lakshman reached the ashram of Darbhanga Rishi. They paid respects to muni and muni in his heart worshipped Ram as his God. He told that Brahma had told him that Vishnu as Ram would come to universe and would come to his ashram. He had been awaiting for that day which had now come. He said, however, that Ram's coming over there was not a favour for him but the God had kept his promise only and should now oblige him to stay with him till he was relieved of this life and joined the God, spiritually. This incident of Ram and Darbhanga indicates :

(1) Ram paying respects to muni as they are respectable to any human being.

(2) Muni gives blessings as munis usually do. Then muni worships Ram as his God particularly since he, as as per Brahma's boon, had been awaiting for Vishnu to come as incarnate as Ram and visit muni's ashram.

(3) Although he felt obliged on Ram's arrival there but the muni expected something more from him and, therefore, told Ram that his visit to the ashram was in fulfilment of his promise and his obligation on him would be to stay there till he, leaving this body, joined him spiritually.

(4) In other words requesting Ram to bless him the paramgati (परमगति).

(5) Ram did wait there and awarded paramgati to his bhakta.

(6) This is Ram's benevolent treatment towards all his bhaktas, like Rishi Darbhanga, who had bequeathed all his yagya, tap etc. for the sake of attaining Ram's bhakti.

(7) Having said all this, the muni burnt himself in yogagni meaning thereby that life and death were in the hands of our rishis by virtue of their attainments through tapasya.

Ram left Darbhanga Rishi's ashram and on his way further, Ram saw a big heap of human skeletons. On enquiry, he came to know that the heap comprised of the rishis' skeletons, which were the remnants of the human beings killed and eaten away by rakshasas. Ram hearing it, announced that he would make the universe free of rakshasas—

निसिचरहीन करउँ महि भुज उठाइ पन कीन्ह,
सकल मुनिन्ह के आश्रमन्हि जाइ जाइ सुख दीन।

As already indicated, Vishnu had come incarnate as Ram with the purpose of :

(1) Annihilating the rakshasas from the universe and.
(2) Granting satisfaction to his bhaktas by his darshan in their respective ashrams.
(3) This was repeatedly announced by Ram and with this purpose in view only he accepted to go to forests
(4) Ram pronounced these jobs by raising his hands. In protocolic parlance pronouncing anything by raising hands signifies confirmation of his promise and making it known to all that he had made this promise in presence of all available there so that he did not have a go back from the promise.

In the forest nearby was Muni Suteekshan's ashram. When the muni came to know of Ram having come nearby, he was very happy. He told all that he did not have so many virtues as may warrant Ram coming to his ashram but the only good thing in him was that apart from Ram he did not believe in any other god and this very thinking may have forced Ram to come to his ashram.

This is bhakta's submission to his God. He was lost in thinking about Ram and although left for receiving Ram, he was not aware of where he was going and for what purpose. Ram had been seeing all this by hiding himself and seeing the muni completely absorbed in his bhakti. Ram appeared in his heart as a raja and subsequently appeared before him but muni did not come to his senses and continued to be lost. Ram then appeared in his heart as Vishnu and then immediately he opened his eyes and saw Ram, Lakshman and Sita standing before him. He paid respects to Ram before Ram could pay respects to the muni as here muni was already lost in bhakti of Ram and having found him the muni had to pay respects to Ram as his God. Ram then picked him up and embraced. Muni took him to his Ashram and worshipped him in several ways and praised him as per spontaneous spiritual protocol between the Bhagwan and bhakta.

जे जानहिं ते जानहुँ स्वामी, सगुन अगुन उर अन्तरजामी,
जो कोसलपति राजिव नयना, करउ सो राम हृदय मम अयना।

Rishi Suteekshan's bhakti for Ram shows that (1) One should serve only one God. In this case Suteekshan was devoted to Ram who was the son of Raja Dasrath and (2) Should have complete submission to him and on his attainment forget every other thing of the universe, including oneself. Ram embraced the muni and told him that he was quite happy with his devotion and asked him to ask for any boon. But here again muni told him that he had never thought of asking for any boon and requested for giving him as considered apt by Ram. Ram blessed him with bhakti, gyan, vairagya and all other virtues but then the muni thought that Ram had given all the above things but not himself as desired by him. So he requested Ram to get seated in his heart alongwith Sita and Lakshman in the shape as they appeared before him. Ram blessed him with his desire and then proceeded further to the ashram of Kumbhaj muni accompanied by muni Suteekshan. Suteekshan apprised Kumbhaj Rishi of Ram's arrival. Kumbhaj (Agast) muni immediately got up and ran to receive Ram and others. Ram and Lakshman paid respects to the muni and the muni embraced them. The muni after asking for the well being asked Ram and Lakshman to have their seats. Here in meeting Darbhanga, Suteekshan and Agast munis one thing is clear that Darbhanga and Suteekshan were over involved and devoted to Ram being comparatively smaller than muni Agast, who had other involvements also. Therefore, muni Darbhanga and Suteekshan paid respects to Ram as their overall Lord before Ram could pay respects to them as munis. But on the contrary Agast gave a chance to Ram and Lakshman to pay their respects for the muni and muni gave them ashirwad. It is also clear that it was munis Darbhanga and Suteekshan, who had to only receive from Ram and not to give anything to him but for Agast, it was otherwise. He was a very deep rooted and knowledgeable muni and Ram had to get from him a lot for fulfilling the purpose of annihilation of rakshasas. Muni Agast gave him proper armaments and mantras for this purpose. Agast muni was, therefore, apart from being a muni wishing to have Ram's darshan, was also a guru to him and, therefore, was subject to the protocol as guru and pupil. Ram, therefore, paid him respects first. Ram was an almighty God also for Agast muni. So in his ashram, the muni also worshipped him as his God—"पुनि करि बहु प्रकार प्रभु पूजा". After the mutual respects and pooja, Ram sat amidst all rishis of the ashram facing each other.

मुनि समूह महं बैठे सन्मुख सब की ओर,
सरद इन्दु तन चितवत मानहुँ निकर चकोर।

Here it is not evident how Ram could sit amidst all rishis and facing towards each one of them because in whatever way one sits, he faces some, on the side of some and behind some. Since Ram can be better known and one can be closer to Ram only when one is face to face with him and not in any other way, Ram had to be face to face to each one of them rather than blessing some and disappointing others as it would have been an action of partiality which Ram could not afford. He was equally benevolent to all the rishis. He, therefore, made out a pose according to which he appeared facing each one.

After this, Ram told muni that there was nothing which was not known to him e.g. the purpose of Vishnu coming as incarnate of Ram and then Ram coming to the ashram of Agast muni. Ram then requested for such a mantra and arms being given to him as may help in the killing of all rakshasas. For a bhakta, it was apt to be proud on Ram himself begging for anything from him. However, Muni Agast mildly told him that whatever he had, had been blessed by God (i.e. Him) only and there was no obligation on his part in giving to Ram whatever was his own only. It would just amount to returning what he had taken from God and kept for him all the time so far. This is the mutual protocol between a guru and pupil and Ram and bhakta. The muni first asked for a boon from him to be with him always alongwith Sita and Lakshman and for granting him his bhakti. He told Ram that he had already been kind enough to grace Chitrakut and Dandak forests and now he should proceed to Panchwati where the rakshasas had been harassing the rishis. For this purpose, he also gave to him his collection of arms from various gods etc. Ram, Lakshman and Sita accordingly went and settled in Panchwati and made it comfortable for munis to live and do their pooja/tapsya free from any fear of rakshasas.

Whenever Ram had settled and was living comfortably, the poet utilises the occasion for the welfare of the people. Here also he had Lakshman to request Ram to tell him about gyan, vairagya, maya and bhakti. Seeing Ram being worshipped by rishis, Lakshman was confused whether he should treat him as his master, elder brother or as God. Such things could be asked when one is comfortably placed. So Lakshman also was in search of such an occasion and he asked for such a deliberation finding Ram sitting peacefully one day in Panchwati :

एक बार प्रभु सुख आसीना, लछिमन बचन कहे छलहीना,
सुर नर मुनि सचराचर साईं, मैं पूछउँ निज प्रभु की नाईं।
मोहि समुझाइ कहहु सोइ देवा, सब तजि करौं चरन रज सेवा।
कहहु ज्ञान विराग अरु माया, कहहु सो भगति करहु जेहिं दाया।
ईश्वर जीव भेद प्रभु सकल कहौ समुझाइ,
जातें होई चरन रति सोक मोह भ्रम जाइ।

Lakshman had so for been serving Ram as his elder brother but seeing the rishis worshipping him and considering him as almighty God, Lakshman found a chance to ask Ram the difference in Ishwar and jeeva and gyan, vairagya and maya. Ram told in brief that the entire universe is run by the almighty on the basis of 'my' and 'yours'.

मैं और मोर तोर तैं माया, जेहिं बस कीन्हे जीव निकाया।

This 'concept' of 'me', 'my', 'mine' and 'you' and 'your' is in other words the 'maya' by which the almighty makes everyone live in this universe. This is my hand, this is my heart, this is my son, this is my wife, this is my money and conversely it is you, yours etc. is the 'maya' under whose influence the man lives and the moment he is above these considerations, he gets salvation (मोक्ष) and becomes a part of the almighty himself. Gyan is when there is no pride and when one sees everyone as a symbol of Brahma himself. Vairagya is the condition of a person when he leaves all ambitions and leisures and pleasures. Jeeva is one, who does not know himself, the God and his 'maya'. The One, who controls 'maya' is 'Ishwar'. One attains vairagya by dharam, and gyan by yoga but what pleases God most is the bhakti. Bhakti is independent and is not dependant on any other cult whereas even gyan and vairagya are under bhakti itself and if one has attained bhakti, he has attained everything. After attainment of bhakti, one becomes dependent only on him by his heart, actions and speech, and he worships him without any consideration.

बचन करम मन मोर गति भजनु करहिं निःकाम,
तिन्ह के हृदय कमल महुँ करउँ सदा विश्राम।

This is the spiritual protocol indicating the protocolic relation between Braham, Jeeva and Maya as pronounced by none else than Ram only. This eradicated the confusion in the mind of Lakshman and Lakshman having heard bhakti-jog from Ram himself paid respects to Ram. In this way hereafter Ram had been pronouncing the ethics of gyan and vairagya to Lakshman.

One day Sarupnakha, the sister of Ravan came to Panchwati and saw Ram and Lakshman. She felt attracted towards them and could not control herself. The poet says that for a rakshasni like Sarupnakha, there was no sense of any relation between her and her father, brother or son and whosoever she found charming, she would fell in love for him. She dressed herself as a beautiful lady and went to Ram and proposed herself for marriage.. On Ram telling that he was already married, she went to Lakshman but then Lakshman told that he was the sewak of Ram and that she would not be happy in marrying a sewak. He also told that Ram was competent even to have more than one wife—

सुन्दरि सुन मैं उन्हकर दासा पराधीन नहिं तोर सुपासा।
प्रभु समर्थ कोसलपुर राजा, जो कुछ करहिं उनहि सब छाजा!

from protocol point of view, the poet has told that :

(1) The social ethics of respect for father, mother, brother, son etc. were not cared for by the rakshasas. The poet has gone to the extent of saying that Sarupnakha had been making love, with whomsoever she liked even if it were her father, brother or son.

(2) Lakshman was a sewak only and he was aware of the sewakdharam. He, therefore, alerted Sarupnakha that a lady like her could not do by marrying a sewak as in that case she would not be able to enjoy the married life.

(3) Ram was the raja of Kaushalpur (Awadh). Although impliedly the poet had indicated at the time of Bharat's meeting with Ram in forests and Ram giving him his shoes (letter of authority) that Ram had been referred by all as the Raja of Awadh and Bharat had been managing the affairs of the kingdom as the lieutenant of Ram only under his authority. Here Lakshman had clearly stated that Ram was the Raja of Awadh.

(4) "प्रभु समर्थ" would indicate that in those days only the raja was competent to have more than one wife. Raja Dasrath had three or even more. In Pandvas also Arjun, Bhim etc. had more than one wife. For others, perhaps, the 'rule of one wife' was prevalent.

(5) In the modern concept of a king, the dictum goes that "king can do no wrong" and the king is "immune from all laws". In Ram Kal too this dictum held good as pronounced by Lakshman in saying that for a raja "जो कुछ करहिं उनहिं सब छाजा।" "Whatever he did is apt for him."

(6) For a sewak, if he observes all protocol, there is no leisure or pleasure.

(7) Taking Sarupnakha as a lady, Ram and Lakshman had not been assaulting her as per laid down dharam but then these ethics could not be withstood when Sarupnakha came to her realself as a rakshas and started frightening Sita. There was no way out for Lakshman except to punish her.

तब खिसिआनि राम पहिं गई, रूप भयंकर प्रगटत भई।

It was then only that Lakshman cut her nose and ears.

(8) Ram knew she was the sister of Ravan and Ram had come to forests to annihilate all rakshasas. There were many rakshasas in that area. Ram wanted to make them know that he had come to finish them all but then he did not want to start war first. On Sarupnakha's behaviour, he was forced to make his presence felt to all the rakshasas in that area.

And as expected, she went to her brothers Khar and Dooshan, who were nearby and aroused them against Ram and Lakshman. Being the rakshas kings of the area, they could not tolerate it and immediately set out to give them a fight. As already indicated, according to Hindu belief good or bad omens tell of the happenings in future. When Khar-Dooshan started for battle, bad omens took place but being the rakshasas, they did not care for these bad omens. Good/bad omens are taken care of by purer persons only. Seeing the force coming, Ram immediately worked out a war strategy. He sent Lakshman with Sita in the closeby cave and himself took position. He told Lakshman to be careful and remain alert in protecting Sita against the rakshasas if anyone reached there as also keep himself aware of what was happening in the battle. Seeing Ram, the rakshasas were also down with his charm and could not straightaway start fighting and said—"वध लायक नहिं पुरुष अनूपा." Khar asked Ram to hand over his wife and they would permit him to go to his house without being killed in the battle, which they thought was imminent if battle took place. He sent his messenger to Ram and asked him to make him aware of what Ram replied. Ram told that he being an kshatri had been searching the chances of such battles and was, therefore, not afraid of giving a fight. He also said in case Khar-Dooshan were not able to face him, then they could return home and as per protocol of war, he would not kill anyone going back from the battle field.

जौं न होइ बल घर फिरि जाहू, समर बिमुख मैं हतउँ न काहू।

Here the poet has shown that before starting war, a messenger was sent for not resorting to war with certain conditions and if those conditions were acceptable the war could be avoided and also in case one of the party to the war phased themselves out from the battle, then the other party would not attack and kill them. So perfect were the laws of war in those days.

On the messenger's return, fierce battle started. In the battle, one side attacks first and the other defends. On Ram's attack, the sainiks of Khar-Dooshan started running back to save their lives. But as per war strategy, Khar-Dooshan warned them that in case anyone ran away from battle field, he would be killed by them.

भए क्रुद्ध तीनिउ भाइ, जो भागि रन ते जाइ,
तेहि वधव हम निज पानि, फिरे मरन मन मंहु ठानि।

Then the running sainiks came back to fight taking it for certain that they had to die either in battle field or by Khar-Dooshan if they ran away from the battle field. Khar-Dooshan and entire force were killed. At the time of their death they said "Ram" "Ram" and because of that Ram granted them 'Nirvan'. The battle was over and the gods were happy. This was the first big battle in which so many important rakshasas had been killed eversince Ram had come to forests. Then Lakshman came back with Sita and paid respects to Ram. Ram continued doing such actions in Panchwati.

Then having seen the rakshasas dead, Sarupnakha went to Ravan and enraged him and through her also the poet has been able to pronounce the successful policy of a ruler.

(1) The king's jobs are to care for the protection of his kingdom and keep on adding to the treasure.

(2) The king should not get lost in drinks or keep lying down.

(3) The king should keep vigil and alertness lest any enemy should suddenly attack him.

(4) One cannot be successful in ruling without ethics; in earning wealth without religious tanets; in doing goo l

works without submission to almighty; in attaining education without proper intellectual development; in becoming sanyasi and at the same time involving oneself in worldly leisures; a raja without good advisers etc.

(5) One should not overlook the enemy thinking that he is quite weak. Similarly one should not ignore ailment, fire, snake thinking that these would do no harm.

On Ravan's asking, Sarupnakha narrated the entire incident that two rajkumars from Awadh had come to forests with the intention of killing all the rakshasas on earth. Under their protection, the munis were doing their pooja fearlessly. They also had a very beautiful woman with them. The younger had cut her nose and ears. She did not tell the entire happening properly that she had proposed herself to them and then only on insisting on the same even without their agreeing to the proposal, the rajkumar was forced to cut the nose and ears. The poet has tried to indicate that such persons should not be believed on their face value without ascertaining the actual facts. Ravan too, being a clever politician laughed it away but only when she told that Khar, Dooshan, Tisira and their army had been killed by one of the rajkumars in battle that Ravan became serious as Khar, Dooshan etc. had been equally brave and could not be easily killed by any ordinary rajkumar.

खर दूषण तिसिरा कर घाता, सुनि दस सीस जरे सब गाता।

Ravan calmed her down by pronouncing his bravery and went to his mahal but he was upset thinking that no god, human being or rakshas could even dare touch his ordinary servant what to speak of Khar, Dooshan etc., who were equal to him in bravery and no body could kill them except the God almighty. If God has come incarnate to annihilate the rakshashas from the earth, then he would perforce develop enmity with him so that by having been killed by him, he could have 'mukti' as he could not worship God having been involved in all vices and if he is ordinary human being then he would defeat him in battlefield. This would indicate that Ravan had prudently understood Ram as incarnate of God almighty and had spontenously become·his bhakta but since it was not possible for him to do traditional bhakti, he adopted the other way of developing enmity with him. Ram had somewhere else also said that anyone who keeps him in mind, attains mukti. Even an enemy, although out of fear, keeps thinking of him in his heart and, therefore, becomes his bhakta and entitled to mukti.

खर दूषण मोहिं सम बलवंता, तिन्हहि को मारइ बिनु भगवन्ता।
तौ मैं जाइ बैरु हठि करऊँ, प्रभु सर प्राण तजें भव तरऊँ।
होइहि भजनु न तामस देहा, मन क्रम बचन मंत्र दृढ़ एहा।

Ravan reached this decision and concluded to abide by this decision by heart, action and speech. Having decided this, he made a plan to proceed further. After one becomes bhakta, next stage for him is to attain bhakti. This could have been possible through some guru only. He could think of Marich. Ever since Marich had been sent away to Lanka by an arrow of Ram from Vishwamitra's yagya bhoomi, Marich had become Rambhakta. Infact Marich was already a Rambhakta and had come to have darshan of Ram in Vishwamitra's Yagya and being in doubt, Ram threw him away by a blunt arrow and did not kill him. Therefore, only a Rambhakta could be engaged as a guru and Ravan could immediately locate him for this purpose. He immediately went to him.

On the other side, Ram had thought of further implications of the killing of Khar-Dooshan etc. as the rakshasas were not going to swallow this defeat, particularly the rakshasas like Ravan, who had even defeated the gods. He could know that Sita's presence with him was a weak point and any time in loneliness, Sita could be kidnapped by rakshasas. He, therefore, told her to get absorbed in fire (Agni) till he annihilated all rakshasas and would there after reclaim her from fire.

सुनहु प्रिया व्रत रुचिर सुसीला, मैं कछु करबि ललित नर लीला।
तुम्ह पावक महुं करहु निवासा, जौ लगि करौं निसाचर नासा।

Sita accordingly got herself absorbed in fire and a semblance of Sita only existed in the ashram. Since at that time Lakshman had gone to bring some eatables and the entire proceeds had been cooked up in his absence, he could not know it at all. This shows that the raja had to keep some of his actions secret even from his closest persons. The concept of secrecy prevails in the government working even on date. As already indicated, Ravan went to Marich's ashram and paid respects and spoke very sweetly :

दसमुख गयउ जहां मारीचा, नाइ माथ स्वारथ रत नीचा।

Here the poet has expressed the fulfilment of following tanets of protocol :

(1) Ravan became Ram's bhakta immediately after thinking that he was God incarnate.

(2) Now he could reach God either after overpowering 'maya' or through the route of bhakti.

(3) This could be advised by a guru only. He, therefore, went to Marich, treating him as his guru in his mind as Marich was a Rambhakta and he could not find anyone better than him to be his guru.

(4) Ravan was a mighty king and could have called him in Lanka but the protocol provided that the pupil should go to guru and guru should not be called to his house, howsoever mighty the pupil might be.

(5) After going to guru's ashram, the pupil has to pay respects to him and not the vice versa, particularly where one's self interest was involved.

(6) Ravan, therefore, paid respects to Marich by bowing down.

(7) The poet warns that bowing down of a mean person ultimately result in causing harm only.

(8) Marich, however, worshipped Ravan as after all he was a very mighty king of the area and the king had to be worshipped when he came to the ashram of his people.

(9) After worshipping, Marich respectfully asked for the reason of his coming there and why he was so upset as also why he had come alone as according to the political protocol the king was always escorted by armymen and others close to him, whenever he went out of the rajmahal. Therefore, Ravan's arrival alone was something unusual. Marich had cleverly asked for all these in one sentence.

Ravan narrated the entire episode to him. While narrating, however, Ravan had expressed his pride too so that Marich could not think that he was a meak man and could handle him in that way. Ravan then explained to him his plan of Marich becoming a golden deer and going to Ram's ashram. Ram would go out to hunt him and in his absence Ravan could kidnap Sita. As already indicated, to reach Braham either one has to overpower 'maya' or through bhakti. Sita was the incarnate of these both. Ravan, therefore, wanted to have Sita as maya or bhakti. Marich told Ravan that Ram, who had thrown him at a distance of 400 miles, killed Tadka and Subahoo and broke Shiv dhanush, is not an ordinary person and if he wished the well-being of his dynasty then he should not develope enmity with Ram and forget about taking any revenge. But the more Marich told Ravan about his divinely actions, the more he was convinced of his thinking of developing enmity with him so that by being killed by him, he attained mukti. Ravan then frightened Marich of death if he did not obey him. Thinking his death as definite, he preferred to be killed by Ram.

उतरु देत मोहि वधव अभागें, कस न मरौं रघुपति सर लागें।
और
मन अति हरष जनाव न तेही, आजु देखिहउँ परम सनेही।

A bhakta cannot wish for anything else than the darshan of his God and would like to be killed by him, only.

मम पाछें धर धावत धरें सरासन बान
फिरि फिरि प्रभुहिं बिलोकिहऊँ धन्य न मो सम आन।

And accordingly he became golden deer and went near Ram's Ashram. Sita on seeing the golden deer requested Ram to kill it so that they could have its Mrigchhala (मृगछाला). Ram knew all behind the golden deer but he got up with a view to make Ravan's planning successful leading to his and his family's annihilation as requested by the gods. As a matter of abundant caution, as any ordinary man would do, Ram asked Lakshman to be alert in his absence as many rakshasas were there around the ashram.

सीता केरि करेहु रखवारी, बुधि बिबेक बल समय विचारी।

Ram asked Lakshman to be alert in the forest and use his intelligence, alertness, force and take action as demanded by the occasion. For protecting anything from the enemy one has only to use intelligence first, then the alertness and if these both fail then use the force. This is how the battle strategy has to be worked out too by a raja in fighting against another raja. Ram went behind the deer. The deer took Ram to a distant place. Ram then killed him by his arrow. While falling down, the deer proclaimed Lakshman and then Ram as per plan to confuse Sita and Lakshman. Sita knew the entire drama and asked Lakshman to go for helping Ram, who seemed to be in trouble. Lakshman, being obedient to Ram and Ram having ordered him to be alert in protecting Sita against rakshasas, could not leave the ashram. Further, he had since known that Ram was almighty God and could not have any fear from a deer. He politely told Sita all this but then Sita alleged Lakshman having some bad intentions. Lakshman had then to think and then entrusting Sita's protection to the forest's god, he proceeded in the direction of the deer.

मरम बचन जब सीता बोला हरि प्रेरित लछिमन मन डोला।

Lakshman having been very obedient to Ram, his duty, as a matter of protocol, was to remain in ashram for the sake of Sita's protection and he was sticking to the same particularly when he knew that Ram could not have fear from anyone. But then on Sita alleging him of bad intention, Lakshman got confused. This again was what Ram wanted and it was only his 'maya' which forced Sita to abuse Lakshman and Lakshman to decide to proceed where Marich (deer) had gone.

As planned seeing none at the ashram except Sita, Ravan came there in the garb of a sadhu. Ravan had already become Ram's bhakta. He first attained gyan, then guru (Marich) and now to attain bhakti, he became a sanyasi as one cannot reach Ram without renunciating the worldly ambitions. So Ravan in the third stage of process, became a sanyasi to overpower maya or attain bhakti through the medium of Sita. Ravan, whose very name upset everyone reached Ram's ashram with great fear lest Ram or Lakshman should come there. It was because although he had become Ram's bhakta and Ram's bhakta did not have to have any fear of anyone, but the entire scheme made out by him to deceive his own God Ram, made him so. In other words Ram's opponent cannot have peace at all and always remains upset. In this process one loses, one's intelligence, alertness and force, which are necessary for any kshatriya to face the enemy in battle. Ram had also advised Lakshman to use these in protecting Sita against rakshasas. On reaching Ram's ashram, he narrated several pauranic stories etc., showed political diplomacy; his affection and ultimately his threat. Ravan at first wanted to please Sita, the bhakti, by affection, prem etc. but when Ravan saw that these did not work on her then he thought of overpowering her, not as bhakti because bhakti cannot be attained by force, but as 'maya'. To reach Braham one has to either have the process of bhakti or maya. So Ravan basically being a rakshas, could not continue to assuage Sita with bhakti as from his speech and actions Sita had known him being a rakshas. Having realised that Sita had since known him, he came in his real form of Ravan. Sita at first got frightened but then took courage and told him that Ram would be coming soon and he would have to pay for his action by losing his life. Ravan became furious (after all the rakshas in Ravana could not withstand all that Sita had said). But then before taking further action he paid respects to Sita in his heart.

मन महुँ चरण बंदि सुख माना।

This showed the bhakta within Ravan. He, as already indicated, found himself unsuccessful to reach Ram through bhakti. As he could not attain Sita as bhakti, the next alternative available was to use force to overpower 'maya'. This process could be easily done by a forceful rakshas. But still before adopting the force process, he paid respects to Sita. He picked up Sita by force and made her sit in the plane and flew in the sky although everytime he was having fear. This psychologically is the position of any person, who tries to deceive God knowing full well that he knew it all, because of his inner guilt. Sita had been crying. Sita could have cursed (श्राप) the rakshas but firstly she was not real Sita but only a semblance and semblance cannot have purity of passing any curse on anyone and secondly this had all been planned by Ram and Sita as already indicated. Her crying was just to show how an ordinary person would feel in the situation. She, while crying said Lakshman was not at fault and she had unnecessarily been angry with him and abused him.

On the way in the sky was Jatayu. He had already met Ram and Sita in the forests. He listened to the cry of Sita and recognised it was Sita only and the rakshas had kidnapped her. Jatayu encouraged Sita and attacked Ravan. Ravan recognised him. On Jayatu's attack, Ravan fell down and became unconscious but when he came to senses, he cut one of Jatayu's wings. Jatayu fell on earth. Ravan proceeded further but he was still not without fear. On the way, Sita threw some clothes seeing some vanars on the hillock. Ravan reached Lanka and made Sita sit under one Ashoka tree. Ravan expressed his devotion as also frightened her. This means he was still not clear whether to adopt the 'marg' (मार्ग) of bhakti or that of overpowering 'maya' to reach the almighty. He was, therefore, adopting alternatively both the methods. Ultimately he made all arrangements for her comfort and established her under Ashoka tree. Ravan's further devotion to the wife of Ram is expressed here in the sense :

(1) On reaching ashram and before picking up Sita, Ravan at first adopted the process of bhakti to reach Ram and accordingly went to her as a sanyasi and narrated several pauranic stories.

(2) When Ravan felt that from his speech and other actions, Sita had known that he was not a sanyasi but was only posing to be so, he adopted the other process of overpowering 'maya', to reach Ram and accordingly to overpower he frightened Sita and showed her his realself.

(3) Since Ravan was guilty of doing all this in the absence of Ram and Lakshman, he had himself been

under fear of either of them coming in. The rakshasas by nature do not have any guilt or fear per se but in Ravan, gyan had developed that is why he was subjected by fear too while doing a wrong thing as a lawyer cannot commit crime as he would always be remembering the particular provision of penal code applicable in having committed crime and caught.

(4) Before picking Sita up and boarding her in his plane, Ravan paid her his respects.

मन महुँ चरन बंदि सुख माना।

and not only paid respects but was happy in paying his respects for her. This anyone would (particularly a rakshas of Ravan's status) do only when one had developed in his heart some devotion.

(5) Even while carrying her in his plane, Ravan had all the time fear of whether what he had done was correct or not. Even when Jatayu met him on way and challenged him, Ravan was feeling shaky otherwise how an eagle could challenge Ravan and Ravan becoming shaky on a challenge from a bird only.

(6) Till he reached Lanka, Ravan had been trying both the processes of bhakti by showing her love and overpowering maya by frightening her as Sita was incarnate of both and Ravan knew by dint of having gained gyan that either of the two processes could make him reach Ram.

(7) Ravan made Sita establish under an Ashoka tree as it is said that under Ashoka tree one forgets all his annoyance and ailments and attains whatever is wished. Ravan having won all the gods did have the luxury of owning Ashoka trees.

(8) Ravan had made all arrangements of comfort to Sita while establishing her under the Ashoka tree even if something was not provided by the sacred tree.

(9) Sita had to suffer because she lost confidence in Lakshman and abused him. Except that Ram and Sita had already planned it like this, how could it be possible that having known Lakshman so long as her

complete devotee, she could lose confidence and rebuke him and send him away leaving her to be alone in the ashram. On the contrary, a lady would feel more unsafe in the forest and would have ordinarily liked Lakshman to stay with her and not to leave her alone.

(10) Sita had known Ram that of all the beings in the universe, how he could have bad time while hunting a mere deer.

(11) Although Lakshman had felt that calling 'Lakshman' 'Ram' by name by Marich was a drama by the rakshasas and Ram would not have been in trouble and he told Sita so but he had to leave the ashram in disobedience of Ram's orders to keep Sita protected in the ashram from rakshasas after weighing whether in the situation he should proceed for Ram's help in disobedience of Ram's order or to bear the abuses of Sita. Being very dutiful and devotee to both Ram and Sita, he preferred to face the fury of Ram by disobeying his order rather than the curse and abuse of Sita and went away from the ashram. But since Sita's protection was primary duty for him and Ram's return after killing the deer was definite, Lakshman should have opted to stay back till Ram's return bearing Sita's abuses and on Ram's return which was certain, Sita would have also felt sorry for what she had thought about Lakshman.

(12) When Ram saw Lakshman coming to him leaving Sita alone, he externally showed fear of Sita having been kidnapped by rakshasas.

रघुपति अनुजहि आवत देखी, बाह्य चिंता कीन्हि विशेषी।

It means Ram knew this all to happen and only as an ordinary human being showed his fear. Poor Lakshman was unnecessarily being pulled between Ram and Sita although they both were doing this as a drama but Lakshman was not aware of all these tactics of God.

(13) Ram also expressed anger on Lakshman by saying :

जनकसुता परिहरिहु अकेली, आयहु तात बचन मम पेली।

This was perhaps, the first time that Lakshman had to disobey Ram but then Ram had indirectly given Lakshman power to act as the situation warranted in the ashram in his absence.

सीता केरि करेहु रखवारी, बुधि विवेक बल समय बिचारी।

So Lakshman took the decision of leaving Sita in ashram alone as warranted by the situation in which Sita started abusing him and alleging something Lakshman could never think of in respect of Sita, whom he considered more than his mother. Lakshman in reply respectfully told Ram also what had happened.

गहि पद कमल अनुज कर जोरी, कहेउ नाथ कछु मोहि न खोरी।

Having gone to ashram and not finding Sita there, Ram became upset and started asking everyone if he had seen Sita or knew her whereabouts. In this quest, he even requested the non-beings to tell about the whereabouts of Sita. Lakshman, who only was available then did not lose courage and persuaded Ram that Sita would be found and not to worry and think of further course of action. Although Ram was doing all this to appear like a human being, Lakshman was actually in for the real sadness. Ram was crying in absence of Sita in such a way that the poet was forced to compare him to a great separatee or very passionate person lost in love of his wife. Poet has also affirmed that Ram had been doing this as any human being would have done in the situation.

मनुज चरित कर अज अविनासी।

On the way Ram saw Jatayu remembering Ram's name. Ram took him up in his lap as protocol would provide for God to act for his bhakta in case of ailment. On Ram's touching him, he lost all his ailment. Jatayu told that Ravan had taken away Sita and he only had put Jatayu to this condition. He told that he was keeping himself alive to tell him all that had happened. Ram offered him further life if he chose so but then a bhakta could never think of living further rather than leaving the universe in the lap of the almighty.

सो मम लोचन गोचर आगें, राखौं देह नाथ केहि खाँगे।

Ram granted him 'mukti' but thought that in swarag, Jatayu would tell his father Dasrath about the kidnapping of Sita. Ram had brought Sita with him to forests despite Dasrath's request to leave her back in Awadh, obviously with the assurance of protecting her against any danger in forests and now knowing that Sita had been kidnapped, Raja Dasrath would feel annoyed and also would come to know of the weakness of Ram in not having been able to protect her. So he requested Jatayu not to tell Raja Dasrath about the incidence and if he really was Ram then Ravan himself would go and tell his end to Raja Dasrath i.e. Ravan and his brothers and sons would be killed by him.

सीता हरन तात जनि कहहु पिता सन जाइ
जौं मैं राम ते कुल सहित कहिहि दसानन आइ।

Such was the protocol of son towards father that the son even feared doing anything wrong in the universe after the death of the father, as would annoy him or as may have not been allowed to be done by the son by the father when he was alive and the fact that Ram had not been able to protect Sita was a matter of great shame for Ram. Ram sent Jatayu to his Loka. While dying, Jatayu paid tributes to Ram and worshipped him. Ram with his own hands performed the last rites on Jatayu's death.

"तेहि की क्रिया जथोचित निज कर कीन्ही राम"

Ram and Lakshman then proceeded further and on the way killed Kabandh rakshas. He had been cursed to be so by Durbasha rishi. On death the rakshas came to his previous form. Here the poet has through Ram himself said that brahmins are respected by him and anyone against the brahmin was not favoured by him.

सुनु गंधर्व कहउँ मैं तोही, मोही न सोहाइ ब्रह्मकुल द्रोही।
पूजिअ विप्र सील गुन हीना, सुद्र न गुन गन ज्ञान प्रबीना।

Here Ram had said that a brahmin had to be worshipped even if he had no virtues and a shudra is not to be recognised even if he had all the virtues. This appears paradoxical as Ram had always been advocating that even mortals or immortals (चर और अचर), who worshipped him were his men. He had accordingly made Nishadraj a shudra, his friend and Ravan, a pandit was now his enemy. Even at the time of Sita's swayambar, the arrangements for seating were according to capability and not according to varan.

उत्तम मध्यम नीच लघु, निज निज थल अनुहारि।

Here the arrangement was not as per brahmin, kshatriya, vaish and shudra. So much was the recognition of capability then how Ram happened to say here that a brahmin is worshippable even without any virtues and shudra, with all virtues, was not to be taken cognizance of. This must have been the reflection by the poet of the condition prevailing in his time when Manas was written. In Mohammedans' rule, brahmins had been insulted and shudras, who got converted to Islam, were given recognition in Muslim rulers' darbar. Accordingly when shudra had risen to high posts in the darbar, they got respect from public at large too, whereas brahmins, who stuck to their religion were dishonoured and punished by Mohammedans and anyone protecting them was also punished. Hakikat Rai was an example. Guru Gobind Singh's sons had been killed, Guru Tegbahadur had been killed too by Mohammedan rulers. People, therefore, had started going against the dharam and dharam protectors for the sake of saving themselves from the clutches of Mohammedan rulers. It was in these circumstances that the poet was forced to let it be known through almighty Ram himself that brahmins had to be respected and shudras had to be treated as such.

Ram and Lakshman then went to Sabri's ashram. A sadhu had given boon to Sabri that she would atttain 'mukti' when God incarnate as Ram would visit her. Now she remembered that boon and recognised Ram as the incarnate of God. She fell in his feet and she, as per protocol, worshipped them both; served food comprising as usual of roots and fruits. Ram took the same praising it as being very tasty because these were served with great devotion. Here itself Ram had gone back from what he had told Kabandh that a shudra, with all virtues, too had not to be recognised. Sabri was a shudra and still Ram (1) visited her ashram, (2) accepted her worship, (3) sat in the ashram, (4) ate the food served by her, (5) ultimately praised her as being one of the best devotees of Ram; and (6) granted her his own bhakti and 'paramgati'. It shows that whatever Ram had said against shudras and in favour of brahmins was managed by the poet as a result of what had been happening at the time Manas was written and with a view to protect brahmins and through them save Hindu dharam in those days as it was being annihilated by shudras getting converted to Islamism and at the same time to develop hatred amongst Hindus against the shudras getting converted to Islamism. Also Ram's appreciation of Sabri was with a view to show that women were equally eligible for worship. In Mohammedan period, as in Islam, the ladies were not considered eligible for bhakti or worshipping God or read religious books. Through Ram, the poet has sent the message that anyone, who is his devotee, is dear to him and even the women were eligible to do bhakti. Meera, who had become bhakta, had to face great difficulty as the women in those days were not allowed to go to temples and worship God. It was Tulsidas's time itself. Therefore, through appreciation to the devotion of Sabri by Ram himself, Tulsidas not only sent a message that women were equally eligible to worship but also encouraged Meera to continue to be Lord Krishna's bhakta.

अधम ते अधम अधम अति नारी, तिन्ह महँ मैं अति मंद अघारी।

कह रघुपति सुनु भामिनि बाता, मानउँ एक भगित कर नाता।

From this, it appears that Sabri was (1) a low shudra and then (2) a woman; and (3) a non-intelligent amongst women. But even then she said Ram had accepted her. Ram told her that for him the relation of bhakti was the only relation recognisable and no other relation worked.

जाति पांति कुल धर्म बड़ाई, धन बल परिजन गुन चतुराई।

भगतिहीन नर सोहइ कैसा, बिनु जल वारिद देखिअ जैसा।

Here Ram has come above the caste, dynasty, religion and greatness, wealth, force, his own family people, or clever persons. All these have no recognition before him unless one had the bhakti too otherwise all these were of no avail.

As already indicated, the poet has found occasion, where through Lakshman, Bharat or anyone else, he has been able to get the pronouncement of Ishwar—bhakta relationship made by Ram himself. Here Ram having told Sabri that he recognised and entertained a bhakta only, the question then arose what bhakti was, which was acceptable to Ram. Ram told nine kinds of bhakti and through anyone of these, one could reach Him. These are :

(1) Company of saints (सन्त);

(2) Getting absorbed in Ram katha (only listening of katha is not enough);

(3) Service of guru;

(4) Praising Ram (राम स्तुति) without any consideration attached;

(5) Have good faith in Ram and remembering everytime Ram's name (मंत्र);

(6) Overpowering all vices; being kind to everyone; getting desiled from worldly engagements (वैराग्य); and being a man of character;

(7) Seeing Ram everywhere in the universe and respecting saints even more than Ram himself;

(8) Being content with whatever one gets and not finding faults in others even in dream what to speak of actual day-to-day life;

(9) Leading a simple life and treating everyone without any deception; having full confidence in Ram and never getting complexed or never to be too happy or too worried. In other words if one has full confidence in Ram then he would be same in moments of great joy and sorrow.

Even if any person has one of these attainments, he would be closer to Ram, irrespective of whether he is male, female, mortal or immortal.

नव महुँ एकउ जिन्ह कें होई, नारि पुरुष सचराचर कोई।
सोई अतिसय प्रिय भामिनि मोरें, सकल प्रकार भगति दृढ़ तोरें।

Here Ram has made everyone eligible to his bhakti irrespective of whether he is male, female, from any religion, caste, dynasty or even mortals and immortals equally. Ram was almighty God knowing everything. Still to pamper his bhakta, he asked Sabri if she could give any news about Sita, even knowing how the poor lady would know it. This, however, perhaps, was with a view to show to the people at large that having attained Ram's bhakti, one attains Ram's formation and in that situation, she/he would know everything which Ram could know. This was proved to be so when Sabri advised Ram to go to Pampasur and meet Sugreev, who would be able to tell everything about Sita. After this, she got herself absorbed in Ram and burnt herself by Yogagni and Ram granted her his dham.

Ram then left that forest and proceeded further keeping Sita's separation in heart. At the same time Ram advised that how much soever one may keep raja, woman and shastra closer to oneself, one cannot have any control on them. This may be for Lakshman's consumption as he had been fully devoted to Sita but still Sita alleged him to be having bad intentions towards her. Similarly by serving raja, one may be feeling that one might get any job done through raja but raja has to weigh many things before agreeing to any proposal. In other words he is bound by religious, economic and public interest etc. before taking any decision. Shastras too one cannot claim to have mastered them as each time one goes through these, one would find newer and newer coachings from these. By crying so much in separation of Sita, Ram wished to show to the people that too much attachment with wife is not desirable as any separation, which is not in one's hands, would be suicidal for him. If there is not much attachment then one would still cross over the separation. Ram has also advised that Kamdev has the force of women in putting the human beings under his control. Therefore, to overpower Kamdev, one has to give up the passion for the women. Similarly, greed can be overpowered if one does not attach any sanctity to his wishes being fulfilled or on vanity. Also one can overpower rage if one has control over his speech. Ram has told that passion, rage or greed are the three enemies of man and these can be overpowered in the way suggested above.

तात तीनि अति प्रबल खल काम क्रोध अरु लोभ,
लोभ कें इच्छा दम्भ बल काम के केवल नारि,
क्रोध कें पुरुष बचन बल मुनिवर कहहिं विचारि।

As already indicated, the poet has chosen the correct person for proclamation of any policy statement e.g. for Ishwar-Jeeva relation, he has got it pronounced by Ram. The policy of control and character, while living in the universe, has been pronounced by some rishi/muni. Here the above policy pronouncement' of control over passion, greed and rage pertains to the human beings' worldly life. Ram has attributed this policy statement to munis (मुनिवर कहहिं विचारि) and does not say it from his authority. Similarly, while consoling Bharat to stand the sad demise of Raja Dasrath, Guru Vashisth had said :

सुनहु भरत भावी प्रबल विलखि कहत मुनिनाथ।
हानि लाभु जीवनु मरनु जसु अपजसु विधि हाथ॥

At other places too such worldly upbearing pronouncements have been made by Rishi Valmiki, Vishwamitra, Vashisth, Atri, Agast etc. This is the protocol, the poet has maintained everywhere with a view to bring confirmation/ confidence in the statement. Shiv had told Parvati, lest she should again develop some doubt about Ram's capability that Ram knew all this but he had by his behaviour shown the helplessness of the men with passion that they would cry on separation from wife which they should not and for the enlightened persons this would bring conviction in their minds that one should not have attachment with wife, which may ultimately put the person in alround despair.

गुनातीत सचराचर स्वामी, राम उमा सब अन्तरजामी।
कामिन्ह कै दीनता देखाई, धीरन्ह कै मन बिरति दृढ़ाई

Or since Ram had said that such is the feeling of munis, the poet has affirmed the same by getting the pronouncement confirmed by lord Shiv, who knew Ram most of all others. Further, seeing that even in bad times, Ram had been giving advice for the sake of benefit of all the people to be aware of passion, greed and rage, these could be controlled by human beings with the blessings of Ram only. Therefore, there is nothing in the universe except Ram.

उमा कहउँ मैं अनुभव अपना, सत हरि भजनु जगत सब सपना।

This Shiv had not just uttered but had said based on his experience. With Ram's blessings, Shiv had been able to overpower Kamdev and with Ram's maya, Sati got the doubt about Ram's bonafides which resulted in Shiv separating from Sati. With Ram's blessings, Shiv again got married to Parvati etc. Therefore all the pronouncements by Shiv were based on his experience only.

On the way Ram and Lakshman sat in comfort under a tree near a lake. Ram went on telling Lakshman many pauranic tales. At that time Narad muni, who had been watching all that had been happening, saw Ram very sad on Sita having been kidnapped and attributed this to the curse he had passed on Vishnu when Vishnu had given him the form of a Vanar as a result of which he could not marry the bride in a swayambar. At that time Narad had passed on the curse that as Narad was sad on not getting selected for marriage because Vishnu did not give him proper form, so would Vishnu on incarnation as Ram suffer and be sad on loss of his wife and vanars only will help him at that time. Thinking this, Narad thought this was the best time for him to remind Ram that this had happened because of his curse and since Ram would now have felt the gravity of such separation, he should be able to tell him why he did not give him beauty enough as to charm the bride to agree for marriage with him. In other words, one feels the gravity of any shock when one has himself to face it and for others' sadness anyone could console easily.

पर उपदेस कुशल बहुतेरे, जे आचरहिं ते नर न घनेरे।

Narad muni went to Ram and paid his respects. As per protocol, Ram should have first paid respects to muni as a human being but here the poet has made Narad to pay respects and Ram picking him up and embracing several times. This is because here Narad muni had not come to meet Ram as human being but as the incarnate of Vishnu as Narad's purpose of visit was to remind Ram of what had happened between him and Vishnu, when Narad wanted to get married.

Therefore, it was for the muni to have paid respects to Ram as incarnate of Vishnu. Ram asked for his well being and asked him to sit closeby. Lakshman, being a human being, washed the feet of the muni in respect as required by protocol between a human being and a muni. As per requirement, Narad at first praised Ram and when he saw him pleased, he requested for giving one clarification. The poet has here told the important protocol that when one goes to a big boss for some obligation then :

(1) He should see that the occasion for broaching the subject is appropriate.

(2) The mood of the person is alright.

(3) He should at first offer prayer/praise to please him.

(4) Then he should ask for permission to broach the subject.

(5) And then only should tell the purpose.

(6) If all this is done, it generally becomes obligatory for the other person to listen to the prayer and do whatever was possible to redress the grievance.

Such protocol/system should be owned by a person for day-to-day requirements.

Since Ram was already pleased when the muni praised him, Ram said that he did not keep any secret from his bhaktas.

जन सन कबहुँ कि करउँ दुराउ।
जन कहुं कछु अदेग नहिं मोरे।

Having got such an assurance, then only the muni said 'Ram' name should be above all and rest in the hearts of all bhaktas. Ram said BE AS DEMANDED (एवमस्तु). Then

Narad asked why when Vishnu himself under his 'maya' made him wish for the marriage did not allow him to get married. What could possibly be the reason for that :

तब विवाह मैं चाहउँ कीन्हा, प्रभु केहि कारन करै न दीन्हा।

Eversince, then, Narad was not successful in getting married, and he had not been able to understand why Vishnu did not permit him to get married. But since he never broached the subject before him after that, the doubt could not be removed. Therefore, Narad thought this to be appropriate time to remove his doubt as Ram was already suffering from his curse and would be remembering everything now. Ram, who is the protector of his bhaktas, then narrated that he is always the well-wisher for his bhaktas, who consider Ram as the only protector. Here the poet through Ram himself have told the relation of Ram and the bhakta, who are fully devoted to him :

सुनु मुनि तोहि कहउँ सहरोसा, भजहिं जे मोहि तजि सकल भरोसा।
करउँ सदा तिन्ह कै रखवारी, जिमि बालक राखइ महतारी।
गह सिसु बच्छ अनल अहि धाई, तहँ राखइ जननी अरगाई।
प्रौढ़ भएँ तेहि सुत पर माता, प्रीति करइ नहिं पाछिल बाता।
मोरे प्रौढ़ तनय सम ज्ञानी, बालक सुत सम दास अमानी।

And—

अवगुन मूल सूलप्रद, प्रमदा सब दुख खानि,
ताते कीन्ह निवारन, मुनि मैं यह जियँ जानि।

Ram told him frankly that if a bhakta had full confidence in him, he too protects the bhakta from all evils. In this case, Narad had already overpowered Kam but after that he became proud of it. To annihilate the pride, therefore, Ram had through his 'maya' created the town on way of Narad and made Narad ambitious to get married to the bride created through 'maya'. In this way, Ram had finished his pride of having overpowered Kam as he fell in the trap of the beautiful bride. Then Ram did not want Narad to get married as Narad was a sanyasi and through his tapsya only attained the position of closeness to Brahma and other gods. Once Narad was married, he would fall in worldly ambitions and vices of passion, rage, pride, and greed (काम, क्रोध, मद, लोभ)। Since Narad was a bhakta of Vishnu and from Vishnu himself he wanted a handsome form so that he could get married and then involve himself in all worldly vices which was not apt for a bhakta, Vishnu had to manage the affairs in such a way that his pride was finished and at the same time he did not fall in worldly vices from which he had absolved himself after great and tough tapsya. In other words, Vishnu wished him to continue in his position and not to get degraded. Therefore, the entire episode, even at the cost of earning his curse, as a result of which Ram had now been wandering in forests, had been formulated. Narad after hearing the above frank facts, was satisfied.

सुनि रघुपति के बचन सुहाए, मुनि तन पुलक नयन भरि आए।

Narad muni was satisfied with what had happened in his case but then since Ram had said that he was always in for the protection of his bhakta from all vices so that he did not go down from sant-hood, Narad asked Ram to tell him the virtues of a sant.

सन्तन के लच्छन रघुबीरा, कहहु नाथ भव भंजन भीरा।
सुनु मुनि सन्तन्ह के गुन कहऊँ, जिन्ह ते मैं उन्ह के बस रहऊँ।

The poet then through Ram himself narrated the virtues of a sant, because of which he remained under his control. Before one becomes sant, he is under the control of Ram's 'maya' but once a person achieves sant-hood, Ram comes under his control as he becomes above 'maya'. The sant is above the vices of passion, rage, greed, love, pride and jealousy. He has no ambitions, and is yogi, gyani and respectful to others. Except for attachment to Ram bhakti, he has no attachment to either himself or his house. After hearing the virtues of a sant through Ram's mouth itself, Narad was fully satisfied and after paying respects to Ram, Narad went to his place.

4

Kishkindha Kand

Since now Ram and Lakshman only were left after Sita had been kidnapped, the poet has in the beginning written two slokas only. The first in praise of Ram and Lakshman and the second in praise of Lord Shiv since, as already indicated Tulsidas had through this book conveyed to the people that Ram and Shiv are complementary to each other. In other words, Ram is the God of Shiv and Shiv is worshipped by Ram. Because Sati had adopted to become Sita to test Ram and Shiv could not have her after that as his wife (Having once become his God's wife), Shiv divorced her. Similarly Ram, before, proceeding to Lanka to fight with Ravan, worshipped Shiv and stablished Shivling as symbol, at present Rameshwaram. Poet, therefore, starts the chapter after worshipping the two.

Ram and Lakshman proceeded further. They reached near Rishimuk hill. There, Sugreev used to live. He saw two very brave persons coming towards the hill. Sugreev had been living at this hill but was always afraid of his brother Bali, who had expelled him from the rajmahal and had been living here on this hill as Bali due to some curse (शाप) could not come on that hill. Seeing the two brave persons coming there, he got frightened and asked Hanuman, his secretary, to go and find out their bonafides after changing himself as a brahmin, and to give him appropriate signal if they were Bali's men so that he could run away from that place rather than facing them. Hanuman accordingly went there as a brahmin. He paid respects to

Ram and Lakshman and then asked them about their introduction. When one wants to know about any strangers, one has to first, as a matter of protocol, pay respects and then only request for their introduction as to who they were and why they were wandering about in the tough terrain of the hills. After seeing them, Hanuman had, of course, thought that they were some great persons. Ram narrated his whereabouts and the fact of Sita having been kidnapped, whom they had been searching in forests. Ram, after having told about himself asked Hanuman about his introduction. Hanuman was already Ram bhakta but he could not think of Ram being in forest in that guise. After hearing about his introduction, Hanuman could easily locate him and immediately fell in his feet and begged to be excused for not having recognised him. Hanuman then told that there were reasons, for his not recognising Ram e.g. (1) He saw Ram after many years and then too in the guise of a tapsavi, which Hanuman could never think of, (2) He was only a vanar and did not have very sharp memory; and (3) He was under Ram's maya and that under maya's influence, he could not recognise Ram but asked Ram as to how he could not recognise his sewak. Obviously Ram could not recognise Hanuman as he did not come in his self but in the guise of a brahmin. Ram too, therefore, became ignorant as Ram recognised his devotee where he is without any deceiving mind (निष्कपट). Hanuman being a full devotee of Ram, begged to be excused for his not recognising him and for having come before him as a brahmin.

एकु मैं मंद मोहवस, कुटिल हृदय अग्यान,
पुनि प्रभु मोहि बिसारेउ, दीन बंधु भगवान।

Hanuman then came to his self and fell in Ram's feet. Now recognising his bhakta, Ram picked him up and embraced him as per usual protocol between a bhakta and Ram. Ram even said that bhakta was closest to him as the bhakta had no dependence upon anyone except him. Having known Ram, Hanuman narrated all about Sugreev living on the hill. He also requested to be friendly with him and with the mutual help, both would be able to cross the difficulty. Sugreev would send the vanars to various corners of universe to find Sita after Sugreev is relieved of the fear of Bali, i.e. if Sugreev becomes the raja of the place. Hanuman brought them to Sugreev and narrated the story of each to each other.

तब हनुमन्त उभय दिसि की सब कथा सुनाइ,
पावक साखी देइ करि जोरी प्रीति दृढ़ाई।

After acquainting each of the other's life history, and having obtained the wish of their mutual help, the friendship was affirmed in presence of fire. At present, agreements are executed between two rajas on stamp paper, under affidavit etc. to bind the two sides to what was contained in the agreement. Similar must have been the practice in Ram's period too. The poet has given the colour of the execution of friendship before fire as fire was considered to be of sanctity. Even now the most important function of marriage in Hindus is held as saptpadi around fire only and this bond is considered to be an eternal bond. Further, the agreement executed was in clear terms and without any ambiguity as any agreement has to be. Now the agreement is ratified by each country with a view to see that no lacunae remained. In the case of Ram-Sugreev agreement too Lakshman notified it :

कीन्ह प्रीति कछु बीच न राखा, लछिमन राम चरित सब भाषा।

It means there was no ambiguity and Lakshman seem to have witnessed it as in the present day each agreement has to be witnessed too with a view to rule out any doubt about their bonafides. Sugreev assured Ram that Sita would be found. He also narrated how Sita had once thrown some ornaments, when being kidnapped by a rakshas. He showed those ornaments to Ram, who recognised the same as those of Sita. Having been assured by Sugreev to help Ram in finding Sita, Ram asked Sugreev to tell why he was living on the hill. Sugreev then explained the entire episode that happened between him and Bali resulting in Bali expelling him from the kingdom and keeping his wife too with him. Ram assured him that he would kill Bali and no one would be able to save him. Since Ram and Sugreev had developed friendship, which had been affirmed before fire, now they had to help each other as the protocol between friends warranted :

जे न मित्र दुख होहिं दुखारी, तिन्हहिं विलोकत पातक भारी।

निज दुख गिरि सम रज करि जाना, मित्रक दुख रज मेरु समाना।

Here Ram had said that a person, who did not feel the ailment of the friend, he is not worth showing his face to anyone. He also said that for a friend, his own ailment, howsoever grave, should be taken as minor and the friend's minor ailment too should be treated as grave and should mutually act like that. Ram had further explained what the friend should feel and do for other friend and if it is not done then there is breach of friendship. Ram accordingly assured his friend Sugreev to pass on his sadness to him as he would be able to help him.

सखा सोच त्यागहु बल मोरें, सब विधि घटब काज मैं तोरें।

Sugreev told that Bali was very brave and he could not think Ram would be able to defeat him in battle. Ram then assured Sugreev of his bravery by throwing one arrow pass through palm trees and also by dismantling a heap of bones by one arrow. Before invading a raja, one has to satisfy whether he was equivalent or not otherwise there would be defeat only and one should in that case avoid attacking. Then one should only act to save oneself against any attack. The doubt in Sugreev's mind was because of Ram's maya. Now that maya was over and Sugreev recognised Ram and became firm in conviction that he would be able to defeat Bali. He developed gyan, with Ram's kindness and then said :

शत्रु मित्र सुख दुख जग माहीं, मायाकृत परमारथ नाहीं।

Enemy, friend, good and bad days are all as per Ram's maya and do not exist otherwise in fact. Then Sugreev forgot everything of defeating Bali, getting kingdom and his wife back etc. as usually happens when one is out of the effect of maya. Maya is caused by passion, rage, pride and greed (काम, क्रोध, मद, लोभ) and when one gets Ram's bhakti, he is above all these vices and then he does not have any worldly desires (ambitions). Ram then brought Sugreev back under influence of his maya and sent him to challenge Bali. Sugreev accordingly went and challenged Bali. Bali defeated Sugreev and Sugreev came back and was not happy. Ram told that he could not enter the battle and kill Bali as he could not differentiate between him and Bali (both resembling each other). He again sent him. Sugreev again went and challenged Bali. Bali's wife persuaded Bali not to proceed as Sugreev was having the assistance of Ram. But then Bali, being a brave vanar, could not stop himself thinking why should Ram help Sugreev against him when he had not done any harm to Ram.

कह बाली सुनु भीरू प्रिय समदरसी रघुनाथ,
जौं कदाचि मोहि मारहिं तौं पुनि होउँ सनाथ।

Bali was convinced that Ram could not be partial to him and even if he killed him, he would attain paramgati. Fighting started and Ram had been seeing the fighting from behind a tree. When Ram saw Sugreev had failed in his attempt to defeat Bali, he killed Bali by an arrow. Bali fell down. Ram and Lakshman appeared before him. With Ram's kindness, Bali was above maya and, therefore, recognised Ram as God. "सुफल जन्म माना प्रभु चीन्हा"। One recognises Ram only when one is out of the influence of maya. But still he was having a bad feeling for Ram as to why he killed him like a hunter inspite of Ram having come as incarnate of Vishnu to protect dharam.

धर्म हेतु अवतरेहु गोसाई, मारेहु मोहिं व्याध की नाईं।
और
मैं बैरी सुग्रीव पिआरा, अवगुन कवन नाथ मोहि मारा।

Although Ram could have managed his dying without raising these doubts but then for the knowledge of people at large, Ram wanted to offer clarification so that later on people might not doubt Ram's integrity and bonafides. One reason in killing Bali like a hunter, as Bali had correctly said, was that Bali was a vanar and for killing a vanar :

(1) The Rule of Law does not apply. The Rule of Law applies to cases where both sides knew the rule and the law.

(2) Bali being a vanar (an uneducated being in forest), could not be faced in battle as per laws of war and could be killed only from a distance. Similar is the case when one goes out for hunting an animal in the forest. One sits on a machan etc. and then fires on the animal. One does not fight with the animal face to face. So Ram had been watching the fight between Sugreev and Bali from behind a tree but one cannot fire an arrow from behind a tree particularly where the arrow had hit Bali's heart.

बहु छल बल सुग्रीव कर, हियं हारा भय मानि,
भारा बालि राम तब हृदय माझ सर तानि।

That the vanars did not fight a battle as per law is clear from the above saying that Sugreev and Bali had been fighting with all cunningness, fraud, deception etc. Therefore, it was not proper for Ram to have fought with such vanaras face to face. Further, Ram's arrow hitting Bali in heart shows that Ram had appeared before Bali and had then hit him. Ram could not have hit from behind the tree. He had only been watching the fighting from behind the tree and had hit from front after coming out from the hiding behind the tree. It is, therefore, not correct that Ram had hit Bali from a hiding.

Regarding the reason for killing Bali, Ram told :

अनुज वधू भगिनि सुत नारी, सुनु सठ कन्या सम ए चारी।
इन्हहि कुदृष्टि बिलोकइ जोई, ताहि बधें कछु पाप न होई।

As per canons of Hindu dharam, younger brother's wife, sister, son's wife and one's daughter, all the four are like daughters and a person, who has evil eye against any of these, deserves to be killed and killing of such a person is not a sin or against law. Still Ram asked Bali if he had any grouse, he could keep him alive but then Bali preferred to die in presence of Ram, hit by him to enable him to attain paramgati rather than living further and then dying as an ordinary man.

"अचल करौं तनु राखहु प्रान।"

और

मम लोचन गोचर सोइ आवा, बहुरि कि प्रभु अस बनिहि बनावा।

Here Ram cleared his position that he had not done anything wrong and he was able to undo what had happened if Bali was not satisfied with the explanation. But then Bali preferred to die in presence of Ram, the almighty. While dying Bali requested Ram to bless him to be his bhakta wherever he might be born. This shows that Bali was convinced of Ram's explanation that he deserved to be killed like that. Bali also entrusted the protection of his son Angad to Ram thinking that :

(1) Since he had not behaved well with Sugreev, Sugreev might take revenge out of his wife and son.

(2) Angad was the eldest son of Bali and was, therefore, the legitimate successor to the throne. After his death, he feared that Sugreev might not recognise him as successor to the throne and make his own son as Yuvraj.

(3) Ram being almighty God, one was safest in his hands and under his protection. None else could provide such protection.

(4) Angad was still young and deserved to be properly brought up and taken care of for anything he did wrong or for any mischief by Sugreev.

(5) Angad being brave like his father, could be of help to Ram in his mission of tracing Sita. In other words, Bali told Ram that he could confide in Angad and Angad would help Ram rather than keeping any ill feeling against Ram, who had killed his father.

यह तनय मम सम विनय बल कल्यानप्रद प्रभु लीजिये,

गहि बाँह सुर नर नाह आपन दास अंगद कीजिये।

After this Bali died. Then his wife Tara came crying. Ram bestowed gyan on her too after absolving her from the effect of maya and also consoled her. Then Ram asked Sugreev to perform last rites of Bali and asked Lakshman to coronate Sugreev.

राम कहा अनुजहि समुझाई राज देहु सुग्रीवहि जाई।

'समुझाई' word may be that Ram would have told Lakshman as to how to coronate Sugreev as also to make Angad his Yuvraj as per Bali's request so that, there was no partiality against Angad later on and also to perform this ceremony in presence of all family men, brahmins and other elders.

लछिमन तुरत बोलाए पुरजन विप्र समाज,
राज दीन्ह सुग्रीव कहँ, अगंद कहं जुवराज।

This shows that there was democracy at work in those days inspite of monarchy although not strictly followed as it is today in as much as the coronation was held in presence of and with agreement of all members of family, brahmins and other socially elders so that there was no dispute later on. Simultaneously, Angad was made Yuvraj so that no injustice was done to him later by Sugreev. It was not the end. Ram then called for Sugreev and coached him about political management. Ram being the eldest in the family, had been coached by the guru how to rule as he was the successor apparent. So while sending Bharat off from the forests, Ram coached Bharat also. Here Bali was versed with the ruling canons but not Sugreev. Therefore, Ram coached Sugreev how to rule.

पुनि, सुग्रीवहि लीन्ह बोलाई, बहु प्रकार नृप नीति सिखाई।

This also shows that the system of rule had been clearly laid down and it was duly taught to the ruler to be. Same continued in the later Hindu Rulers so much so that in Maurya Rule, Chanakya Niti is well known universally till date how he could make Chandra Gupta Maurya, the ruler of India. His philosophy is regarding all aspects of the ruling ethics—political, economic, administrative, religious, social etc. Such was the comprehension on the subjects in ancient India. While sending Sugreev off, Ram blessed him to have perpetual rajya along with Angad but he should not forget his job too.

अगंद सहित करहु तुम्ह राजू, सतत हृदय धरेहु मम काजू।

This couplet is full of protocolic teachings :

(1) Sugreev was blessed to rule without any fear now.

(2) Sugreev was told that while ruling, he should not forget that Angad was the Yuvraj. Therefore, Ram blessed Sugreev to rule along with Angad since Ram had made him Yuvraj on the request of his father Bali to protect Angad's interest, who being the son of Bali, was successor apparent to the kingdom.

(3) He had entered into an agreement with Ram. According to this agreement, Ram had undertaken to kill Bali and restore kingdom and his wife to Sugreev. Sugreev was to help Ram in finding out the whereabouts of Sita and assist him in securing her back. Ram had done his part of the job and reminded Sugreev to always remember the job to be done by him.

Having sent off Sugreev, Ram and Lakshman settled in a cave on the hills. Raining season started and no job was done in rainy season. This period, therefore, was to rest. Ram and Lakshman passed these days saying various pauranic stories etc. on bhakti, vairagya, politics etc.

कहत अनुज सन कथा अनेका, भगति विरति नृप नीति विवेका।

During talks between Ram and Lakshman, all matters of principle and philosophy were discussed such as

(1) बूंद अधात सहहिं गिरि कैसे, खल के बचन सन्त सहें जैसे।

Meaning thereby that as the rain drops cannot effect the mountains so the abuses by bastards do not effect the minds of saints.

(2) Similarly as lightening lights and is then off like wise the affection by a bastard is not perpetual. It is momentary. The rains-stream flow like a bastard, who feels big even if he gets a small amount.

(3) The water of the river joins the ocean like a jeev, who becomes eternal after getting closeness to the almighty God. There is no dust available during rains, particularly in hilly area as one loses one's sense and the ethics of dharam in rage.

(4) Due to heavy rains, the water flows out of the farms like the women, who gets spoiled, if let loose. Here again the poet favours the women to be kept under control otherwise she would be lost. This had been written at the time when there was Muslim rule in India and during Muslim rule, there was no safety for the women. They were kidnapped by the persons of Muslim rulers, if found wandering about in the streets. It is in this context that the poet had written that given the freedom, the women gets spoiled. In the modern concepts too whereas on one side there is talk of grant of liberty to women, at the same time it is resulting in the matrimonial relations between husband and wife getting spoiled and subsequent increase in the number of divorce cases whereas divorce cases were not heard of in the past. Now with the westernisation, the tolerance is lost in women and the couple resorts to divorce on petty matters.

(5) Because of the storm, the clouds get dispersed as the entire wealth and dharam gets annihilated with the birth of a spoilt child in the family.

(6) After rains, winter gets in and the weather becomes very pleasant. In the ponds, the water gets crystalised as the heart of the saint becomes clean when he gets rid of greed and pride.

(7) In winter, there is rain but very seldom, as the bhakti of Ishwar is not attained by all but by some only.

(8) In winter, the fish gets worried because of the shortage of water but wherever there is ample of water, the fishes are without any fear like there is no fear to a person, who has the protection of God.

(9) The lotus blossoms in pond like a believer in Nirgun (निर्गुण) Brahma shifting to Sagun (सगुण). With the shifting of a devotee from Nirgun, in which case he always remain quiet and restrained, to Sagun when one becomes jubilent with the darshan of God in his life.

(10) The small insects on land vanish with the winter setting in like the doubts in the mind of a person vanishing on finding a good guru.

भूमि जीव संकुल रहे गए सरद ऋतु पाइ,
सद्गुरु मिले जाहिं जिमि ससंय भ्रम समुदाइ।

While coronating Sugreev, Ram had reminded him to keep his part of the job (finding Sita) in mind. But now the rainy season was over and still Sugreev had not cared for locating Sita. This had been upsetting Ram. Here Ram has advised people that like Sugreev, who forgot to fulfil his commitment of finding Sita on attaining his raj, wealth, and wife, one should not get involved in these things after attaining them as the raj, wealth and women are enemies of the dharam in a person otherwise one would have to pay for these heavily. Ram had said that he would kill Sugreev too with the arrow with which he killed Bali if he continued to get so much involved in raj, wealth and women. Seeing Ram in rage, Lakshman got ready with his dhanush-ban. Then Ram consoled Lakshman and told him he should not get ready for the battle but only show some rage to Sugreev, so that he remembered to fulfil his part of the agreement. In modern concept also, the agreement has to be fulfilled by both the sides to the agreement and if one fails to do so, he will have to face consequences. This principle applies to the agreements between individuals, groups, corporates, governments and public and amongst different governments at international level. At international level, we have the UNO and international court of justice, whose judgements, though not strictly binding become morally so in face of pressure from various other countries. Ram was furious for Sugreev not having fulfilled his part of the agreement but then as a matter of protocol, one has to first check up what he had been doing in fulfilling the agreement; issuing a show cause notice and then given one chance, if possible to do it now rather than start pecuniary action against the defaulting party as a fight does not yield good results for either party.

तब अनुजहि समुझावा रघुपति करुणा सींव,
भय देखाइ लै आवहु तात सखा सुग्रीव।

Here Ram's thinking of knowing the facts first rather than starting action against Sugreev paid dividend.

Although Sugreev had got himself much involved in wealth and women after getting the same and had forgotten Ram's job but then as per bureaucratical protocol, the secretaries have to remind the ruler of such jobs to be done. Here in Sugreev's kingdom, Hanuman was the common link between Ram and Sugreev as he had made them friends and was a witness to their entering into an agreement of mutual help. He, therefore, reminded Sugreev and Sugreev became alert and sent for all the petty nobles under him for entrusting the job of finding Sita by sending vanars to various parts of the universe. All were accordingly despatched telling them that they would be killed if they did not return within a fortnight after getting the job done.

"भय और प्रीति नीति देखराई"

All were frightened of death sentence; they were also told affectionately and also were told about the importance of the job in fulfilling the agreement entered into with Ram.

As advised by Ram, Lakshman came to the capital and threatened Sugreev. Sugreev being guilty of not having paid any heed to Ram's job, could not face Lakshman. As a matter of strategy he,therefore, sent forth Angad to pacify Lakshman because Angad was innocent and Ram had given special protection to him as per Bali's request. Angad paid respects and praised him. Lakshman became cool. Even then Sugreev was frightened of Lakshman's rage. He again, as a matter of strategy, sent forth Tara (Bali's wife) as one does not show rage to a woman, and Hanuman as he was the mediator between Ram and Sugreev's friendship as also he could pacify and tell Lakshman the action already taken by Sugreev in sending vanars in various directions. Tara and Hanuman paid respects to Lakshman and praised him. They escorted Lakshman to rajmahal where Sugreev paid respects and Lakshman embraced him. Sugreev himself admitted that in passion one forgets everything. Lakshman then consoled him. Hanuman narrated the action already taken. Then Sugreev happily went to Ram along with Angad and other vanars. Lakshman was in front and they followed him. They followed Lakshman with a view to :

(1) see that Ram, if violent, would get pacified seeing Lakshman first and they following him;
(2) show that they were all through obedient to Ram and Lakshman;
(3) indicate to Ram that Lakshman was satisfied with the action already taken in the direction.

रामानुज आगें करि आए जहँ रघुनाथ।

Sugreev came and paid respects to Ram and accepting his guilt stated that he had forgotten the job under the influence of Ram's maya only, which gets lessened only on Ram's kindness. Here Sugreev stated that even rishis and munis and gods were under maya's influence then what to speak of Sugreev, who was a vanar and poor animal. Here Sugreev has been stated to be an animal. This would confirm the contention that Bali, being an animal, had to be killed by Ram as an animal is killed during hunting and not in a face to face fight.

"मैं पसु कपि अति कामी"

Sugreev also accepted here that passion, rage and love are the enemies of human beings. Ram felt consoled and embraced Sugreev and asked him to make attempts with a view to locate Sita. Meantime many vanars came there and they were all sent in different directions. Ram responded to each of them paying respects by making himself in as many forms. Sugreev gave them a month's time within which they had to return. The orders were given by Sugreev as he was the king of the place and they recognised Sugreev only.

"कह सुग्रीव सबहि समुझाई"

Sugreev threatened them that anyone coming without search after the one month's time, would be killed by him. The vanars set on their journeys to all directions in groups. Since it was expected that Ravana would have taken Sita to Lanka, Sugreev proposed to send most trustworthy and capable amongst them to Lanka e.g. Angad, Nal, Hanuman and Jamvant. He, therefore, called them and asked them to go to Lanka and make efforts by heart, action and speech (मन, कर्म, वचन) to find out Sita with a view to do the job of Ram. Ram being the master had to be served by all means as per ethics :

भानु पीठि सेइअ उर आगी, स्वामिहि सर्व भाव छल त्यागी।

Similarly God be served after getting absolved from all forms of maya. Hanuman bowed before Ram in the last. Ram called him as his own man; blessed him and handed over a ring to him. Ram knew that he only would be able to reach Sita. He, therefore, gave the ring to him and asked him to console Sita in every way possible and tell her about Ram's force and the sadness, he was facing in Sita's separation. Although it showed that Ram knew everything but he was working as an ordinary human being and in accordance with the canons of politics.

All left in search of Sita. On the way they felt thirsty. Hanuman climbed up a hill and saw some birds coming out from a distant place. Birds' coming from there showed that there must be water available. Hanuman, therefore, took all of them there. They saw a sarovar, a temple and a lady tapsavi there. They told their purpose etc. The lady asked them to take bath and take rest and have meals. The vanars were sent by her out to sea shore and she herself went in search of Ram. She paid respects to Ram and after getting his blessings, went to Badrinath. By now many days had passed and the vanars were worried that in case they did not go back within a month after having searched Sita, they would be killed. Angad was particularly worried as he being the son of Bali, Sugreev would take revenge and find an excuse to kill him. Even uptil now it was Ram, who had saved him from Sugreev's clutches. Jamvant, who was older amongst them told that Ram was not an ordinary human being. He was God almighty and had come incarnate to serve the purpose of gods, brahmins and rishis. Then sampati, an eagle, who was living nearby came and was happy that he had got so many vanars to eat for many days as due to his wings having been burnt, he was not able to move about in search of food. They all got frightened. It is, however, not clear as to how after seeing an eagle only, the brave Angad, Hanuman etc., who could fight with great rakshasas in Lanka got frightened. Then Angad made some pondering and said "Jatayu had been lucky to have died doing Ram's job". Sampati hearing this, came closer to vanars and asked all that they knew about Jatayu as Jatayu was his brother. As per tradition, Sampati performed last rites of Jatayu and could see from the hill Sita sitting in the garden in Lanka. He told vanars that eagle with his sharp eyes could see Sita but vanars could not.

मैं देखउं तुम्ह नाही गीधहि दृष्टि अपार,
बूढ़ भयउँ न त करतेउँ कछुक सहाय तुम्हार।

He asked vanars that only remembering Ram he got his wings back so they could also be successful in their mission with Ram's kindness. Then there was the problem of crossing the sea and reaching Lanka. Everyone was doubtful about crossing the see. Angad said he could go but he had doubt about his safe return. Then Jamvant turned to Hanuman and apprised him of his bravery. Hanuman was very brave but as a result of some curse by saints, he had not been aware of the same. On Jamvant reminding him of all his bravery and the incident how he had forgotten it, he became aware of his force and said yes he would go and come back after finding Sita's location. Till then they should wait there. He even said that he was brave enough to kill Ravan and bring Sita but Jamvant, who was a great philosopher, and politician, told that his job at present was only to search Sita and then Ram, the almighty, would himself kill Ravan and others.

एतना करहु तात तुम्ह जाई, सीतहि देखि कहहु सुधि आई।
तब निज भुज बल राजिव नैना, कौतुक लागि संग कपि सेना।
और
कपि सेन संग संघारि निसिचर रामु सीतहि आनिहैं।

Jamvant told that Ram had come incarnate of God only to kill rakshasas and bring relief to gods and rishis etc., whom Ravan had been causing annoyance.

5

Sundar Kand

Here again in the beginning of the chapter, the poet remembers his God Ram and then Hanuman, who had now come in picture. Hearing Jamvant, Hanuman came in form and with confidence asked them to wait till he returned after searching Sita. He paid respects to all and started remembering Ram. It is from here that Hanuman became real bhakta of Ram. On the way, Mainak hill attracted him to take rest but then he thought without completing the job, he could not have rest. This is the extent of devotion, a bhakta should have for the Bhagwan.

राम काजु कीन्हे बिनु मोहि कहां विश्राम।

The gods thought of testing Hanuman's bravery and see whether he would be able to do Ram's job. They sent Sursa. She said God had sent vanar for her meals. Being a lady, Hanuman did not fight with her and requested that he was going to do Ram's job and after he had done the job, he himself shall offer for being taken as meals.

राम काज करि फिरि मैं आवौं, सीता कइ सुधि प्रभुहिं सुनावौं।

तब तव बदन बैठिहउँ आई, सत्य कहउँ मोहि जान दे माई।

But when she did not agree, Hanuman offered himself for being eaten. She opened her month. Hanuman became double of that; she again further opened and Hanuman further got-enlarged; she then further enlarged her mouth. Then Hanuman, went in and came out of the month, and then asked permission to go further. She then told of her mission and blessed Hanuman to go and he would be able to do the job. On the way Hanuman killed another rakshasani in the sea and reached Lanka. On reaching Lanka, Hanuman adopted a strategy to search Sita in Lanka during the night and for that he should become very short so that he could not be seen by others. He surveyed Lanka from all sides first. It was an island in the sea with a protection wall all around like a fortress and protected by very brave persons. He framed himself in small size and entered Lanka remembering Ram. On the way there was Lankani Rakshasani. She would not allow any one to enter Lanka without proper permission. This shows that the protection of Lanka was managed in such a way that even a mosquito could not enter and how much Ravan was vigilant to protect his fort/kingdom. This also is an advice to all rulers to arrange so much protection for their kingdoms. Hanuman thrashed her. She fell and blood oozed out of her. She remembered that when Brahma had given boon to Ravan, he had told her that when Ram's messenger would burst her, she could make out that annihilation of Ravan's dynasty was quite close. She blessed Hanuman and permitted him to get in after having attained gyan. Hanuman again became in a short form and started searching Sita from one house to another. He searched Ravan's mahal too but could not see Sita anywhere. Then he saw one house where a temple was also constructed and a tulsi plant grown. He was surprised to see such an environ in the town of rakshasas. Then Vibheeshan woke up and he remembered Ram. Hanuman could make out that he was a Rambhakta. He thought of making friendship with him as a sadhu would not interfere in the fulfilment of his job.

एहि सन हठि करिहउँ पहिचानी, साधु ते होइ न कारज हानी।

This is a protocol i.e. advice that one should find the weak corners in enemy's place so that one could get all information from there. Hanuman too was successful in locating some such place in Ravan's town and finding Vibheeshan, he considered him of his affinity and, therefore, decided to develop friendship with him with a view to get some hint about the whereabouts of Sita, particularly when Hanuman had failed to find her out having searched all houses in Lanka. He became a brahmin and started uttering praise of Ram. Vibheeshan too immediately placed him as one of Ram's bhaktas and came closer to him. He paid respects (as a person would do to a brahmin) and asked Hanuman his introduction and well being.

'तब हनुमंत कही सब राम कथा निज नाम'

They both got absorbed in Ram's thoughts and lost their senses for sometime. This was natural for Vibheeshan on having seen a bhakta in Lanka after a long time and for Hanuman in having been able to locate a Rambhakta in the kingdom of rakshasas and having then felt that his job would now become easier as being Rambhakta, Vibheeshan would help him tell Sita's whereabouts.

Vibheeshan told Hanuman that he had been living in Lanka amongst the rakshasas like tongue amongst teeth. The tongue is always worried in case there is any ailment to teeth but the teeth cut the tongue, whenever a chance is available. He requested if Ram would ever be kind to him. He, however, had satisfaction on meeting Hanuman as the meeting of Rambhakta could be only with the grace of Ram only.

अब मोहिं भा भरोम हनुमतां, बिनु हरि कृपा मिलहिं नहिं संता।

Hanuman also told Vibheeshan that, based on his experience, Ram, as a matter of habit, loves his bhaktas.

सुनहु विभीषण प्रभु कै रीती, करहिं सदा सेवक पर प्रीती।

और

अस में अधम सखा सुनु मोहू पर रघुबीर,
कीन्ह कृपा सुमिरि गुन भरे विलोचन नीर।

This is the protocolic affection/devotion between Bhagwan and the bhakta. Vibheeshan then told how Sita had been living in Lanka and told him the way out how he could meet her. Hanuman then departed and set off to meet Sita again in a short form. He paid respects to Sita in his heart and waited for the night to pass. Hanuman was upset on seeing Sita in a very terrible condition. At that time, Ravan came there with many ladies.

He persuaded Sita to only see him with kidness and he would make all his queens serve her. Ravan was quite a learned person. He used the four principles of conciliation, offering wealth, threatening and division, Sam, dam, dand and bhed (साम, दाम, दंड, भेद). These are the four policies adopted by any king to control the people, to control the enemy and to win over any person. These principles are even today accepted and adopted by the rulers. English are said to be using these very principles in ruling over India. In the first instance they settled in India by the first principle of 'साम' conciliation with the then ruler of Bengal and the Mughal ruler of India for the purpose of trade only. Then they offered wealth and purchased some territory and made forts. They started collecting the taxes by giving punishments and created fear in the minds of Indians after they suppressed the first war of independence in 1857 (Mutiny). By the principle of 'भेद' division, English were winner in the first battle they fought on Indian land i.e. the battle of Plassy in which they created dissension in the army of Saraj-ud-Daula, the ruler of Bengal by winning over his commander-in-chief. Subsequently they used the policy of भेद (division) amongst Hindus and Muslims so that they continue fighting amongst themselves and do not think of fighting with the English, the rulers of the day and they were successful in ruling India with this policy. Again in India in the present day the so called national parties do not care for the national interest and have been creating differences not only amongst the Hindus and Muslims but also amongst various castes within Hindus too. Presently the elections are practically held on communal and caste basis. Subsequently too the privileges are given to certain people causing discrimination against others. In Pakistan where there are only Muslims, the policy of division and differentiation is adopted in creating differences between Shias and Sunnis and the originals and Mohajirs. In other countries too where they boast of equality, there is some discrimination amongst the people from various religions, countries, castes etc. Ravan adopted these policies in winning over Sita.

बहु विधि खल सीतहि समुझावा, साम दाम भय भेद दिखावा।
कह रावन सुनु सुमुखि सयानी, मंदोदरी आदि सब रानी।
तव अनुचरी करउँ पन मोरा, एक बार बिलोकु मम ओरा।

Ravan even offered that Mandodri etc. all his queens would be under her if she only once looked toward him with grace. Here Ravan has acted quite according to protocol between :

(1) Bhagwan and bhakta. For reaching Ram, Ravan could either go via bhakti or by overpowering 'maya'. Sita was the incarnation of both. He, therefore, requested her and adopted all methods of bhakti (conciliation) to be kind to him. When she did not agree with this method then he also used the principle of punishment (threat) to overpower Sita i.e. 'maya'.

(2) He offered her that all his queens would be under her. It means that he was prepared to surrender everything for her if she became kind to him.

(3) What is the wish of a bhakta is to have the grace of the Bhagwan. Ravan, therefore, requested Sita only to show kindness to him.

(4) Ravan addressed her as सुमुखि and सयानी meaning thereby that she being a सुमुखि could grace him only by looking towards him. In this way she would be able to make use of her kind, benevolent look. Further, Ravan had used all methods to make her grace him and since she was intelligent (सयानी) enough, she could opt to grace him keeping all his requests and persuasions in view.

Sita, however, had been briefed by Ram that entire drama was being performed with a view to annihilate the rakshasas from the earth. She, therefore, could not agree to Ravan's request. Further, since Ravan had kidnapped her and Sita had been acting as an ordinary human being, she could only hate him in that capacity. Sita, therefore, continued to act as an ordinary person and continued hating him. Further, in Hindus the pativrata ladies do not show their face to a stranger and do not talk to a stranger directly. Sita was, however, face to face with Ravan in Ashok

Vatika and there was nothing available for her to hide herself. Symbolically, she picked up a straw and talked from behind it. She told Ravan that he should remember Ram and not think of overpowering her as it will annihilate him. Sita used very tough words for him as a result of which Ravan got provoked and took his sword. This he thought was the way out to overpower 'maya'. But it was only a threat as Ravan could not have actually done it for the wife of his almighty God. He then gave her some time to agree to his request otherwise he would be forced to adopt force to overpower 'maya'. Mandodri also coached Ravan of the niti "मयातनया कहि नीति बुझावा". Here the word 'Niti' would indicate that Mandodri must have told him :

(1) Not to kill a lady as it was against the ethics of a brave man to have killed a mild lady.

(2) Not to do any harm to the wife of his almighty God himself and to continue to adopt the method of bhakti only and not overpowering 'maya'.

(3) Since Ravan had already given a time limit to Sita to agree within that to accede to Ravan's request, Ravan should abide by that.

(4) Mandodri must also be honouring Sita as the wife of almighty God, otherwise an ordinary lady would prefer her co-wife (to be) being murdered rather than bringing her to administer the present queens as Ravan had been proclaiming in front of all those queens themselves. Mandodri, therefore, forbade Ravan from killing her and rather than overpowering maya, he should resort to bhakti.

(5) Ravan gave her a month's time within which to decide whether she would be gracious enough or would have to be overpowered.

(6) As per protocol, a king has to apply the policy of both frightening and appeasement. Ravan had been doing so. Even after he threatened Sita and asked the maids deputed with Sita to keep her frightened, Ravan had also deputed one Trijata there knowing full well that she was Rambhakta to keep Sita pleased by her bhakti.

त्रिजटा नाम राच्छसी एका, राम चरन रति निपुन विवेका।
सबन्हौं बोलि सुनाएसि सपना, सीतहिं सेइ करहु हित अपना।

It is not that Ravan did not know Trijata being Rambhakta but he would have intentionally posted her there to keep Sita pleased so that Ravan could reach Ram through bhakti, if Sita could be pleased. Then all the maids started serving Sita.

(7) Sita, however, could not be pleased and she too thought that it was not possible for her to accept Ravan as Ram's bhakta as he had not behaved with her well. Ravan, therefore, deserved only to be killed by Ram as a rakshas enemy and was not fit to reach Ram either through bhakti or by over powering her as 'maya'. Sita, therefore, asked Trijata to bring fire from somewhere to enable her to burn herself. Trijata, however, knew it as a momentary phase and was convinced that Ram would come and overpower the rakshasas. She, therefore, showed her inability to bring fire at that time. Also it was her job as a head-maid to Sita to see that Sita did not resort to anything not desired by Ravan.

Sita then requested the stars in the sky to come and help her in burning. Just then Hanuman threw the ring given by Ram to be handed over to Sita to make her believe that Hanuman was really Ram's representative and not one planted by rakshasas. Ram could anticipate this difficulty. He, therefore, as a matter of protocol, gave Hanuman the ring or say some letter of credence in modern language. This helped Hanuman to convince Sita of his bonafides. Otherwise Sita could not have believed and rightly so, that a vanar could be Ram's friend/ representative.

कपि करि हृदय विचार दीन्हि मुद्रिका डारि तब,
जनु असोक अंगार दीन्ह हरषि उठि कर गहेउ।

Sita recognised this to be Ram's ring but was surprised how it came there as without defeating Ram one could not get it and Ram could not be defeated by anyone. Also it could not be manufactured dubiously.

जीति को सकइ अजय रघुराई, माया तें असि रचि नहिं जाई।

It is not clear how Sita could think that a ring could not be manufactured dubiously by Ravan, who was all competent and later during the war he actually made Ram's head by 'maya' and told Sita showing the head that Ram had been killed. It must, therefore, be not ring but some letter of credence, signed by Ram. The signature, it would not have been possible to make forged one. Also if we go back to the incident where the boat man enabled Ram, Lakshman and Sita cross Ganga, Ram looked towards Sita to give some ornament to be handed over to the boatmen as labour charges and at that time Sita had given Ram her ring for this purpose. If Ram had his own ring, then why he should look for assistance from Sita. Further, Ram had put off all his ornaments etc. in the rajmahal at Awadh itself and had left Awadh as a tapasvi in tapsavi's clothes. Then how could Ram have his ring. The only possibility can be that Sita had given a ring to Ram to be handed over to the boatman and the boatman did not accept the same. That ring would have remained with Ram and that ring might be with Ram's name carved on it "राम नाम अंकित अति सुन्दर". This couplet can also mean that on the letter of credence given to Hanuman by Ram, reference might be to Ram's signature, which were very charming and 'मुद्रिका' also means a printed order. Therefore, 'मुद्रिका' might be referring to a letter of credence only. When Sita was in confusion, then Hanuman introduced himself. As usual, Sita did not believe him to be Ram's man although he narrated the whole story. Then Hanuman appeared before her but Sita not believing him turned her face.

फिरि बैठी, मन विसमय भयऊ।

Then Hanuman said 'सत्य सपथ करुनानिधान की'। Then only Sita could believe as the word 'करुणानिधान' could be used by Ram's men only. He also referred to the Mudrika/letter of credence given by Ram in confirmation. Then Sita accepted the bonafides of Hanuman. Then Sita asked about Ram and Lakshman's well being and why they had been cruel to her as not to get her released so far. Hanuman told that Ram and Lakshman were alright except that they were sad because of her separation and assured her that Ram did have double the love, Sita had for him. 'तुम्ह ते प्रेम राम के दूना' How Hanuman said Ram's love was double to that of Sita may be possible because :

(1) Like Sita, Ram was also sad in separation but Sita was just sitting there and Ram had to make all arrangements to fight with rakshasas to get Sita released.

(2) Without thinking what would happen to Ram if Sita resorted to killing herself, she was making efforts to kill herself and Hanuman was a witness to it. Ram had never in disgust thought so and had always been making sincere endeavour to have Sita back.

(3) Sita was herself to be blamed for this condition as Sita made false allegations against Lakshman of having bad intentions leading to her having been kidnapped.

(4) Sita had under-estimated Ram in having believed that Ram was in trouble while chasing the deer (Marich) to kill him and this under-estimation was the key root of having sent Lakshman out from the ashram.

(5) Hanuman had only seen Ram's anxiety and sadness in having been separated from Sita on having lived with him for several months but had not lived with Sita and as such did not have occasion to know the extent of her love for Ram rather he had only seen Sita making efforts to kill herself not being able to bear the separation.

(6) Ram's sadness had been narrated by Hanuman to Sita which would indicate that Hanuman was fully aware of the same and on the basis of this knowledge only Hanuman would have said that Ram's love for Sita was double to that Sita would have for Ram and Hanuman did not actually know Sita's grievance and consequent love for Ram.

Hanuman consoled Sita that Ram would have come much before but her whereabouts were not known. Now, all rakshasas shall be killed without any loss of time. He also said that he would have himself taken her with him but he does not have Ram's permission for that.

अबहिं मातु मैं जाउँ लवाई, प्रभु आयसु नहिं राम दोहाई।

The question of protocol gets into the matter here.

(1) Ram/Sugreev had ordered the vanars to locate Sita and come back within a month's time. Ram had not desired Sita to be brought because the entire drama was to annihilate the rakshasas under the pretence of Sita having been kidnapped.

(2) For attacking any king, some excuse is necessary and here Sita's kidnapping was a valid reason.

(3) The matter whether Hanuman could bring Sita with him had already been discussed when Hanuman departed to cross the sea and Jamvant had told that Ram's orders were only to trace where Sita was. Hanuman therefore, told Sita accordingly.

(4) To reassure Sita that Hanuman was not pretending in saying so, he even swore by Ram.

(5) Hanuman knew that Ravan had already done a wrong thing in having brought Sita in absence of Ram from the Ashram. Now by taking Sita again with him, Hanuman did not want to repeat the same wrong.

(6) Hanuman knew that Sita was a pativrata and she would not allow any other person to touch her as it was against the ethics of pativarta dharam. Hanuman was, therefore, unable in doing that.

(7) Hanuman also indicated that Ram would come soon along with the army of vanars and get her released from Lanka after killing the rakshasas.

कछुक दिवस जननी धरु धीरा, कपिन्ह सहित अइहहिं रघुबीरा।

(8) Hanuman had intentionally mentioned to assure Sita that Ram would come with a large army of vanars so that Sita could know that Ram was not alone to face the rakshasas. Although Sita knew that Ram alone could

do the job but Hanuman, as a human being, had thought of assuring Sita about Ram's force to fight with rakshasas.

(9) Hanuman also mentioned about the army of vanars to remove the doubt in Sita's mind about the strength of vanars which he subsequently showed when Sita questioned it, by adopting a large figure of himself.

हैं सुत कपि सब तुम्हहिं समाना, जातुधान अति भट बलवाना।
मोरे हृदय परम संदेहा, सुनि कपि प्रगट कीन्ह निज देहा।
सीता मन भरोस तब भयऊ, पुनि लघु रूप पवन सुत लयऊ।

To assure Sita about Ram's strength along with vanars' army was something Ram had asked Hanuman to do. Hanuman, therefore, did the job in a very wise manner. So that she may not feel Hanuman being proud after having shown his large body, Hanuman immediately advised that although the vanar is a small animal yet they had the blessing of Ram, with which one becomes very forceful.

Then Sita having been assured of his being a Rambhakta by heart, action and speech (मन, कर्म, बचन), Sita blessed Hanuman to be the treasure of strength and modesty. One becomes a person of character if strength is accompanied by modesty otherwise with only strength one can become rakshas. Sita's blessings to Hanuman were, therefore, quite apt at that point of time when Sita had seen the strength only of rakshasas. She also blessed him to be ever young and ever–alive. Sita knew that this ashirwad was necessary for Hanuman as he had to do a lot of Ram's jobs facing all sorts of situations. Such blessing could be given only after Sita had known that Hanuman was fully devoted to the cause of Ram. Hanuman was happy with Sita's blessings and then treating her as mother, (a son would ask the mother to feed him) Hanuman also told Sita that he was hungry and knowing fully well that Sita could not give him anything to eat, he immediately stated that she should not worry for that and he only wanted her permission, as a matter of protocol, to enable him to pluck fruits from the garden and eat. Sita could not withhold her permission when a son was hungry and who stated so before the mother. She, however, warned him that very strong rakshasas had been protecting the garden. Hanuman should, therefore, beware of that. One of the jobs entrusted by Ram to Hanuman was to show his strength to Sita to reassure her of vanars' strength. Hanuman, therefore, wisely thought of seeking mother's permission to pluck fruits from garden and on his being challenged by the guard to show his strength too.

तिन्ह कर भय माता मोहि नाहीं, जौ तुम्ह सुख मानहु मन माहीं।

Hanuman told that he was not afraid of the guard and rakshasas and would face them if his quenching the hunger in that way pleased her as a mother. Hearing this and having known the intelligence, strength and his manoeuverability to face the situation, Sita permitted him to pluck and eat fruits. As anticipated, the guard challenged Hanuman and he killed them. Some went and told about the incident to Ravan. Ravan sent his brave persons but they were also killed by Hanuman. They again went and told Ravan about what happened. Ravan then deputed his son Akshay Kumar but he too was killed by Hanuman. Then Ravan deputed Meghnad with instructions not to kill but bind him and present him in his court so that he could know the purpose of Hanuman having done all this and also to see for himself how a vanar had killed so many rakshasas including his son. This was necessary from diplomatic point of view to know the root cause of any concern to the king.

मारसि जनि सुत बांधेसु ताही, देखिअ कपिहि कहां कर आही?

Hanuman faced him too and killed many of his followers and made him unconscious. Meghnad resorted to all sorts of 'maya' but could not win over Hanuman. Then he used 'Brahmastra'. Hanuman could have faced that too having Ram/Sita's blessing with him but thought that in case he did not yield before the Brahmastra, it would be against the religious ethics in not having accepted the superiority of Brahma over him and others. He, therefore, yielded before the Brahmastra. Meghnad having bound him presented before Ravan in darbar. Hanuman too desired to have a chance to face Ravan and yielded otherwise with Ram's blessing even Brahmastra would have been of no avail. Ram had himself told Hanuman to obtain all information about the strength etc. of Ravan as according to war strategy it was very necessary to know the enemy's strength so that the preparations to fight with him were made commensurate with the strength of the enemy.

"प्रभु कारज लगि कपिहिं बधाँवा।"

Hanuman saw Ravan's darbar, where even the gods and digpal had been standing in all humiliation before Ravan but Hanuman did not have any fear of what he saw in the darbar.

After Ravan turned into Rambhakta when Sarupnakha came to him and Ravan realised Ram was not an ordinary person but Braham himself, the poet rather than calling him Ravan has started saying him as Lankesh, Dasmukh etc. as Ravan was the symbol of a rakshas and the other names were not those of a rakshas. When Hanuman was produced before Lankesh, he asked him as usual :

(1) Who he was?

(2) On whose behalf he had created the trouble as a simple vanar could not have dared doing all this in Lanka where Dasanan was ruling?

(3) Had he not heard his name?

(4) How is it that even before Ravan, Hanuman was without any fear?

(5) Why had he killed the rakshashas?

(6) Does he not have worry that he would be killed?

Hanuman answered that he had come on behalf of the almighty God i.e. Ram who creates, bears and kills the beings and who comes incarnate to annihilate the rakshasas like Ravan and has already killed Khar-Doosan etc. He also reminded Ravan how he had been defeated by Sahasbahu and Bali. He was hungry and, therefore, tried to pluck and eat fruits. His people started fighting and he had killed only those, who had been fighting with him.

On this, his son had tied him and brought here. His only anxiety now was to tell Ram about Sita and if Lankesh wanted his and his family's welfare, he should go and seek refuge under Ram. Ram would still excuse him.

प्रनतपाल रघुनायक करुना सिंधु खरारि,
गएँ सरन प्रभु राखिहैं तव अपराध बिसारि।

This was the protocol amongst rajas at that time that if even an enemy went to him and begged for being pardoned, he would forgive him for the crime committed by him. Hanuman coached him still to leave his pride and seek refuge under Ram but he would not agree and duly raged, he ordered him to be killed. At that time Vibheeshan entered Ravan's darbar with his assistants. He paid respects to Ravan and told him that killing of a raja's representative was against the international ethics.

नाइ सीस करि विनय बहूता,
नीति विरोध न मारिअ दूता।

This couplet indicates that like the present day international law granting immunities to the ambassadors of other countries by dint of which the country cannot only not kill him but have to provide full security to him inspite of any guilt/crime committed by him. The country can only ask the parent country to call him back. Similar must have been the laws/traditions/policies/at that time quoting which Vibheeshan requested Ravan not to kill Hanuman, who was immune, being the representative of another Raja Ram/ Sugreev and his pleading had been duly accepted by the House unanimously indicating that even in Ravan's darbar there was a semblance of democracy (though limited).

''सबहीं कहा मंत्र भल भाई।''

And it was decided that since vanar had special love for his tail, the same might be burnt after putting cloth and oil around it. Ram would also realise his mistake when he saw Hanuman without tail. Hanuman was also happy on this decision. He enlarged his tail so much that most of the cloth and oil in Lanka got consumed. It was then burnt.

Hanuman climbed up at one house after another and burnt entire Lanka except Vibheeshan's home which had been spared by Hanuman. He soaked himself in sea water and then went to Sita to say bye. He turned himself in shorter form and paid respects to Sita and asked for something which he could show to Ram in confirmation of his having met Sita. Sita gave him her chudamani (ornament) which Hanuman took gladly. Here again the ornament might be some letter of confirmation given by Sita to be shown to Ram to confirm that Hanuman had met her in Lanka. Although Hanuman's telling Ram that he had met Sita should have been enough but Hanuman thought it fit, as a representative, to go to Ram with some confirmation. From Ram it was essential as Hanuman was to meet Sita for the first time and, therefore, some authority was necessary but here Ram had already known Hanuman as his devotee and his word should have been enough. It shows that some exchange of letters, besides verbal confirmation, was very much in vogue in those days like it is now that everything is taken in writing only.

मातु मोहि दीजे कछु चीन्हा, जैसे रघुनायक मोहिं दीन्हा।

Sita conveyed her respects to Ram and requested for her being got released from Lanka at the earliest. Hanuman in turn consoled Sita and left Lanka. He returned to the other side of the sea and met all others, who were very happy to know that Sita's whereabouts had been known and the job entrusted to them had been done. Hanuman narrated all that he did in Lanka. They all returned to Kishkandha and started eating fruits in Madhuban. The guard complained to Sugreev that Yuvraj Angad had been destroying the garden. Sugreev could make out that Ram's job had been done otherwise Angad would not have dared to destroy the garden.

"सुनि सुग्रीव हरष कपि करि आए प्रभु काज"

Then all came to Ram and explained, where and how Sita had been located. Ram met all with affection and asked for their well being as per tradition. Ram embraced Hanuman and asked about Sita as to how she had been living and protecting herself in Lanka. The purpose in asking was to confirm that Sita was still alive and alright and had been waiting for Ram to get her released from Lanka. Hanuman also handed over the ornament given by Sita. Ram recognised and embraced. Hanuman also explained whatever Sita had told to be conveyed. Hanuman then requested for hastily going there and bringing Sita back. Ram felt obliged to Hanuman for the job done by him and recognised it but could not at that time offer any reward for it. Giving reward/award by the kings to their men for having some job done, as present now, was also prevalent in Ram's period to give recognition to the job done and for others to have an example for encouraging them to do good jobs. It is on this principle that the award of Bharat Ratan, Padam Sri, Param Virchakra, President's medal etc. have been introduced by government and their occupants are seen with special respects by the people. Hanuman fell in Ram's feet. A devotee feels ashamed on hearing his own praise by the master. So was Hanuman. Ram then asked how Hanuman entered Lanka, met Sita, and finally burnt it. Hanuman narrated all and attributed it to Ram's blessing. He did not have pride at all as to be proud is against Ram's dharam. Tulsidas has, therefore, particularly said :

''बोला बचन बिगत अभिमाना''

सो सब तव प्रताप रघुराई, नाथ न कछु मोरि प्रभुताई।

Also as per protocol, a devotee does not take credit for any job done by him and accepts it as ordained by God. Ram awarded Hanuman his bhakti, which could not be attained by anyone.

Ram then called in Sugreev and ordered him to make preparations for departure to Lanka. As per protocol, the army of vanars was under the control of Sugreev, the raja of that place. Ram, therefore, called him and asked him to order the vanars to set off for Lanka. As per protocol, the command lies in the commander only and not in anyone else, howsoever great he might be. Ram also gave recognition to this theory of command.

अब विलम्ब केहि कारन कीजे, तुरंत कपिन्ह कहुँ आयसु दीजे।

The army got collected there and they all paid respects to Ram on Sugreev's askance. Ram then started proceeding to Lanka. All good omens happened as per Hindu mythological beliefs followed by all nations. Even Sita could know by omens that Ram had set off for Lanka. Ravan accordingly got the hint by bad omens faced by him. The army of vanars was all jubilant and in good form. On the other hand all in Lanka were still not out from the shock of Lanka having been burnt by Hanuman and were thinking that a representative could do so much harm then what would happen when the master came. Mandodri was particularly more tense and requested her husband to forgo the enmity with Ram; return Sita and beg to be excused. Ram would forgive him as he was quite benevolent. Ravan laughed away whatever Mandodri had said that ladies were temperamentally fearful and they would have fear even when something good was going to happen.

सभय सुभाउ नारि कर साचा, मंगल महुँ भय मन अति काचा।

The couplet that "मंगल महुँ भय मन अति काचा" would also confirm that Ravan had turned into a bhakta of Ram and what was going to happen was the attainment of paramgati of the entire family by virtue of having been killed by Ram, the almighty. Ravan, therefore, correctly said that for a good cause, he was developing .the fight with Ram and even then Mandodri was feeling bad about it. Ravan showed all love for her and proceeded to his darbar. After going to darbar, Ravan came to know that Ram had come on the other side of the sea. Ravan 'came to know' would indicate that Ravan had full team of spies, who had been telling him of all that had been happening. Following the tradition of limited democracy, Ravan asked all his secretaries and advisers to tell what they felt about that was happening. This would indicate that even the most autocratic king like Ravan had in those days kept a Council of Secretaries/Advisers for consultation on all important matters and would not just do whatever he wanted to do. All advisers laughed and said that Ravan had already won so many battles then why this anxiety now. It indicates that although after Hanuman had burnt Lanka, everyone was tense but no one could speak frankly about it. There was constant fear from Ravan in the minds of all and although he had many advisers, they would speak only whatever was demanded by the master. This was bad for running government. The advisers should be given freedom of speech so that they were able to give correct advice. It is with this purpose in view that our constitution has provided safeguards to public servants in service conditions so that no severe action could be taken against them in the discharge of their duties unless a proper charge had been framed and requisite disciplinary procedure is followed giving him reasonable opportunity to defend himself against the charges levelled against him in the charge-sheet; and holding enquiry into the charges. The employee is given full opportunity to defend himself and then the disciplinary authority applying his mind before awarding punishment and even thereafter there are several ladders in the bureaucratic heirarchy for appeals. Such freedom, it seems, was not available in the darbars of the rajas. They could not, therefore, talk and advise fearlessly. Such advice bound by fear could not be correct advice too.

Even the poet has subsequently said :

सचिव वैद गुर तीनि जो प्रिय बोलहि भय आस,
राज धर्म तन तीनि कर होइ वेगिही नास।

If the secretary, doctor and guru talked as the king/ master desired either due to some fear or due to some expectation, then very soon the kingdom, the religion or the body would get destroyed e.g. if the secretary had fear, he would not give correct advice as in the case of the darbaris of Ravan. They did not dare say that he should compromise with Ram, returning Sita as this would have annoyed Ravan, who would have either expelled the person from his kingdom as he did with Vibheeshan or got him killed or he would lose all he had got including the seat in the darbar. Similarly if a guru is under some pressure of expectation or fear from the pupil, then the guru would only tell of good things to happen and would not alert him of the ensuing bad things or his doing irreligious things. In Mahabharat, the Daropdi's nuding episode happened in the presence of Guru Dron and Bhishampitamah because they could not stop it due to fear of Duryodhan. This led to the kingdom of Dharatrastra having been destroyed and his having been defeated by Pandavas in Mahabharat. The doctor too have to be given freedom to advise correct treatment. If he does not advise an operation in time or does not serve bitter medicines, the patient shall have to suffer more. Also if the doctor, out of fear, does not tell the correct ailment at the correct time like if a cancer patient is not told of existence of cancer in the initial stage, the ailment might become incurable.

In the Ravan's Darbar too all councillors had been only praising Ravan for his bravery and chivelerian acts in the past and none was able to warn him of the ensuing danger due to the enmity with Ram. It could also be possible that since Ravan had designed to get killed by Ram after developing enmity with him, he wanted the designs to be endorsed by his darbaris too so that he might claim that he had developed enmity with the concurrence of all. It was only Vibheeshan, who opposed and he had been given a beating and expelled from the kingdom. This again had been a wrong action for any king to have expelled his brother, who was aware of all about the kingdom to disclose to the enemy, if he happened to join him. When the matter was under consideration, Vibheeshan arrived. He paid respects to Ravan and sat. He obtained Ravan's permission to express his thinking which he said would be in his best interest. If we go back to Sita swayambar, when all rajas failed even to move the Shiv dhanush and Ram came forward to try it, Janak's queen had said that none in the good books of raja was advising him correctly as all were there only to please him and not advising him of the bitter truth that Raja Janak should give up his promise of Shiv dhanush breakage and not allow Ram, who was too mild for the dhanush, which could not even be moved by strong rajas. None, however, could dare advise raja to give up his promise. Vibheeshan advised Ravan that in his own interest, he should give up Sita and be a bhakta of Ram leaving passion, greed, rage etc, which only harmed the people. He advised that Ram was not an ordinary person but Braham himself and had come incarnation for the benefit of gods, cows and brahmins by annihilation of rakshasas. Ram might forgive him if he sought his refuge.

बार बार पद लागऊँ विनय करउँ दससीस,

परिहरि मान मोह मद भजहु कोसलाधीस।

Even Malyawant, who was an elderly adviser, agreed with what Vibheeshan had said. But, as already said, all the courtiers were only praising Ravan out of fear and expectations and were not tendering correct advice. Ravan in rage said the two, Vibheeshan and Malyawant, be removed from the darbar. Malyawant then went to his house if Ravan was not prepared to listen to him and Vibheeshan again repeated his advice saying—

सुमति कुमति सब के उर रहहीं, नाथ पुरान निगम अस कहहीं।

Nothing is good or bad but thinking makes it so. In bad days, the thinking too gets polluted and one gets convinced of the correctness of his wrong thinking and wrong actions. So thinking is important as both good and bad notions are always there but actually it is thinking which converts them into bad or good, eventually. Here Ravan knew that Ram was Braham but in his mind he was convinced that enmity with Ram only could result in his goodness ultimately. So he was not prepared to listen to any advice to the contrary. He, therefore, got enraged and expelled Vibheeshan from his kingdom not agreeing to his modest request—

तात चरन गहि माँगउँ राखहु मोर दुलार,

सीता देहु राम कहुँ अहित न होइ तुम्हार।

Vibheeshan then along with his secretary went to the other side of the sea, where Ram had arrived. While going, he did not go and join Ram quietly but proclaimed in the darbar itself that Ram was God and he was forced to go to Ram and that no one should subsequently blame him of being a traitor, who left his brother and joined the enemy to help him in the war against his brothers. Vibheeshan's departure from Lanka caused innumerable loss to Lanka e.g.

(1) Ravan lost a correct, frank and valuable adviser;

(2) Ram got a man from the enemy to help him in telling all secrets of Ravan and in fighting against the enemy.

In fact it was Vibheeshan, who alerted Ram when Meghnad was performing a yagya after which it would not have been possible to defeat him. Again it was Vibheeshan, who advised Ram of the way Ravan could be killed by throwing fire arrow in his abdomen. Similarly he chalked out the strategy of dividing Ram's army in four parts before attacking Lanka as he knew which was strong front to be faced by braves and which was weak to be handled by juniors.

Vibheeshan was happy that he would be able to serve the almighty.

जिन्ह पायन्ह के पादुकन्हि भरतु रहे मन लाइ,
ते पद आजु बिलोकिहउँ इन्ह नयनन्हि अब जाइ।

Thinking like this, he reached the other side of the sea. The vanaras thought he was some enemy's man. They caught him and reported the matter to Sugreev. After checking up from him, Sugreev told Ram that Ravan's brother had come to see him. Ram asked for his advice. Sugreev advised that rakshasas were quite illusionary and possibly Vibheeshan had come to know their secrets. He should, therefore, be kept as captive. Ram told him that according to the diplomacy, he was correct but as Ram, he would provide refuge to anyone, who sought it. This shows that in Ram's period, the institution of spies was there and the spies were deputed to mix up with the enemy's force and convey all secrets to the master. Such persons, like the present concept of prisoners of war, if caught, had been kept captive as a rule. Ram, therefore, took cognizance of that rule and appreciated Sugreev's advice but on the other side, spiritually, Ram could not deny refuge to anyone. Ram supported his conviction by saying—

सरनागत कहुँ जे तजहिं निज अनहित अनुमानि,
ते नर पाँवर पापमय तिन्हहिं बिलोकत हानि।

For kshatriyas this was also a conviction that they could not deny refuge to anyone even if he was from enemy's side. Ram also told that in case Vibheeshan was having some illusions then he would not be able to even see him. Vibheeshan, therefore, could not do any harm to him. Even otherwise Ram was sure of his strength. He even said that it was only a leela otherwise Lakshman is enough to kill all the rakshasas in the universe.

निर्मल मन जन सो मोहि पावा, मोहि कपट छल छिद्र न भावा।
जग महुँ सखा निसाचर जेते, लछिमनु हनइ निमिष महुँ तेते।
जौं सभीत आवा सरनाई रखिहउँ ताहि प्रान की नाईं।

Here the poet has also told of the protocol between the Bhagwan and bhakta. Ram never liked a bhakta with illusions like the dictum that one who comes for equity, should come with clear hands and mind. Similarly, the bhakta must go to God with clear mind as God would know of the ill-feelings of the person. If Vibheeshan had come due to his brother's misbehaviour with him then he was quite welcome.

This was the protocolic feeling amongst the kshatriyas of that time. Ram, in a democratic process, had asked for Sugreev's advice and since he did not accept it, he gave reasons to convince him of his decision, which had been welcomed by all.

उभय भान्ति तेहि आनहु हँसि कह कृपानिकेत,
जय कृपाल कहि कपि चले अगंद हनु समेत।

Ram, therefore, convinced all that in either case, there was no harm in welcoming Vibheeshan. There was other side of the policy too. Enemy's man could also be of use as he would be able to tell all secrets of that side. Such person could, therefore, be accepted and a watch kept on his day-to-day behaviour. Ram did test Vibheeshan's integrity from time to time and he had been rather helpful in the war. At the time of Ram's battle with Ravan, Ram was not able to kill him as whenever Ram cut his heads and hands, these would again grow up. Although Ram knew what to do in the situation yet he had been awaiting for Vibheeshan to tell and ultimately Vibheeshan did tell to thrash a fire arrow in Ravan's abdomen after which the heads and hands would not grow. From his side, Ram was also firm in protecting Vibheeshan even at the cost of his life. In the battle with Ravan when Ravan threw shakti on Vibheeshan to take revenge on his having joined the enemy and having betrayed him, Ram threw Vibheeshan away and offered himself to face the effect of the shakti, which virtually made Ram unconscious as it was very powerful. Such were the reciprocal ethics in accepting the enemy's man in one's force.

After having decided to welcome Vibheeshan, Ram deputed his men with Angad and Hanuman to escort him to Ram's place. Here again the deputation of Angad and Hanuman was fully as per even present day protocol of receiving the persons of other countries by an equivalent on the receiving country's side. Vibheeshan was Ravan's brother. He could not, therefore, be escorted by any ordinary person. At the same time, since he was not a raja, Sugreev too could not be sent to receive him. Ram, therefore, deputed Angad, who was the yuvraj and of the same status as Vibheeshan. Hanuman was also sent along as he had already met him, while searching for Sita in Lanka. So Hanuman could recognise him and also show him that since Vibheeshan had helped Hanuman in finding out Sita and then in saving him from being killed by Ravan in Lanka, so had Hanuman helped Vibheeshan in welcoming him to Ram's Darbar. They brought Vibheeshan to Ram's Darbar. He paid respects to Ram and Lakshman and introduced himself as per protocol.

नाथ दसानन कर मैं भ्राता, निसिचर वंस जनम सुरत्राता,

सहज पापप्रिय तामस देहा, जथा उलूकहि तम पर नेहा।

He did not conceal anything and told that he was Ram's enemy Ravan's brother and belonged to rakshas dynasty. He was a sinner temperamentally but had come to seek refuge in Ram's darbar having heard of his habit of welcoming the refuge seekers from Hanuman. He fell in Ram's feet and Ram picked up and embraced him. Ram asked him to sit alongwith him and Lakshman asked about his well being in living with the rakshasas. Vibheeshan told that now he was alright with Ram having accepted him as his man. Ram told him that even if a person, who had done all wrongs, within mortals and even immortals, came to his refuge leaving all other alternatives, he would convert him into a sadhu.

जौ नर होइ चराचर द्रोही, आवै सभय सरन तकि मोही।
तजि मद मोह कपट छल नाना, करउँ सद्य तेहि साधु समाना।

Some persons interpret it that anyone having misbehaved with mortals or immortals if comes to Ram's refuge after leaving pride, love, illusion etc, Ram would convert him into a sadhu but the meaning could also be that if a man had already left pride, love and illusion, then he automatically became sadhu but Ram's grace lies in the fact that he, on any one having come to his refuge, makes him leave all pride, love, illusion etc. and converts him into a sadhu. This also appears more logical in the context of Ram's magnanimity, which he had shown to Vibheeshan when he said that he was from rakshas dynasty and temperamentally a sinner, full of all vices. Ram said—

सगुन उपासक परहित निरत नीति दृढ़ नेम,
ते नर प्रान समान मम जिन्ह के द्विज पद प्रेम।
और
सुनु लंकेश सकल गुन तोरें, ताते तुम अतिशय प्रिय मोरे।

This is the broadmindedness of great people to appreciate the virtues of the other man. So, Ram recognised all virtues in Vibheeshan so that he did not feel small in Ram's darbar and welcomed him. Vibheeshan then requested for grant of Ram bhakti, which Ram granted. Ram also performed raj tilak ceremony making Vibheeshan the king of Sri Lanka. Complete devotion to Ram does lead to a lot of attainments, socially, spiritually and politically. Vibheeshan got the kingdom. That was the worldly and political gain. He was recognised by Ram and included in his force, inspite of his belonging to a rakshas community, that was social gain and attainment of Ram bhakti was spiritual gain. After these, nothing is left for a man to seek for. This also shows that there was the rule of vassalage. Awadh's Raja was a Chakravarti Samrat having so many smaller rulers under him. Bali was one under Awadh as confirmed by Ram that Bali had not behaved well with his brother and such persons had no place in Awadh's rajya, and, therefore, deserved to be killed. Similarly Nishad was another ruler under Awadh. After defeating Bali, Ram did not establish his rajya over there but made Sugreev the ruler of that place, of course, as a vassal under Awadh. Similarly, Lanka, though not vassal under Awadh, was not occupied by Ram after defeating Ravan, but had been handed over to his brother Vibheeshan. By designating Vibheeshan as the ruler of Lanka even before Ravan was defeated, Ram had shown Vibheeshan that he did not have any ambition over the rajya and that he had to fight with Ravan as he had himself developed enmity with him by kidnapping Sita. Had Ravan not kidnapped Sita, Ram would not have invaded Lanka. This shows that generally the Chakravarti rajas did not, without any cause, invade another kingdom simply to enlarge their kingdoms and each kingdom had freedom to exist, of course, in many cases as vassals, where it was incumbent on the principal king to keep such vassals under protection from any other invasion. Similar is the position today in the institution of vassalage.

जो सम्पत्ति शिव रावनहि दीन्हि दिएँ दस माथ,
सोई सम्पदा विभीषणहिं सकुचि दीन्हि रघुनाथ।

All vanars also praised Ram for his benevolence. Now Vibheeshan having joined Ram and belonging to that area, Ram asked for his advice as to how to cross the sea to reach Lanka. Vibheeshan told Ram that although his arrow could dry up the ocean but it was better first to request the ocean to give path. This was as per peaceful approach to any problem in Hindus. Ram too accepted it. Such an approach is in existence even today in India that is why even when Pakistan the aggressor was vacating Kashmir,

India approached UNO and resorted to cease-fire with a view to finding a peaceful solution to the problem although this approach had been a blunder for India as proved by subsequent developments. Here also although Ram requested for several days but the ocean did not provide any path. Lakshman was already against such an approach and was of the view that—

कादर मन कहुँ एक अधारा, दैव दैव आलसी पुकारा।

'for a brave warrior everything should be obtained by force and not depend on the things as ordained by God. This was the view kept by Lakshman. Ram knew it but he wanted to wait for sometime and ultimately he might have to resort to the ultimate step of using force only. As per Ram, we must exhaust all channels available before resorting to the ultimate use of force.

On the other side, Ravan deputed his spies to check up what was happening on Ram's side. The vanars recognised them as enemy's spies. They bound them and brought before Sugreev. Sugreev ordered for the parts of their body being broken. They started crying. Then Lakshman took pity on them and released them. He also gave a letter addressed to Ravan to again tell him either he returned Sita and begged to be excused otherwise he would have to face the consequences. It would be observed that from Ram several chances had been given to Ravan to give up his stubbornness and submit to Ram's authority. The spies explained, all that had happened, to Ravan. They also told that there were crores of vanars as brave as the one, Hanuman, who killed Akshay Kumar and burnt entire Lanka. They praised Ram but Ravan could not swallow it and abused the spies. Then they handed over the letter given by Lakshman. Ravan took the letter in left hand meaning thereby that he did not care for such brothers and did not even give any cognizance to such letters. That is why he took the letter with left hand and rather than reading it himself as that would have amounted to giving recognition to the letter, he asked the secretary to read it for him.

बिहसि बाय कर लीन्ही रावण, सचिव बोलि सठ लगा बचावन।

When the letter was read to him, Ravan had all the fear in his mind but outwardly he only laughed it away—

"सुनत सभय मन मुख मुसुकाई"

The spies coached Ravan to hand over Sita and seek Ram's refuge. On this, Ravan kicked them off and they also joined Ram's force and got nirvan.

Ram had been requesting the ocean to give path but there was no effect for three days. Then Ram said—

"सठ सन विनय कुटिल सन प्रीति, सहज कृपन सन सुन्दर नीति।
ममता रत सन ज्ञान कहानी, अति लोभी सन बिरति बखानी।
क्रोधिहिं सम कामिहि हरि कथा, ऊसर बीज बएँ फल जथा।

The effect of (1) request to a fool; (2) affection to a thick headed person; (3) narration of gyan to a person involved in worldly leisures; (4) detachment to a greedy person; (5) to keep quiet to a raged person; and (6) God's praise to a passionate person, is like sowing seed in barren land i.e. there would be no effect of all these efforts. Ram got prepared to fire the arrow to dry up the ocean. Then ocean appeared in person and paying respects to Ram begged to be pardoned. Ocean came with a lot of oceanic wealth comprising of gold, pearls, diamonds etc. to offer as presents. He stated that ocean was also lost in Ram's 'maya' only and did not pay any heed to Ram's request but then it was for Ram only to save all the creatures in the ocean as they too are the creation of Ram only. Here the poet has through the ocean proclaimed the important controversial couplet.

ढोल गँवार सूद्र पसु नारी, सकल ताड़ना के अधिकारी।

People say that the poet has done great injustice to the women in saying that they are kept fit by beating only whereas he was most respectful for the women at other places. But the poet's saying has to be interpreted keeping other environ in view, viz. :

(1) This had been said by ocean and not by any rishi, muni or Ram etc. and that too when the ocean was under great fear psycho from Ram, who was going to dry up

the ocean. Further, the ocean had himself too stated to be 'गंवार' illiterate/uncivilised/stupid. Such a person's saying is not to be taken cognizance of in the parlance of educated people. But then why did Tulsidas cause this couplet uttered even by the ocean, particularly in respect of the woman.

(2) Obscurely, it can also be treated as telling Ram that a woman too is to be kept under control and in case she revolted then by beating her. Although Ram, while going for hunting the deer (Marich), had warned Lakshman not to leave Sita alone, yet Sita made Lakshman leave the ashram alleging his bad intentions. If Sita had been under full control, she would not have dared say this to Lakshman, particularly when she knew that Ram was not to be defeated by anyone and she too knew that Ram had not allowed Lakshman to leave Sita alone. If she had been kept under control, the entire tranquility leading to the war with Ravan would not have arisen.

(3) Ramcharitmanas had been written in 16th century when there was Mughal rule in India. Due to Muslims' fear of kidnapping the Hindu ladies, they were not allowed to go out. They also could not go to schools etc. for education. They, therefore, could not weigh the advantageous or disadvantageous positions. And, therefore, they had to be kept under proper control since they could not take proper decisions. It was in this context that the poet had alerted the people to keep the women under proper control lest they should go astray leading to all sorts of complications.

(4) Further, 'ताड़ना' word does not denote that ढोल, गंवार, शुद्र, पशु और नारी all should be beaten with sticks etc. Such beating has been milder with each word used. At first is ढोल (drum). This has to be beaten by sticks to create noise. Next comes गंवार (an illiterate person). He may have to be occasionally slapped to keep him on correct path. So this occasional slapping is milder than the beating by sticks. Next is शुद्र (shudra). A shudra is all

understanding but at times, he may go astray. At that time he has to be shouted upon to bring him to correct path. So this is milder than beating by sticks or slapping. Next is पशु (animal). One does not have to even shout at him but has to signal to behave. Only at some occasions, one has to be rude to set the animal alright. Next is नारी (women). For a women, if she happens to go astray, one may only warn her to behave. In the case of woman, she, by and large, behaves alright and is obedient to the husband but sometimes she has to be warned too seeing that she was not acting in a prudent manner. This much alertness was made even by Shiv, when his fully devoted wife, Sati insisted on going to her father's house to attend a yagya being performed by him and where Shiv had not been invited. Shiv told Sati not to go as one is not honoured if goes uninvited to any function but Sati insisted and went there resulting in her committing suicide there having found Shiv dishonoured. So in the case of a woman even alertness or a warning is considered to be a 'ताड़ना' although it is not so and may be justified in keeping the family hegemony cordial. The head of the family, the male person, considered to be more prudent than any other in the family based on his experience etc., has to have an upper hand and veto in the affairs of the household for smooth running of the family. In the present day, whenever ladies have been given more liberty and a better say in the affairs of the family, there has been dissolution of marriages or an unpleasantness in the family.

The ocean offered to be dry but then the benefits of the ocean to mankind would get marred. Therefore, such an action be taken so that ocean was not dried up and Ram's army too crossed it. The ocean told that Nal and Neel, two vanars, were good engineers in his army and they could construct a bridge over the sea. This plea was accepted and all vanars brought stones from the mountain and Nal and Neel constructed the bridge. This shows that at that time, there were very good engineers in India and the job does was superb as is comprehensible even today. Rather than saying so in Manas, the poet has mentioned that Nal and Neel had in childhood got a boon from the rishis that the stones thrown by them in water would not sink.

नाथ नील नल कपि द्वौ भाई, लरिकाई रिषि आसिष पाई,

तिन्ह के परस किएँ गिरि भारे, तरिहहिं जलधि प्रताप तुम्हारे।

Here the construction of the bridge has been attributed to—

(1) Nal and Neel having got a boon in childhood from the rishis that stones thrown by them in ocean would not sink. They could thus throw stones and the army could pass over the sea.

(2) The stones thus thrown would not sink due to the kindness of Ram, the almighty. This was with a view to show to the universe that with Ram's grace even the stones could cross the ocean then why human being would not cross the worldly ocean with his grace.

(3) Nal and Neel may be good engineers, whc constructed a bridge on the sea, a technical feat.

This has been given colour of boon or Ram kripa so that people might digest that way and may not believe a bridge having been constructed on the ocean which is an improbability even today. A bridge was accordingly got constructed. The ocean went back paying his respects to Ram and having praised him.

6

Lanka Kand

As usual, in the beginning, the poet worships Ram and then Shiv. Since in this chapter, Sita meets Ram and Ram, Lakshman and Sita get together, there are three slokas in the beginning of this chapter as per Tulsidas's tradition.

Jamvant, who was the oldest adviser with Ram, knew about the boon having been granted by rishis to Nal and Neel that stones thrown by them in sea would not sink. He, therefore, narrated the entire episode with a view to make Nal/Neel remember it. Then all vanars brought stones. Nal and Neel used these and interconnected them so that they grew in a bridge on the sea.

सैल विसाल आनि कपि देहीं, कुदंक इव नल नील ले लेही।
देखि सेतु अति सुन्दर रचना, बिहसि कृपानिधि बोले बचना।
करिहउँ इहां सँभु थापना, मोरे हृदयं परम कलपना।

Here too it has been stated that the vanars brought the stones and handed over to Nal and Neel, who took them like the balls, as is done in construction these days, when bricks are thrown from ground to upper floor and are caught like balls by another person. After that these stones were used in construction of the bridge. "सेतु रचना" indicates that Nal and Neel had constructed a proper bridge and it was a marvel of the time. Then comes spiritual protocol from which even Ram is not spared. He too have Shiv as his God. Ram, before leaving for the big job of annihilating the rakshasas, desired to instal the Shiv idol at that place. Here the poet has wished to convey :

(1) Every one have to remember the God almighty before starting any job as all jobs can be carried out with the grace of God only.

(2) Even gods are not above it. They too have some God to grace them. Ram worshipped Shiv and Shiv worshipped Ram. Ram had even said—

सँकर प्रिय मम द्रोही, सिव द्रोही मम दास,

ते नर करहिं कल्प भरि घोर नरक महुँ वास।

One, therefore, cannot be against Shiv and be worshipper of Ram or vice versa. One may be having any of them as his God but should not oppose the other.

(3) This might be in view of the fact that at the time Ramcharitmanas was written, there was great division between vaishnavites and shaivites and even between the followers of Ram and Krishan. Therefore, with a view to bring about a reconciliation between the two, the poet has made both inseparable. It is even said that the brahmins of those days spread rumours against the Manas seeing its popularity and with a view to test its bonafide, a copy of the Manas was placed in Shiv temple in the night and next morning the book was found containing the signature of Shiv on it approving the contents of the Ramayan, including the inseparability of Ram and Shiv. Ram had even said that the persons, who had darshan of Rameshwar would after death go to his loka i.e. Shiv Bhakti is recognised not only by Shiv but by Ram too—

जो रामेश्वर दरसनु करिहहिं, ते तनु तजि मम लोक सिधरिहहिं।

To make the installation a success, Ram had invited many rishis, and munis of the area. Now the rishis and munis have to be given dakshina. This too was readily available with Ram as was given by the ocean when he appeared before Ram. So all those pearls etc. had been given to brahmins, rishis etc.

Ram's army crossed the sea through this bridge and reached Lanka. Ram gave permission to all in his army to eat whatever they found there. Here Ram had been made the commander of the force. So far Sugreev had been the commander as the raja of the land but when the army started for Lanka, Ram became the commander and, therefore, the vanars started eating in Lanka only on Ram's permission. As per protocol and laws of war, there has to be unity of command to which all have to obey.

सिंधु पार प्रभु डेरा कीन्हा, सकल कपिन्ह कहुँ आयसु दीन्हा।

खाहु जाइ फल मूल सुहाए, सुनत भालु कपि जहँ तहँ धाए।

When Ravan came to know of the bridge having been constructed on sea and Ram's army had reached Lanka, he could not first believe as it was a tremendous task. He became worried but outwardly laughed and went to rajmahal. Here Mandodri again persuaded Ravan to leave his ego and there was still time to hand over Sita and ask for Ram's pardon. She said that one should have enmity with a person, whom one can win over by intelligence or force. Here Ram was above Ravan in both these and, therefore, enmity would only result in his disaster. Mandodri also told the basic fundamental of Hinduism according to which in the last quarter of the life's span, one should hand over the charge of household/kingdom to the son and should himself go to forest for tapsya. Ravan also being in that span of age was advised to follow the canon of Hinduism; hand over Sita to Ram and had over kingdom to his son and proceed to forest for tapsya. Ravan told her not to have any fear as he was quite strong enough to defeat Ram as he had already overpowered all gods etc. Saying this, Ravan went to his darbar. He asked his advisers and secretaries as to how now should they face the enemy. The secretaries showing their anxiety asked why His Lordship had been asking the way to fight with Ram's army from time to time when each one of the rakshasas was capable of killing the entire army of Ram. But Prahast, a son of Ravan, after hearing what the secretaries had said, told Ravan that he should act according to international ethics and not depend on the advice of the secretaries as they were not as capable as the king.

नीति विरोध न करिअ प्रभु मंत्रिन्ह मति अति थोरि।

This shows—

(1) there was some law of war and international relation, (नीति) to be followed in all such cases and

(2) the secretaries of a king, specially of status of Ravan, would not give correct advice as firstly they did not have as much brilliance and secondly they gave advice suiting the king due to fear and expectation. They, therefore, were not to be believed and the king should act as per rule :

"कहहिं सचिव सठ ठकुरसोहाती"

Even one vanar burnt the entire Lanka then why these so called strong persons could not face him. Prahast had told the correct thing but he was taken by Ravan as a coward, not prepared to face the enemy, for the sake of kingdom. But Prahast told that :

प्रिय बानी जे सुनहिं जे कहहीं, ऐसे नर निकाय जग अहहीं।
बचन परम हित सुनत कठोरे, सुनहिं जे कहहिं ते नर प्रभु थोरे।

There are many people, who speak suiting others and who are prepared to hear such talks but there are few, who can tell the things of well being but which are hard to be heard and still few, who take such things in that spirit too. In other words, it is very difficult to tell and to listen the non-amiable talks although these may be of advantage but everyone wants to listen to sweet and suiting talks. People, who have no fear or consideration can only talk rude but suitable, and not others. He, therefore, advised that as per law he should return Sita to Ram and if he goes back getting Sita, it is alright, otherwise they should fight tooth and nail to defeat the enemy :

नारि पाइ फिरि जाहिं जौं, तौं न बढ़ाइअ रारि,
नाहिं ते सन्मुख समर महि, तात करिअ हठि मारि।

Prahast accordingly told the position as per law. He admitted that a wrong had been committed in kidnapping Sita. Therefore, the wrong should be set right by returning Sita if that could save the war otherwise they should fight with the enemy with all force. But Ravan could not accept and rather abused his son.

सुत सन कह दसकँठ रिसाई, असि मति सठ केहि तोहिं सिखाई।

Prahast then left the sabha and went to the rajmahal. Ravan also went to rajmahal in the evening. He went to the pleasure house at the top of the rajmahal, where there were dances and all leisures and pleasures although an enemy of Ram's status was at his head.

On the other side, Ram's army settled on this side of the sea in Lanka. A proper place was found for Ram's darbar. For such purposes, a place at a height is to be found as from there the leader of the show could see all what was going on in his army as also in the battle. Lakshman made out a stage for Ram to sit there.

सिखर एक उतंग अति देखी, परम रम्य सम सुभ्र बिशेषी।

Ram was sitting on his asan surrounded by all. He saw moon in the sky and asked why there were black spots in the moon. Such humorous talks are also necessary to keep everyone in good mood. This also shows the intelligent reply by everyone. Sugreev said it was earth's reflection in moon which is scientifically correct. This shows the astrological knowledge in India at that time. Someone said these were Rahu's attack's remnants in moon. This is a mythological fact. Ram told poison is the brother of moon (both having born from ocean) and moon has given place to his brother poison, which is of dark colour. Hanuman said moon is Ram's sewak and, therefore, Ram's dark complexion is reflected in moon. This appreciation was liked by Ram and shows that a bhakta sees his Bhagwan in everything.

Ram saw some bright place and asked Vibheeshan as to what it was. Vibheeshan told it was Ravan's pleasure house. It glittered and was full of music and dances. Ram threw an arrow in that direction to kill the pride of Ravan. It is necessary to demoralise the enemy. With this arrow, Ravan's crowns and Mandodri's ear-rings were cut off and fell on ground. No one knew the basis of this happening as the arrow was not seen by any one nor was there any other apparent reason for it. Ravan, however, laughed it away. Mandodri, got afraid and again requested Ravan to surrender to Ram, who was not an ordinary human being. But Ravan would not agree as he himself was also aware that Ram was not an ordinary person and he had developed enmity intentionally with God only.

Next morning, Ram called all advisers and asked what should be done further. Jamvant advised that one more effort be made for resorting to peace rather than attacking the enemy and starting battle. This shows, how much peace loving Indians have been since ages and war is resorted to only when inescapable. Same thing happened during Mahabharat too, when even Krishan had gone to Kaurvas as a peace-harbinger and requested to avoid war even by just giving five villages to Pandavas but Duryodhan could not agree leading to Mahabharat. Here too Ram agreed to give one more chance to Ravan to surrender by deputing Angad as peace messenger. Ram told Angad to persuade Ravan that it was to the advantage of both sides to compromise rather than resorting to war.

काजु हमार तासु हित होई, रिपु सन करेहु बतकही सोई।

Ravan should return Sita and surrender in his own interest. Angad was happy to have been entrusted with a job by Ram. This was the devotion. Angad paid respects to all and departed. On the way he met Ravan's son. He developed quarrel with Angad, who killed him. Everyone thought same vanar (Hanuman), who had burnt Lanka, had again come. Everyone gave way in fear.

बिनु पूछे मगु देहिं दिखाई, जेहि बिलोक सोइ जाइ सुखाई।

He went to Ravan's mahal and one messenger told Ravan of his arrival. Ravan called him in. Angad saw the fearful Ravan sitting in darbar but he did not have any fear. Seeing Angad, all in darbar got up in honour. Such an honour is given when a very high personality, king etc. comes and not for an ordinary messenger as Angad presently was. But all had got up in honour in fear of the vanar. Ravan could not digest giving such honour to Angad by his darbaris and got enraged. Angad bowed before the king, as per protocol while meeting a king and sat there. Ravan asked about his identity. Angad narrated all and told him that he had come for his well-being as his father and Ravan had been good friends. He told that Ram could even now excuse him if he returned Sita and accepted Ram's overlordship. Rather than accepting Angad's advice, Ravan started explaining his bravery and told Angad that he was able to defeat Ram but accepted the bravery of Hanuman, whom Angad said was only a minor messenger in Ram's army. Angad showed his surprise that Hanuman had burnt Lanka without Ram's permission. He, therefore, out of fear, had not so far gone back. Without fear, Angad disclosed in the darbar the weaknesses of Ravan, captured by Sahasbahu; one arrested in Patal; and one remained in the under arm of Bali (under control of Bali). This showed the fearlessness granted to a representative of another king in the darbar of a king similar to the present day immunities granted to ambassadors.

एक कहत मोहिं सकुच अति रहा बालि की कांख
इन्ह महुँ रावन तैं कवन सत्य बदहि तजि माख।

Then Ravan started telling the stories of his bravery. A talk between Angad and a king like Ravan is unthinkable if there was no fearlessness. Ravan also deprecated Ram in his talks, which annoyed and enraged Angad, who told him that he had not come for any compromise but to warn him either to surrender or face a war and even he alone could have defeated Ravan and taken Sita back but this was not the wish of Ram. When Ravan started talking against Ram, Angad got enraged and put his foot on earth challenging if anyone could even move it, he would advise Ram to return back. Such was the authority given by the Lord to the representative in those days. Inderjeet and others tried to move the foot of Angad but failed. Then Ravan got up but Angad said :

गहत चरन कह बालि कुमारा, मम पद गहें न तोर उबारा
गहसि न राम चरन सठ जाई, सुनत फिरा मन अति सकुचाई।

This shows the intelligence of the representative. How he dealt with in Ravan's darbar and degraded Ravan and his people morally. In war strategy, the killing of the enemy morally, is half victory. Ram achieved the same through Angad and Hanuman. Angad still persuaded Ravan to surrender before Ram but he did not agree. Angad came back to Ram. Ravan went to rajmahal where Mandodri again persuaded Ravan to seek Ram's refuge in view of what he had seen from Hanuman and Angad, who are Ram's juniors. Ram had sent the messenger as a matter of grace and it was a chance for Ravan to agree to what Angad had said. Ravan, however, did not buzz. Mandodri even said :

काल दंड गहि काहु न मारा, हरइ धर्म बल बुद्धि विचारा।

Bad time is not apparently known as it does not quarrel or beat the person but deprives the person of his religion, strength, intelligence and thinking power meaning thereby that the person only is convinced in his mind that he was doing correct thing although apparently it was wrong. That is what the poet has said at another place :

"तुलसी जस भवतव्यता तैसेइ मिलहिं सहाय"

Whatever is in store for a person, the circumstances make it so. Ravan, after hearing Mandodri, went to his darbar.

Ram called in Angad and asked him to narrate all that had happened and how he had got hold of Ravan's crowns and sent them there. Angad told that these were not the four crowns but the four policies of ruling, viz. love, wealth, punishment and division (साम, दाम, दंड, भेद). These have left Ravan and have come to Ram. So Ravan was bereft of all these four virtues.

सुनु सर्वग्य प्रनत सुखकारी, मुकुट न होहि भूप गुन चारी।

Such intelligent and learned were the juniors and vanars in those days what to speak of the actual pandits and other caste persons. Angad also narrated all about Lanka, and management and strategic preparation made therein. After hearing this, Ram called all his advisers to draw the strategy of attacking Lanka. Although Ram was supreme commander and he knew how to manage the affairs yet he wanted to keep into confidence his advisers too as required by war protocol because even a junior person could give good advice. This also shows that although supreme commander, the king should not consider himself as perfect and should run the show in consultation with all his lieutenants. Accordingly Ram called all and asked :

लंका बांके चारि द्वारा केहि विधि लागिअ करहु विचारा।
तब कपीस रिच्छेस विभीषण, सुमिरि हृदय दिनकर कुल भूषण।
करि विचार तिन्ह मंत्र दृढ़ावा, चारि अनी कपि कटकु बनावा।
यथायोग सेनापति कीन्हे, जूथप सकल बोलि तब लीन्हें।

The first and foremost war strategy is to know all about the enemy's capital. Here Angad and Hanuman had told that Lanka had four gates of entry. The attack should, therefore, be at all the four gates. Ram had consulted Sugreev, the king of vanars, Jamvant, a senior secretary and Vibheeshan who knew all about Lanka. The entire force was then divided into four parts to attack from each gate. A commander was deputed with each part according to the importance of the gate on which he was being deputed. So Ram also selected and deputed four commanders, each in-charge of a force to attack at designated gate and the army accordingly attacked Lanka from four sides.

When Ravan heard of the attack, he also called his commanders and ordered his army to kill all vanars. The rakshasas proceeded as ordered. They mounted on the walls on all sides of Lanka. On one side was the slogan praising Ram and on the other praising Ravan. There was fierce battle. Ravan's soldiers started retreating. Then Ravan ordered that whosoever retreated from the battle would be killed by him. Thus it became fear of death in either way. Ravan's force then started fighting with more involvement.

जो रन विमुख सुना मैं काना, सो मैं हतब कराल कृपाना।

This too was a war strategy to put in fear within army's mind from retreating and fighting with more devotion. This worked and when the rakshasas fought with more devotion, the vanars started retreating, Hanuman came to their rescue. Angad heard of Hanuman having gone alone. He also joined him. This shows the alertness in the commanders to fight out together, wherever help was required. The two, Hanuman and Angad, fought with great zeal and involved a great loss to Lankan army.

भुज बल रिपुदल दलमलि देखि दिवस कर अंत,
कूदे जुगल विगत श्रम आए जहँ भगवंत।

Angad and Hanuman killed lot of enemy's people and seeing the fall of night, came back and reported to Ram. In those days even in big wars the battle lasted during the day and was stopped during the night. This is what is heard in the case of Mahabharat too in which case it is said that after the closure of the battle on sunset, the enemies used to sit together and talk together. When Abhimanyu was killed, both Kauravas and Pandavas were there to attend the funeral. So was in the case of Bhisam etc. also. In Ram-Ravan war also, the battle was during the day and rest at night. Ram appreciated the bravery of Hanuman and Angad which gave them satisfaction. Appreciation of the braves in the army is also a strategy to keep up the morale of the jawans. Next day again the battle started and Angad and Hanuman were there. There was again fierce battle. Rakshasas created darkness all through so that none could see the other. Ram, however, recognised it and with one arrow finished the maya. This shows that Ram, as commander-in-chief, had been very alertly watching all that was happening in the battle field from his stage and had been taking preventive measures as warranted. The commanders in the war should accordingly be very alert and be a part of the battle even though sitting in the headquarters. Angad and Hanuman went to the battle field and the rakshasas ran away. Again during night they came back and reported to Ram.

On the other side, Ravan saw that half of his army had already been killed by Ram's sena. He called darbar and asked for advice as to what to do further. Malyawant, a senior person, advised him to still seek Ram's refuge. Ravan got enraged and expelled him from the darbar. Meghnad, however, assured of defeating Ram next day. Next day again battle started. Meghnad challenged Ram, Lakshman, Angad, Hanuman etc. in the battle field. He killed many vanars. Hanuman then faced him in battle. Meghnad, rather than fighting with him, went to Ram and challenged him. Ram destroyed all Meghnad's armaments. He then spread his maya. Ram, however, with one arrow finished the maya. Then with Ram's permission Lakshman went along with Angad and others to fight with Meghnad. Ram had drawn proper strategy as to who would fight with whom. At first the juniors like Angad, Hanuman etc. were put to fight and then Lakshman. After that only the turn of Ram came. So to fight with Meghnad, Ram deputed Lakshman.

Fierce battle started between the two. None was able to defeat the other. Lakshman perplexed Meghnad. When Meghnad thought that now he would be killed. To save himself, Meghnad fired Brahmshakti and hit Lakshman, who became unconscious. Meghnad tried to pick him up but failed. Then Hanuman easily picked him up and brought to Ram. Seeing Lakshman unconscious, Ram was upset. Jamvant told that there was one Sukhain Vaid in Lanka. Someone should bring him from there. Hanuman went and brought him alongwith his house. Hanuman was very intelligent. He thought if he requested Sukhain to accompany him, he might refuse to serve the enemy and time was also very short. He, therefore, took away the entire house. On reaching Ram's side, Sukhain told the medicine available at Himalayas and should be brought before the next day started. Hanuman immediately left to bring the requisite medicine.

On the other side, Ravan too was not keeping quiet. He, through his spies, came to know of Hanuman having proceeded to bring medicine. He went to Kalnaimi, a rakshas, and deputed him to keep Hanuman engaged during the night so that he could not reach before morning. Kalnaimi was afraid of facing Hanuman but then there was fear of Ravan too. He, therefore, proceeded and created a temple and garden on the way. Hanuman seeing the temple asked for muni's permission to take bath and have rest. He went to take bath in the pond nearby. In the pond a crocodile caught Hanuman but Hanuman killed him. The crocodile was actually a muni and had become so with an other muni's curse. He again came to his original self and warned Hanuman to be alert of the muni in the temple as he was a rakshas. Hanuman came and killed the rakshas and proceeded further. Ravan had further got fire spread on mountain so that Hanuman was not able to recognise the Sanjeevan booty. This shows Ravan's alertness as a commander-in-chief of his army. He had been creating one obstacle after the other in Ram's jobs. Hanuman, however, brought a big piece of mountain having not been able to recognise the medicine as the time at the disposal was short. While passing through Awadh on way, Bharat saw him and thought that some rakshas had been coming. He fired a blunt arrow. This shows that the rajas were quite alert in their respective kingdoms in protecting the same. Bharat was vigilant to see Hanuman. He fired blunt arrow as he had learnt from his father Dasrath to fire a blunt arrow if one does not know the bonafides of the person fired upon. Dasrath had fired a sharp edged arrow on Shravan Kumar, taking him as an animal and killed him resulting in having earned the curse of his parents. Since then all were careful. While protecting Vishwamitra's yagya, Ram was not sure of Marich's bonafides, as it is said that rather than disturbing the yagya, he had come for Ram's darshan but having been a rakshas, Ram could not take a chance of allowing him to come closer and fired a blunt arrow which threw him near Lanka. Ram's purpose of protecting the yagya was served and at the same time Marich was not killed. Here too as Bharat had only assumed Hanuman to be a rakshas, as rakshas, only would carry hills like that to attack someone, he fired blunt arrow. Hanuman came down on earth on arrow having struck. He proclaimed 'Ram'. Hearing that voice, Bharat came closer and asked all about Ram telling that he was Bharat. Hanuman told all that had been happening e.g. Sita having been kidnapped and Lakshman being unconscious in the war with Ravan. After this, since there was shortage of time, Hanuman requested for permission to go. Bharat offered to send him quickly through his arrow. Arrow taking Hanuman quickly to Lanka would indicate that there must have been some sort of rockets, like the present ones, which, when fired, would go with great speed. Hanuman took permission and proceeded for Lanka.

Here a question of protocol arises as to why Bharat, having known the complexity and magnitude of Ram having been engaged in war with Ravan, Sita's kidnapping and Lakshman being unconscious, did not proceed or sent Shatrughan or army to assist Ram, he being a very devotee of Ram and also knowing what Ram would think after learning from Hanuman that Bharat had known all about war but still did not come for assistance. Whereas Tulsidas had been very alert in redressing all such doubts wherever arose, he is silent here e.g. —

(1) At the time of Shiv's marriage with Parvati, they performed Ganesh pooja whereas Ganesh is said to be the son of Parvati and Shiv. Tulsidas wrote that one should not develop any doubt as Ganesh had been Adidevta besides being the son of Parvati and Shiv and Shiv and Parvati had worshipped Ganesh as the Adidevta.

(2) When Nishad got worried seeing Ram and Sita sleeping on santhri, Lakshman removed the doubt saying that Ram was Braham and, was, therefore, above the griefs or pleasures.

(3) When Ram arrived at Ayodya after the 14 years living in forest, he met everyone in a moment. Immediately Tulsidas stated that Ram had made as many forms, as the attendants at that place, were.

(4) Dasrath while starting to attend Ram's marriage from Ayodhya, he remembered Ram. Here Dasrath would not have remembered his son Ram but Adi Ram.

But in the context of Bharat not having cared to go to Lanka for helping Ram is unanswered. Also when Lakshman was fighting a battle of life and death, Bharat does not appear to have cared to know as to what happened to his treatment; whether Hanuman was able to reach in time and whether the medicine worked or not. Similarly, when Hanuman would have told Ram his meeting with Bharat, he also does not appear to have been anxious to inform Bharat of his well being. For a brother, whom Ram thought will not live for a day if he did not reach Awadh after 14 years, such omission appears amiss. There is nothing in

Manas in this regard. It is, however, said that elsewhere it is written that Bharat did raise the question but then Kaushalya told him not to worry as it was all lila (लीला) and nothing would happen ultimately. But seeing from the angle of Ram's lila itself, who had been crying hoarse on Sita having been kidnapped and on Lakshman having been injured in battle left it for his divine power to be associated and did not care to tell Bharat as an ordinary human being would have done.

Further while crying on Lakshman having been injured in battle Ram said—

जौं जनतेउँ बन बंधु बिछोहू, पिता बचन मनतेउँ नहि ओहू।

A person of the entity of Ram could have left courage on Lakshman having been injured in battle so much so that he had even repented on having agreed to carry through father's order of going to forest if this had to happen. But father had only ordered Ram to go to forest and it was Ram only who agreed to take Lakshman along. He, therefore, could have repented on having committed the mistake of bringing Lakshman along and not abiding by Dasrath's order of going to forest, is unthinkable. Like ordinary human being, Ram had been crying in the battle field, where he was the commander-in-chief of the army. Such crying only demoralises the army and is never advisable ethically in the tenets of war (प्रभु प्रलाप सुनि कान विकल भए बानर निकर). Further, Ram, who had not worried at all when Dasrath, rather than coronating him, ordered his living in forests for 14 years, and kept equilibrium (neither happy nor sad), how he was so much worried on that occasion is unexplained. Ram even remembered here his responsibility of returning back in alright condition with Sita and Lakshman. This is what Lakshman's mother Sumitra had expected. Thus Ram could have been worried for that and not for having carried out Dasrath's order.

सौंपेसि मोहि तुम्हहि गहि पानी, सब विधि सुखद परम हित जानी।

Tulsidas has only said through Shiv—

उमा एक अखंड रघुराई, नर गति भगत कृपाल देखाई।

That Ram was Braham and was crying here to show what an ordinary person would have done in the situation.

At that time Hanuman reached there. Sukhain served the medicine and Lakshman became alright. Here the poet has tried to show that in Ram's period even the medicinal treatment was at the top so much so that Lakshman had been saved even when he had been injured by Brahmastra. Such treatment is shown on the basis of the (जड़ी बूटी) ayurvedic treatment. Even today ayurvedic treatment (by जड़ी बूटी) exists in India only which has been recognised by the world at large. Sukhain was sent to Lanka from where he had been brought as demanded by protocol exactly in the same way as he was brought :

कपि पुनि बैद तहां पहुँचावा, जेहि बिधि तबहिं ताहि लइ आवा।

So that the Vaid did not feel awkward in having gone to treat the enemy. With Lakshman having been alright, the vanars became happy but Ravan was upset.

Ravan then went and got Kumbhkaran awakened. He narrated all that had happened to Kumbhkaran. The first reaction of Kumbhkaran, after having heard entire episode, was that Ravan had committed a blunder in having kidnapped Sita, who is Jagdamba and not an ordinary lady and Ram was the Braham.

सुनि दसकंधर बचन तब कुभंकरन बिलखान।
जगदम्बा हरि आनि अब सठ चाहत कल्याण।

This shows that Rambhakti was in the blood of all rakshasas. Vibheeshan was known Rambhakta; Ravan too, immediately after Sarupnakha narrated about her ears and nose having been cut and Khar-Dooshan's death, proclaimed Ram was not an ordinary human being but God incarnate and he should develop enmity with Ram so that by having been killed by Ram, he could attain salvation. Also before kidnapping Sita, Ravan had paid respects to her. That way even Ravan himself was a Rambhakta and now the third brother Khumbhkaran too admitted the authority of Ram as almighty God. He rebuked Ravan that he had not done correct thing and now have sought for his help. But since there was affinity of brotherhood, he offered himself for help whatever be the consequences as is called for in unity although Ravan should have atleast consulted him before doing all this—

प्रथमहिं मोहि न सुनाएहि आई।
कीन्हे प्रभु विरोध तेहि देवक, शिव विरँचि सुर जाके सेवक।

Kumbhkaran as a bhakta was happy that he would have close darshan of Ram in the battle field.

राम रूप गुन सुमिरत मगन भयउ छन एक।

This is the devotion for God even in rakshasas, an instance of Bhagwan-bhakta protocol. Kumbhkaran proceeded for the battle field. At first Vibheeshan came in front and paid respects to his elder brother, Kumbhakaran. He embraced Vibheeshan and praised for his being Rambhakta. Vibheeshan explained that Ravan had hurt him by kicking him when he advised Ravan to seek refuge under Ram. Because of that humiliation, he had come and joined Ram, who accepted him taking pity on him. He again appreciated Vibheeshan for having become Rambhakta but since at that time he was under the influence of being killed, he was not able to differentiate between good or bad. So better he went away from there. Vibheeshan came to Ram and told him about the arrival of Kumbhkaran for battle. The vanars attacked him with trees and stones but there was no effect on Kumbhkaran. Kumbhkaran made Angad, Hanuman, Sugreev etc. unconscious by his attack. Here again Shiv comes forward and tells Parvati, lest she should again develop any doubt about Ram's capability that Ram was doing lila like ordinary human beings.

उमा करत रघुपति नर लीला।

Sugreev etc. came to Ram and sought his help. Ram had given chance to Sugreev etc. :

(1) as a matter of war strategy to send juniors first and then only the commander should go if the juniors fail to handle the situation; and

(2) the juniors should not become proud if they only win

and are not defeated also. Ram, therefore, told Lakshman, Sugreev and Hanuman to fight with the army and he would handle Kumbhkaran.

Division of army and commanders need a lot of knowledge of war strategy which Ram did have and demonstrated from time to time. Ram fired many arrows. The arrows were such that after hitting the target they would return back to Ram for reuse.

छन महुँ प्रभु के सायकन्हि काटे विकट पिसाच,
पुनि रघुबीर निषंग महुँ प्रबिसे सब नाराच।

These days rockets are fired and unmanned planes too are flown but these only attack and do not come back. Science and technology in those days appear to be more perfect as the arrows fired came back for being reused. There was fierce battle between Ram and his army and Kumbhkaran and his army. Ram cut his arms but still Kumbhkaran continued fighting with his body only and was shouting which threatened the gods. Ram then cut his head from the body. Kumbhkaran then fell on earth, dead. Somewhat of the proceedings of battle have been narrated here with a view to have an idea of the fierceness of the battle being fought between Ram and Ravan in those days. Kumbhakaran's head fell before Ravan, who felt aggrieved. The gods were happy and praised Ram. Ram gave Kumbhakaran his Lok as —

(1) Kumbhkaran was killed by him, and

(2) Kumbhkaran was in his heart a bhakta of Ram;

In the night the two forces returned to their respective places, on stoppage of battle. Defeat of Kumbhakaran by Ram raised the morality of Ram's force. In Ravan's camp, there was all sadness amongst gents and ladies. Protocol required someone to encourage the people at that time. This job was done by Meghnad, who indicated that he had got a chariot from God on which he could win the battle the next day.

Next day accordingly Meghnad went to the battle field. On the other side, Lakshman, who had been hurt by the kshatriyas, had come with Sugreev, Vibheeshan, Hanuman etc. Meghnad bound Ram in Nagpash. After injuring Lakshman, Sugreev and Hanuman. Although Ram is Braham and could not be bound but it was lila and to recognise the sanctity of Nagpash, Ram got himself bound. This doubt has been removed by Shiv by saying :

गिरिजा जासुनाम जपि मुनि काटहिं भव पास,
सो कि बंध तर आवइ व्यापक विश्व निवास।

In the absence of Ram, Lakshman, Sugreev etc., Jamvant came to fight with Meghnad. He caught hold of his leg and threw him in Lanka. On the other side, Narad sent Garud to get Ram released from Nagpash. Garud ate away all nagas and Ram was released from Nagpash. When Meghnad became conscious in Lanka, he felt much in having been thrown by Jamvant like that. He went in cave to perform some enemy-killer yagya. Vibheeshan came to knew of it. He alerted Ram that in case the yagya was finished, it would be difficult to defeat him. This shows that from Ram's side the spying was full and he could know everything that was happening in Lanka particularly with the know-how of Vibheeshan. Ram was happy to know of the forewarning by Vibheeshan, who though from enemy side, had been proving to be quite devoted to Ram. Ram deputed Lakshman and others to disturb the yagya and to kill Meghnad.

तुम लछिमन मारेहु रन ओही, देखि सभय सुर दुख अति मोही।

On Ram's order, Lakshman readily proceeded for the battle swearing that he would not report back if he is not able to kill him as ordered by Ram. Such was the confidence in the Kshatriyas of that time. Lakshman and others disturbed yagya and forced Meghnad to join the battle. Fierce battle started. Meghnad was in rage for not having been able to complete the yagya. He attacked the vanars. Ultimately battle started between Lakshman and Meghnad. Meghnad had been using all sorts of rakshasi maya in the battle. Lakshman then remembering Ram fired one arrow which hit his heart and he died. At the time of his death, Meghnad uttered the words "where is Ram,", "where is Lakshman". This shows that from the heart Meghnad was also a bhakta of Ram like Ravan, Kumbhkaran and Vibheeshan as already indicated. Hanuman picked him up and left at Lanka dwara. This was the humane action done by the fighters that the dead body of the killed commanders, if not of all soldiers, was handed over to the people of his side. So Hanuman handed over the body to Ravan's men. Gods were happy as usual knowing the death of Meghnad. Ravan's people—men and women—were all very sad as Meghnad was one on whom they were dependent. Now there was none else in Lanka but Ravan only, who calmed them down saying—

तब दसकंठ विविध विधि समुझाई सब नारि,
नस्वर रूप जगत सब देखहु हृदयँ विचारि।

This shows the extent of brahmgyan, Ravan possessed. After Ravan spoke the above brahmgyan talks, the poet was forced to write:

तिन्हहि ज्ञान उपदेसा रावन, आपुन मंद कथा सुभ पावन।
पर उपदेस कुसल बहुतेरे, जे आचरहिं ते नर न घनेरे।

Ravan having all the brahmgyan had done a very wrong thing in having kidnapped Sita and not agreeing to surrender to Ram inspite of every one having persuaded him to do so. Now on son's death, he told everyone down with sadness that this body was mortal and since one had to die, death should not cause any sadness. Here the poet has also told that one is apt in advising others but does not follow the same himself like a father himself a smoker and drunkard asking his son to be non-smoker and teetotaler. The father, to be more effective in what he says, has to first give up smoking and drinking himself. Ravan's preaching was, therefore, not effective since everyone knew that the entire killing had been due to the bad deeds of Ravan himself.

Next day again the vanars went for the battle and attacked. On the other side now only Ravan was left. He warned his people that only those, who did not have fear of war, should accompany him otherwise he would himself fight it out since it was his own creation. Ravan's saying that it was his creation must be on the basis of what everyone was saying on so many deaths having taken place that all this was because of wrong deed of Ravan. Ravan, therefore, proceeded for the battle with his faithful sepoys. There were bad omens but Ravan did not take cognizance of the same. Ravan and his force started killing the vanars, who duly frightened went and reported to Ram. Ram went to fight with Ravan. Vibheeshan became anxious that Ravan was on chariot and Ram being on foot, how could he engage Ravan in fighting. Ram, however, discounted his fear and told it was not chariot but other aspects in war which counted e.g. intelligence, courage, strength, fairness and being religious minded. Anyone, who had these qualities, could win the battle easily. Vibheeshan was convinced. It is the duty of the commander to keep the morality of his juniors high. So when Vibheeshan got doubt, Ram mitigated the same intelligently. The poet has also found an excuse of teaching the above aspects to public through Ram himself :

सुनि प्रभु बचन बिभीषन हरषि गहे पद कंज,
एहि मिस मोहि उपदेसेहु राम कृपा सुख पुंज।

It is not the advice to Vibheeshan but to the people at large to adopt the said qualities to win over any difficulty in the universe. Fierce battle had started. The gods, including Brahma and Shiv, had come to witness the battle in their vimans.

"एक एक सन भिरहिं पचारहिं"

This indicates that there were rules of fighting in battle. One could fight with one and not that one was attacked and killed by many. Vanars had killed many rakshasas. Then seeing his force being killed, Ravan came to that side and attacked the vanars. Vanars too fought with bravery but could not face Ravan. They sought refuge under Hanuman, Angad and Ram. To save the situation, Lakshman went to fight after taking Ram's permission. Ravan got enraged seeing Lakshman, the killer of his son, and threw many arrows on him, which Lakshman destroyed.

Then Lakshman fired hundreds of arrows on Ravan and he became unconscious. After he became conscious, Ravan threw 'Brahma Shakti' on Lakshman. Lakshman became unconscious and fell. Ravan went to pick him up but was unsuccessful. Then Hanuman came to fight, he made Ravan unconscious with his attack. Hanuman brought Lakshman to Ram and with Ram's grace, after some time, Lakshman gained consciousness. Immediately thereafter he again took his dhanusban and came to engage Ravan in fighting as any kshatriya would do. He broke the chariot and killed the sarthi and made Ravan unconscious with his attack. Another sarthi brought Ravan to Lanka. To keep his juniors' morality high, Ram had been giving them chance again and again to fight with Ravan. Ravan was ashamed finding himself in Lanka, away from the battle field. He, as a true fighter, rebuked his sarthi as to why he brought him from battle field like a coward. Lakshman reported back to Ram. Ravan started performing some yagya to attain victory over Ram but Vibheeshan immediately came to know of it through his spies. He told Ram about the yagya being performed. Ram sent Hanuman and others to disturb the performance of yagya. They rebuked Ravan to have come from battle field like coward and was shielding himself in mahal. After destroying the yagya, the vanars reported back to Ram. On the other side, rakshasas again came to the battle field.

On Ram's side, the gods requested Ram that rakshasas had already had enough of playing in the battle field and now Ravan should be brought to a finish. They told Ram for their request to be more effective that Sita had been quite upset about the war not coming to an end. Ram laughed how Sita had been brought in and proceeded to fight with Ravan. Gods were happy. Fierce fighting again ensued. Inder sent his chariot for use by Ram so that he could fight in a better way with Ravan. The chariot had very efficient horses, which walked as desired by the occupant in his mind. Might be there was so much advancement in electronics at that time that even horses could be controlled by remote control through mind/wish only. Ravan thought that in view of huge army of vanars, he should do some maya and he accordingly made many Rams and Lakshmans. Such maya was spread by Ram also at the battle with Khar-Dooshan etc., where he made every rakshas appearing like Ram and then the rakshasas fought amongst themselves and finished killing each other. Ram recognised the maya and finished it by firing an arrow. Ram then proceeded for a dual fight with Ravan and brought his chariot near Ravan. As a matter of protocol, he paid respects to brahmins in his mind. Ravan said he would give a big fight to Raja Ram and could not be killed like Khar-Dooshan, Kumbhkaran etc. Here Ravan addressed Ram as a raja. So far he had been addressing Ram as tapsavi only. This might be due to—

(1) Now Ram was not fighting on foot like the tapasvi but was having the chariot of Inder. Ravan having already captured Inder and other gods, could well recognise the chariot. Such chariot could be had by rajas only.

(2) Having seen so many brave rakshasas killed, such strategy and war manoeuvrability could be shown by rajas only.

(3) Ravan being a big king thought it was not apt for him to fight with a tapsavi. He could fight with a king only being worth his position.

आज बयरु सबु लेउँ निबाही, जौं रन भूप भाजि नहि जाही।

Seeing that because of this being his last day, Ravan had been uttering all that, the poet here through Ram tells the people on Ravan's utterances that there are three kinds of men :

(1) Like rose, who only gives the flower and is not of any other use. Such men speak a lot but are not capable of doing anything or do not do anything.

(2) Like mango, who give both flower and fruit. Such persons both say and see that it is done too.

(3) Like jack fruit (कटहल) which only gives fruit and no flowers. Such persons do not utter but only believe in getting the job done.

Ravan, however, said that battle field was not the place for coaching but for fighting only. Ravan thereafter threw many arrows and other arms which Ram made ineffective. Ravan then fired arrows on sarthi, who became unconscious. Ram got enraged. He fired many arrows. At first he killed the horses and the sarthi. Then he cut his arms and heads but new heads and hands would crop up (this was due to some boon Ravan had when he cut his heads and worshipped Shiv with those heads). Again and again Ram would cut his hands and heads but they would again crop up. Then Ravan fired many arrows so much so that Ram's chariot disappeared amongst the arrows. The gods became afraid. Ram, however, made all this ineffective. All the heads cut by Ram were floating in space and uttering "where is Ram". This even made the vanars afraid. Ravan then saw Vibheeshan standing before him. He did not want to see him at all after Vibheeshan had left Lanka. Seeing him along with Ram, Ravan got enraged and he fired a 'Shakti' to kill Vibheeshan. But seeing the Shakti aimed at Vibheeshan, Ram came forward and took the effect of Shakti on himself as a result of which Ram became unconscious. This, however, shows that as a matter of protocol, a person had to save his friend or a refugee to whom refuge had been granted even at the cost of his own life itself. Ram had granted refuge to Vibheeshan; he had made him his friend; and had already coronated him as the raja of Lanka. Ram, therefore, threw Vibheeshan aside and faced the attack of Shakti on himself. This enfuriated Vibheeshan, who came forward to fight with Ravan. He attacked Ravan, who fell unconscious. He again got up and a fierce battle ensued between Ravan and Vibheeshan. How could Vibheeshan, a very mild person, who could not even speak before Ravan, fight with Ravan, was unthinkable but then the poet dismantles this thinking by telling through Shiv that it was the effect of Ram's grace which pumped in so much force and morality to enable Vibheeshan to fight with Ravan.

उमा विभीषण, रावनहि सन्मुख चितव कि काउ,
सो अब भिरत काल ज्यों श्री रघुबीर प्रभाउ।

Then Hanuman came to the rescue of Vibheeshan. He killed the sarthi and broke the chariot of Ravan. Fight ensued between Hanuman and Ravan and Vibheeshan went to Ram. Meantime Ram attained consciousness and came again to fight with Ravan. Ravan again started spreading his maya of disappearing and then appearing. He also made several Ravans by maya. The gods got afraid and vanars were also fearful. Ram then eliminated all mayavi Ravans with one arrow. Angad then came and fought with Ravan and after attacking him went to Ram. Ram again cut his hands and head but they again cropped up. All vanar commanders, Hanuman, Nal, Neel, Angad etc. had been fighting with Ravan's cropped up heads but Ravan could not be controlled. Then Jamvant came and attacked. Sarthi took him to Lanka in unconscious condition for the night.

Trijata told Sita about Ravan's new cropping of heads and she was worried. On Sita's asking how Ravan could be killed, Trijata told that Ravan could be killed if an arrow is fired hitting his heart but Ram is not firing such an arrow as in Ravan's heart there was Sita and in Sita's heart there was Ram and in Ram's heart, the entire universe lived. If, therefore, Ram fired in Ravan's heart, the entire universe would get annihilated. Now by repeatedly cutting his heads, Ravan would lose the memory of Sita by diversion and then Ram would fire in the heart of Ravan, causing his death. How intelligent the logic was by a Rakshasni Trijata from which the intelligence of other rakshasas could be imagined. This also shows that Sita was in the heart of Ravan as Ravan had converted as a bhakta of Ram and Sita. This was a logical as well as humorous reply by Trijata to bring Sita out of the worry and also to show that ultimately Ravan would be killed. Indirectly Trijata had told Ram through Sita that Ravan could be killed by firing an arrow in his heart. This also subsequently got proved when Vibheeshan told Ram of the way how Ravan could be killed.

On the other side, Ravan attained consciousness in midnight and finding himself in Lanka, he felt ashamed (of having been brought from the battle field like a coward). He got enraged on sarthi as usual. Ravan again went to the battle field and the battle started as usual first with vanars, who gheraoed Ravan. Ravan then used his maya creating pisachas etc. The vanars in fear started running away.

Even Lakshman and Sugreev became unconscious on Ravan's present attack. Ram dismantled the maya with one arrow. Ram fired arrows and again cut hands and heads of Ravan but the same cropped up again. Infact Ram had been waiting to test the loyalty of Vibheeshan, who knew how Ravan could be killed, as to when Vibheeshan would come out with method for killing Ravan leaving the affection of his brother and being faithful to Ram, whom he had joined against Ravan but who could still be said to be having some affinity with Ravan, after all being his brother and wishing not to be the means of killing him.

उमा काल मर जाकीं ईछा, सो प्रभु जन कर प्रीति परीछा।

Ultimately when maya disappeared, Vibheeshan came forward and told Ram that there was an Amrit Kund in the abdomen of Ravan, which did not permit Ravan to die. Ram was glad to know this from Vibheeshan. This is how the man of an enemy remains a matter of doubtful integrity always but can be helpful too as Vibheeshan had been in alerting Ram when Meghnad and Ravan had been performing yagya and now telling the way Ravan could be killed. There are, therefore, both risk and help in giving refuge to enemy's man. One, therefore, have to be very vigilant in dealing with such persons. Ram then fired arrow in the abdomen as also cut Ravan's heads and hands which did not crop up again now. While dying Ravan proclaimed "where is Ram", "where is Ram". This way having proclaimed Ram while dying, he became entitled to mukti besides his having already become entitled for mukti because of having been killed by Ram as was the entire design of Ravan in having developed enmity with Ram.

गर्जेउ मरत घोर रवभारी, कहां रामु रन हतौं पचारी।

Ram by his arrows sent the heads and hands of Ravan before Mandodri as required by protocol. Gods were happy as all rakshasas had been killed with the killing of Ravan. They praised Ram as per spiritual protocol observed even in God's Darbar. Ravan's queens started crying in dismay on Ravan's death and said while crying that it was because of Ravan's anti-Ram feelings. But on Ram having granted Ravan his Lok, Mandodri paid respects to Ram. Infact she was never against Ram and had always been persuading Ravan to seek his refuge. Mandodri said :

अहह नाथ रघुनाथ सम कृपासिंधु नहिं आन,
जोगि बृंद दुर्लभ गति तोहि दीन्ह भगवान।

Hearing Mandodri saying this in praise of Ram, all gods appreciated Ram. Seeing all queens crying, Vibheeshan went to Lanka and requested them to be courageous. Then Ram asked Vibheeshan to perform last rites, which Vibheeshan then performed. Mandodri etc. queens went to rajmahal praising Ram.

Vibheeshan after performing last rites of Ravan reported back to Ram, who called Lakshman, Sugreev, Hanuman, Angad etc. and asked them to coronate Vibheeshan. Due to Raja Dasrath's orders, Ram could not enter any town for 14 years and had to live only in forests. He, therefore, expressed his inability in going there for the purpose and stated that on his behalf, he was sending Sugreev and Lakshman to represent him. They all went and coronated Vibheeshan with all protocol and a raja after coronation is praised as per tradition so that praise had also been done by them. Then Vibheeshan and others reported back to Ram. Ram called all vanars and praised them stating that because of them all, he had been able to defeat Ravan and coronate Vibheeshan as appreciated by the entire universe. Where all vanars had put their lives at stake in the battle, the recognition of the same was necessary by the commander-in-chief. This not only boosted the spirit of the army but also made them more submissive to Ram.

किये सुखी कहि बानी सुधा सम बल तुम्हारें रिपु हयो,
पायो बिभीषण राज तिहुँ पुर जसु तुम्हारो नित नयो।
प्रभु के बचन श्रवन सुनि नहिं अघाहिं कपि पुंज,
बार-बार सिर नावहिं गहहिं सकल पद कुंज।

Then Ram called in Hanuman and asked him to go and tell Sita about Ravan's defeat and come back after seeking her well-being. As a matter of fact, Ram should have after having defeated Ravan, immediately straight-away called in Sita but he did not do so and acted as per protocol according to priority. Priority required the coronation of Vibheesan first as the kingdom could not be left without a raja even for a single day. In modern democratic set up also the Prime Minister on losing the confidence of House, resigns but the President, while accepting the resignation, asks him to continue till alternative arrangements were made and the previous government continue in office till next election/next-elected government etc. and the country is not kept without a government for a single day as anything untoward can happen during that time and there would be none to administer the management of the state in the absence of the government if after losing confidence the previous government is not asked to continue in office till alternative government steps in. Therefore, the first priority was to coronate Vibheeshan and then to give recognition to the job done by the army. After this only Ram could think of Sita or say his personal matters. Here too Ram did not straight away call for Sita. He first sent Hanuman to check up about the well-being of Sita. Hanuman had been sent for this purpose as he had already met Sita and Sita recognised him. If it were anyone else, then Sita might have thought some maya by the rakshasas, who already had been playing many tricks of maya with Sita. The purpose of first checking about the well-being was also to know whether after staying in Lanka for about an year, Sita would at all wish to join Ram or she was having some other idea in view. As a matter of abundant caution and protocol, therefore, Hanuman was first sent to check up about the well-being of Sita. Also the Raja of Lanka had kidnapped Sita and she was in his possession. It was therefore, necessary to first establish a Raja of Lanka and then only ask for the well-being of Sita and to know that the present raja did not have any objection to Sita coming back and if not, she should be sent with all state honours.

समाचार जानकिहि सुनावहु, तासु कुसल लै तुम्ह चलि आवहु।

Hanuman went to Lanka. All rakshasas/rakshasnis worshipped him and took him to Sita. He paid respects to Sita, who recognised Hanuman as Ram's representative. As per protocol, she asked for the well-being of Ram, Lakshman and the army. Hanuman advised that Ram was well and had won the battle with Ravan and Vibheeshan had been coronated. Sita was happy to know it. Now for giving such a good news as per protocol, commensurate reward/award is given to the incumbent but Sita told him that she could not think of anything in the entire universe, which could be commensurate with the news given by Hanuman. When Hanuman came in search of Sita and found Sita, Hanuman broke the important news about Ram and Sita should have rewarded at that time too but she herself was in a kidnapped position at that time and had nothing to offer. But now with Ram having defeated Ravan, Ram was the overall Lord of the place and accordingly Sita was in a position to give anything in the universe in reward to Hanuman in recognition of the news given by him but the reward had to be commensurate with the occasion otherwise it would only be belittling the importance of the news. Sita was not able to lay hand on any such thing which could be offered to Hanuman and, therefore, showed her inability to reward him commensurately. Hanuman, however, consoled by stating that with Ram's victory, he had attained everything (the rajya of the universe). She still gave Hanuman the boon, he could have wished, that he would be owner of all virtues and that Ram and Lakshman be always favourable to him. This is the greatest reward for a bhakta. Then Sita expressed her desire to make arrangements so that she was able to see Ram; the job for which Hanuman had been sent to know the intention of Sita. Sita too could understand that and without askance she told about it. Hanuman then went and told Sita's intention to Ram. Now fully in accordance with the protocol, Ram called in Angad and Vibheeshan and asked them to go with Hanuman and bring Sita. Since Sita was in Lanka, the raja of that kingdom had to arrange for Sita being brought with state honours and Angad was also sent to escort her. They were sent with Hanuman as he only was known so far to Sita.

"सादर जनक सुतहिं लै आवहु"

Vibheeshan went to Sita and ordered for her being adequately adorned and made up for being taken to Ram. A palki was brought and Sita gladly boarded it. She was taken to Ram duly escorted from all sides. All vanars etc. came to see Sita, naturally so. Ram, therefore, ordered Sita to be brought on foot and not in palki so that all in army might have the satisfaction of seeing her and paying their respects to her as a mother and at the same time Sita to know the extent of the army gathered for her sake. Sita had, it seems, accepted to come by palki as Sita knew that Ram had by defeating Ravan, become the overall raja of Lanka and accordingly as the rani of the place, it was apt for her to come in a palki duly decorated as a queen. But on reaching close to Ram, Ram wanted to tell her that she was the wife of Ram as a tapasvi and not a raja and, therefore, had to travel on foot only. Ram, therefore, ordered her to come on foot. Further, Ram was yet to accept her as his wife as already indicated the real Sita was in fire and she was only an image of Sita.

Ram then desired to have the real Sita out of the fire. For this, he wanted to have an excuse to submerge the image of Sita taken from fire for the time being and take back real Sita out of fire. Further, Ram also wanted to show to the people that he did not just accept Sita, who had lived in Lanka for such a long period without putting her integrity to test. The most sacred test at that time was "fire test" (अग्नि परीक्षा) to show that she had been sincere to Ram even during the period of her stay in Lanka. This was, however, objected to by all, including the rakshasnis, living in Lanka and who were with Sita all the time as they atleast knew with how much difficulty Sita had maintained her sincerity and integrity and did not succumb to the pressure by Ravan.

तेहि कारन करुनानिधि कहे कछुक दुर्बाद,
सुनत जातुधानीं सब लागीं करैं बिषाद।

Ram must have questioned Sita's integrity and said

something in that regard which led to an alround anxiety. Sita could, however, know Ram's intentions as she was pure by her heart, action and speech and belonged to Ram only. But then Sita would have thought that such a question could be raised in Ayodhya also when she would go there and become Maharani. She, therefore, picked up Lakshman out of the gathering and asked him to help her in her 'agani preeksha' as she knew :

(1) all the others were from various other kingdoms and would go back to their respective places and only Lakshman would be left to testify her bonafides later on in Ayodhya ;
(2) Lakshman being a Styavrat (others being either vanars or rakshasas there), his testimony only would carry weight ;
(3) Lakshman was living as a tapsavi and dharmatma. A tapsavi would never say anything wrong ;
(4) Lakshman being obedient to Ram and Sita would only carry out the job, which was rather tough to be carried out and others were not capable of carrying out such a job.

लछिमन होहु धरम के नेगी, पावक प्रगट करहु तुम्ह बेगी।

In modern times too for testifying any action, a witness, who had actually been present at the time, is required to confirm the incident. Some such provision in law might be available at that time too. Sita, therefore, cited Lakshman to be witness to the action to fulfil the legal requirement. Lakshman was reluctant to do the job as he was actually not prepared for such an action, particularly since he was not aware about Sita having been submerged in fire.

"प्रभु सन कछु कहि सकत न ओऊ"

But he could not oppose the order of Ram apparently and seeing Ram serious about his order being carried out, Lakshman gathered some firewood and made out a chita.

देखि राम रुख लछिमन धाए पावक प्रगटि काठ बहु लाए।

Lakshman had also to carry out Ram's order, as subsequently seconded by Sita, who asked Lakshman to be a witness and helpful in carrying out Ram's orders as Sita's secondment of Ram's orders was rather intelligent, prudent and covering legal implications and necessary from religious angle too.

सुनि लछिमन सीता कै बानी, बिरह बिवेक धरम निति सानी।

Sita while jumping into fire requested the fire god to be cool if she was only for Ram by heart, speech and action during the period of her separation from Ram. Sita accordingly entered the fire and came out unburnt. Such was the extent of pativrata dharam at that time and a tough test like agani preeksha was in vogue for this purpose. This way Ram could have real Sita out of fire leaving the imaginary one and at the same time proving to the universe Ram's following dharam in proving Sita's purity and the extent of control a lady should have in such difficult times. Having proved her integrity and a right to be Ram's wife, she took her seat on the left of Ram. As per tradition wife sits on left of the husband leaving the husband free to take care of his other worldly jobs by his right side. All became very happy and resounded "Jayakara".

Ram then allowed Matul, Inder's sarthy to return to Inder. All gods came to praise Ram. Gods too had their part of protocol as well. Although they rejoiced Ram's victory over Ravan throwing flowers from the sky, they did not come to Ram. They had been waiting to come and pay respects to Ram, when Sita also joined him as Sita had played a very important and very tough part in gods' job of annihilation of rakshasas being done through Ram. She only had to sacrifice herself in staying away in Lanka for so much period with the attached sufferings. The gods, therefore, came to pay respects to Ram and Sita, when they were together. They paid their respects; conveyed their obligation; praised Ram for such a tough job of annihilation of rakshasas, who had been annoying the gods all though, having been carried out at the cost of so much suffering for the sake of the gods only. Even Brahma and Shiv had come and praised Ram for the job done.

Here the poet has brought Raja Dasrath too. Raja Dasrath in swarag had been seeing all the achievements of

Ram in the universe. In fact it was on Dasrath's orders that Ram had gone to forest and subsequently facing all these events. It was for the sake of Ram having gone to forest that Dasrath had to give up his life. It was, therefore, incumbent for him now to rejoice and share the achievement of his sons, Ram and Lakshman. Here Dasrath had come to bless Ram on his achievements as his son as also to have blessings of Ram and his bhakti as a God incarnate so that he could achieve mukti. How could a father stay behind, when Ram's successful achievements were appreciated even by Brahma, Shiv and the other residents, of swarg along with other gods etc. Since Dasrath had died in love for Ram i.e., he could not absolve himself from worldly desires (maya), he could not get nirvan and, therefore, it was necessary for him to have Ram's bhakti as God Ram and not by son Ram so that he could attain nirvan. When Dasrath came, Ram and Lakshman paid their respects to a father and the father too blessed them with ashirwad. Ram attributed the entire success to his father and father hearing this was overjoyed. When one attributes the achievement to someone else, and that someone also knowing that it was not because of him, he only appreciates the greatness of the person, who attributes so. Ram then realised that Raja Dasrath, because of his bias toward him in the universe and hatred against Kaikayee at the time of his death, could not get nirvan. Ram, therefore, acting as God now absolved Raja Dasrath of the worldly maya as a result of which he attained gyan and bhakti of Ram. Ram then granted him his bhakti enabling him to attain mukti. Now Dasrath paid respects to Ram as God. He was no more a father but a bhakta of Ram, and went to Surdham.

Inder too came and praised Ram, Lakshman and Sita. He admitted that he was proud of his position, thinking there was none above him but now he had known his position and is out from his pride. He requested for Ram's bhakti being granted to him, which Ram happily awarded. Inder then asked if he could be of any help to him. Ram asked Inder to enliven all the vanars etc. lying in the battle field duly killed as they had sacrificed their lives for his cause (actually for the cause of gods only). Ram could have himself done it but then he had to follow the protocol existing in gods. Even Ram, therefore, entrusted the job to the god responsible for such jobs or in modern time we may call it the job being got done through proper channel, so that Inder could feel elevated for having done something for Ram and that Ram although capable of doing the job himself asked Inder to do it so that Inder could get the credit for it.

प्रभु सक त्रिभुअन मारि जिआई, केवल सक्रहिं दीन्हि बड़ाई।

This has to be learnt from the great people how they show their greatness in doing a job and then giving credit for the same to others. There was spray of amrit and all, except the rakshasas, became alive—

"जिए भालु कपि नहिं रजनीचर।"

The rakshasas did not become alive as Ram had already granted them the mukti whereas the vanars etc. were also gods incarnate and had ,therefore, become alive. After Inder and other gods had gone back, Shiv could not resist coming and paying his respects to Ram, who was his God almighty. He paid respects and praised Ram, God almighty.

अनुज जानकी सहित निरंतर बसहु राम नृप मम उर अन्तर।

Shiv had praised Ram as a raja here. Previously in the forest when Sati was there with Shiv, Shiv had addressed him as "सच्चिदानंद" but here Shiv addressed Ram as raja in view of the fact that at that time Ram, although "सच्चिदानंद" had been performing like ordinary person, crying for Sita, whereas now Ram had defeated Ravan as a result of which he became an overall Lord/Raja of Lanka and with the expiry of 14 years in forest, Ram was now going to be the Raja of Awadh too. So Shiv already started saying him as a raja, though virtually he already was a raja of Awadh. He also sought for Ram's approval for his having Ram's darshan at the time of his coronation in Awadh. Since Shiv had to seek this approval, this too led him to already addressing him as raja. When Shiv had also departed, then Vibheeshan came to Ram and urged him to take bath, have rest from the cajole of war and come to Lanka to see the wealth available there and distribute the same amongst the vanars etc. Here Vibheeshan has performed the fulfilment of political protocol in :

(1) entrusting the entire kingdom and wealth to Ram as he was the overall Lord of the kingdom after having defeated Ravan; and

(2) The army too had a share in the wealth of the conquered territory. So the wealth available was placed at the disposal of Ram for being distributed amongst the army men at his discretion.

देखि कोस मंदिर सम्पदा, देहु कृपाल कपिन्ह महुँ मुदा।

He requested Ram to own him i.e. to keep him as his vassal and then proceed to Awadh. Ram accepted that the wealth and kingdom of Lanka was his but he was getting late in reaching Awadh and if he delayed by even a day, Bharat would give up his life as had been told by him while departing from Chitrakut. Ram, therefore, requested Vibheeshan as a raja to arrange for his reaching Awadh in time. Ram blessed him with happily ruling Lanka and then attaining mukti. Vibheeshan hearing this fell in Ram's feet. He then went to Lanka and brought a lot of pearls, gems, clothes etc. in aeroplane and threw the same for the vanars etc. Vanars picked them as they wished. Such was the jovial environ created by Ram, the commander of the army after the victory in the war. They all wore the clothes, ornaments etc. and came to Ram, who again thanked them and said that because of them, he won the battle with Ravan and was able to fulfil his promise to coronate Vibheeshan. He then asked them to go to their respective homes, remembering him and not having any fear from anyone.

"सुमिरेहु मोहि डरपहु जनि काहूँ"

Here Ram has through the talk to vanars etc. told the universe that anyone remembering Ram, would not have any fear from anyone as Ram would be there to help him always in times of distress. The vanars, however, praised Ram in turn and felt obliged that he had given a chance to serve him. They then left that place for their respective houses. Nal, Neel, Sugreev, Angad and Vibheeshan could not say any thing, when Ram ordered all vanars etc. to leave for their respective houses. Ram seeing their intention, asked them all to board the plane. Ram paid respects to brahmins in his heart and started in plane for Awadh. Ram and Sita sat at the singhasan provided in the plane. There was 'Jayakara' when the plane started. Ram on the way showed to Sita, the battle field and the bridge constructed for coming to Lanka etc. Then Ram showed the place where Shivling had been established (रामेश्वर) and Ram and Sita paid their respects to Shiv, who was their God. Ram showed all other places also on the way where he had stayed after Sita had been kidnapped. The plane then reached near the ashrams of Agast muni etc. Since he had given several arms to Ram, which were helpful in war with Ravan, Ram had to express his obligation and have their blessings. He, therefore, met all the munis and had their blessings, now along with Sita. Then they saw Yamuna, Ganga etc. and passed over Awadh. They paid their respects to Awadh. They did not descend there but went to Prayag. Had bath there and met Nishad because Ram had promised to meet him on his return. Also one protocolic difficulty was there in straightaway going to Awadh. Although Ram knew Bharat was sincere and would have been waiting for the completion of 14 years period to handover singhasan to Ram, but protocol necessitated that Ram should first check up the position of Awadh and to know secretly if Bharat was prepared to hand over the kingdom and waiting for Ram or he had got used to ruling and was not prepared now to descend from the throne. If so, then rather than disturbing and developing quarrel with Bharat, he could have thought of some other way. Ram, therefore, asked Hanuman to go in the guise of a brahmin and check up the position of Awadh as also to tell Bharat about their well being and intention to return to Awadh as demanded by the situation. Since Bharat had said that in case Ram delayed in arrival back to Awadh by even a day, he would give up his life, Ram's intention in sending Hanuman, therefore, was to know the condition of Bharat, as to whether he was waiting for Ram to come; and to apprise Bharat of Ram's well being and his arrival. Ram had picked up Hanuman as —

(1) He was perfect in adopting other guises. He had adopted the guise of a brahmin when he met Ram also.

(2) Hanuman had already seen Bharat and Awadh. Ram could not send anyone else for this purpose.

(3) Hanuman had the capability to fly over the area quickly and come back.

(4) He was very intelligent for doing intelligence jobs. Therefore, Ram picked up Hanuman for this job.

प्रभु हनुमन्तहि कहा बुझाई, धरि वटु रूप अवधपुर जाई।

भरतहि कुसल हमारि सुनाएहु, समाचार लै तुम्ह चलि आएहु।

Hanuman's job was to check up everything and return with a view to enable Ram to decide further course of action. Hanuman went to Awadh. Meantime Ram met Bharadwaj. Here also Bharadwaj had double role from protocol point of view—one he was Ram's bhakta and in that capacity, he worshipped Ram and uttered his praises, other as a muni. From worldly point of view, Ram paid respects to him and he gave him his blessings. Then after seeking muni's permission, Ram boarded the plane. He then met Nishadraj in Sringverpur. Sita worshipped Ganga there. On her outward journey, Sita had requested Ganga to bless her to return safe with Ram and Lakshman and then on return she would again have bath there and express her obligation. Ganga had at that time blessed Sita that she would return safe and with all praises. Ganga gave her blessings.

Nishad came and fell in Ram's feet in love and devotion. Ram picked him up and embraced and enquired about his well-being as designed by protocol. The poet seeing Ram's love for Nishad is forced to say—

यह कलिकाल मलायतन मन करि देखु विचार,

श्री रघुनाथ नाम तजि नाहिन आन अधार।

7

Uttar Kand

Here again the poet starts with manglacharan. Since now Ram, Lakshman and Sita all the three were there, the poet has written three slokas. Again at first he praised Ram and then Shiv. Since Ram had not so far descended at Awadh, the poet has paid his respects to Ram, Sita and Lakshman sitting in plane itself. This chapter mostly revolves around spiritual protocol.

The people in Awadh had been counting days and now when only one day was left in the expiry of the 14 years period, the people were upset whether Ram would at all come or not. They were all very weak in view of the long separation from Ram. Then good omens appeared and everyone felt happy that these omens gave the intimation of Ram's arrival back in Awadh. In view of the purity in the minds of people, the omens, good or bad, were never false. Mothers had been happily waiting for someone to break the news of the arrival of Ram. Bharat too was having good omens but was sad that only one day was left and there was no intimation about Ram's arrival. He cursed himself saying :

कपटी कुटिल मोहि प्रभु चीन्हा, ताते नाथ संग नहि लीन्हा।

और

जौं करनी समुझैं प्रभु मोरी, नहिं निस्तार कलप सत कोरी।

Bharat thought that Ram had taken him as a fraudulent and crooked person that is why at first Ram did not agree to take him with him and now he has not arrived after the expiry of the period. Ram would have considered him fraudulent and crooked as at first when he was going to be coronated, Ram was sent to forests for 14 years because of him and subsequently when he had known that Ram was at war with Ravan and Lakshman was fighting life and death situation, at that time too Bharat did not go to his help meaning thereby that by such fraudulent means, Bharat wanted to continue as the raja of Awadh if Ram did not win over Ravan or Ram would not come back if Lakshman had not recovered or Ram was not able to take Sita back. When Bharat was having all such thoughts in his mind, Hanuman appeared as a brahmin. Hanuman had come to check up if Bharat had been waiting for Ram to come and to find out the situation in Awadh. Seeing Bharat as a very thin and weak person and remembering Ram, he could make out that Bharat was still in for Ram's welcome and was eagerly waiting for his arrival—

बैठे देखि कुसासन जटा मुकुट कृस गात,
राम राम रघुति जपत स्रवत नयन जलजात।

Seeing Bharat in this condition, Hanuman was happy and told him that Ram, whom he had been constantly remembering, was coming along with Sita and Lakshman after winning the war. Bharat became very happy and asked for his introduction. Then Hanuman told his introduction. Bharat got up and met him very affectionately and asked about the well-being of Ram and others. As a matter of protocol on giving such news the raja gives costly things as reward but Bharat said that he could not locate any thing in the universe commensurate with the good news given by Hanuman. Same thing had happened in the case of breaking the news of Ram's victory over Ravan to Sita. She also said that she was not able to locate anything for reward commensurate with the news given by Hanuman.

बार बार बूझी कुसलाता, तो कहुँ देउँ काह सुनु भ्राता,
एहि सन्देस सरिस् जग माहीं करि विचार देखेउँ कछु नाहीं।

Hanuman paid respects and narrated all about Ram. As usual for a bhakta, he asked Hanuman if Ram ever remembered him. Hearing this, Hanuman fell in his feet seeing him so much humble and told Bharat :

"राम प्रान प्रिय नाथ तुम्ह सत्य बचन मम तात"

Ram loved him more than his life even and this was correct as he had seen so. He paid respects to Bharat and departed and reported back to Ram telling all that he had seen in Awadh i.e. Ram was being eagerly awaited there and all was clear for him to go. Bharat was happy. He came to Kaushalpuri and, as per protocol, first told the news to Guru Vashisth. Then he informed the mothers etc. in rajmahal about Ram coming back to Awadh—

"पुनि मन्दिर महँ बात जनाई"

This would indicate that since Bharat had taken an undertaking not to visit rajmahal till Ram returned, he could not go to rajmahal himself and only sent the news there through someone. All mothers ran up on hearing the news and came to Bharat. Bharat narrated to them about Hanuman's arrival and the news of Ram being well and coming with Sita and Lakshman duly defeating Ravan and others. The people of the town came to know of the news and they too ran to see Ram coming. The ladies (सुहागिन) went singing appropriate songs and carrying the gold basins full of curd, fruits, flowers, tulsi leaves etc. as considered of good omen to receive some V.I.P. As per protocol, a raja is received by another raja and other seniors of the kingdom. Therefore, Bharat went to receive Ram alongwith Guru Vashisth, Shatrughan, family members, and brahmins.

हरषित गुर परिजन अनुज भूसुर वृंद समेत,
चले भरत मन प्रेम अति सन्मुख कृपानिकेत।

The gods were in their vimans in the sky waiting to receive Ram in Awadh and to witness the Ram-Bharat milap.

Ram was coming to Awadh after hearing from Hanuman. He showed Awadh to all accompanying him and told that even Baikunth, which is said to be best to live in, is not comparable to Awadh, which was supreme in his mind. Here the poet through Ram has tried to convey that one should have utmost affection for his birth place and his country as Ram had for Awadh. All became happy and conveyed their wishes for Awadh as explained by Ram. The plane landed near the town as per Ram's direction. Ram got down and sent the plane back to Kuber from whom Ravan had taken it away. The plane went to Kuber—happy as well as sad. Happy because it was going to his master, Kuber and sad because he had to leave Ram behind.

Now starts the meeting of Ram with the people of Awadh, who had come to receive him, all as per protocol.

(1) At first Ram saw Bharat, Bam Dev, Vashisth, munis and seeing them he placed his bow and arrow on earth. As per protocol one cannot have arms when meeting the respected ones. This custom exists even today.

(2) Then Ram first of all met Guru Vashisth along with Lakshman and fell in his feet.

(3) Guru Vashisth picked them up and asked about their well being as is the tradition. Ram told that with his grace all was well.

(4) Ram and Lakshman paid respects thereafter to all Brahmins by bowing their heads.

(5) Then Ram met Bharat, who fell in Ram's feet. He would not get up from Ram's feet. Then Ram per force picked him up and embraced.

परे भूमि नहिं उठत उठाए, बर करि कृपासिंधु उर लाए।

Tears fell from Bharat's eyes and he was quite sentimental. Ram asked Bharat's well being but Bharat was not able to speak and ultimately told that since Ram had come back, he was happy.

(6) Then Ram met Shatrughan and embraced him.

(7) Then Lakshman met Bharat. Lakshman being younger, he met Bharat and paid respects.

(8) Then Shatrughan met Lakshman and embraced each other.

(9) Bharat bowed his head in respect before Sita.

(10) Shatrughan paid respects to Sita.

(11) The residents of the town were happy to see Ram. Everyone wanted to have a close darshan of Ram. Then Ram made his as many images as the people were there and met all as per requirement within a minute and graced them.

अमित रूप प्रगटे तेहि काला, जथा जोग मिले सबहि कृपाला।

(12) Ram after gracing all people, saw Kaushalya etc. mothers coming. Ram met the mothers and consoled them.

(13) Sumitra met Lakshman, not as her son, but as a bhakta of Ram.

(14) Kaikayee was hesitant in meeting Ram but Ram met and consoled her.

(15) Lakshman met and paid respects to all mothers, who gave him their blessings. He met Kaikayee several times but he could not forget that Kaikayee was responsible for their having to go to forests.

(16) Sita met all mothers-in-law and touched their feet. They blessed her to live for ever with the husband (सुहागिन रहो). To a married lady, this is the best blessing by any one as per Hindu tradition as a lady's importance in society is till her husband is alive and she is suhagin (सुहागिन). They also asked about her well being.

(17) All mothers were happy to see Ram and performed his aarti, a tradition to receive the incumbent. Kaushalya was surprised as to how her so mild sons would have killed the strong rakshasas like Ravan. For a mother the son is always a weak, poor, mild and humble person—psychologically. All mothers were happy to see Ram with Sita and Lakshman.

(18) Vibheeshan, Sugreev, Nal, Neel, Jamvant, Angad, Hanuman etc. vanars had guised as human beings and were appreciative of Bharat's love/affection for Ram. Ram called them all and told them to pay respect to Vashisth muni by touching his feet and introduced to them that Vashisth muni was the family guru and the

victory in war with Ravan was as a result of his blessings. He introduced them all to muni saying they were all his friends and had devoted themselves to him during war for his cause. Ram praised them and told they were dearer even compared to Bharat. They were all happy to hear their praise from Ram.

(19) They all thereafter touched the feet of Kaushalya. She blessed them and told they were as dear to her as Ram himself i.e. they were all like his sons.

(20) Thereafter all started for the town, which was extremely decorated with all Hindu traditions like 'bandanwars', flags, gold flower-bases etc. in front of each house. Scents were sprinkled on roads and bands were playing.

(21) The ladies were performing aarti with material in golden bases.

(22) Ram, having seen Kaikayee feeling ashamed on her action in having sent Ram etc. to forests, went to her mahal first to eliminate her shyness. He encouraged her and then went to his mahal.

(23) Guru Vashisth called in all senior pandits and told them that it was good day and if all agreed, then Ram could be coronated that day itself.

सब द्विज देहु हरषि अनुसासन, रामचन्द्र बैठहि सिघांसन।

Here the poet has tried to show that for fixing the good day for Ram's coronation, even Guru Vashisth was not competent. Such was the institution of democracy at that time existing in India. Guru Vashisth had considered that day as good for this purpose but still he asked the opinion of all other pandits as well. Might be Guru Vashisth would have been feeling that pre-viously day was fixed by him only when Ram had to go to forests. Also guru had fixed the marriage day of Ram and Ram and Sita had a bad time in forests. So Guru Vashisth now thought it better to consult all other pandits as well if his calculation about fixing that day for coronation was alright. All pandits appreciated this initiative by the muni and recommended not to delay the coronation now and should be done that day itself because previously the coronation was not done on the day Raja Dasrath decided it and the situation changed during the night. The people of Awadh did not want to take that risk now again.

(24) Guru Vashisth called the secretary, Sumant and asked him to arrange to bring the requisite samagri for coronation. This was arranged within no time. This shows that for each job, there were separate persons (officers). Sumant was incharge of such house-hold jobs and was very close to the raja. He had approach to rajmahal also by virtue of his holding that seat. One such secretary was always appointed by the rajas as their confidant. Satanand was with Raja Janak for similar jobs.

(25) Ram called in the servers and ordered for arranging his friends taking bath and getting ready. Here again the things started moving as per protocol. Ram first arranged for serving the guests, who are above self in Hindus.

(26) Then Ram called Bharat and opened his hairs by his hands.

"निज कर राम जटा निरुआरे"

(27) Then Ram arranged for all three brothers taking bath.

(28) Then only Ram untied his hairs and took bath with Guru's permission. Guru's permission was required as his bath was not an ordinary one. It was to be a formal bath before coronation with the sacred water of all rivers etc. Ram took bath and beautifully adorned.

(29) The mothers arranged for the bath of Sita as her's was also a special bath. She was to take seat by the side of Ram on Singhasan. She was properly adorned. She sat with Ram on left side as per rule.

(30) All gods including Brahma and Shiv came to witness and enjoy Ram's coronation.

(31) Guru Vashisth became very sentimental seeing Ram fully ready for the occasion. He immediately called for the Singhasan.

(32) Ram sat on Singhasan after seeking everyone's permission and after paying respects to all. This reflects the democratic approach and the raja taking all with him.

(33) All formalities of pooja etc. were performed by pandits.

(34) The first Tilak ceremony was performed by Guru Vashisth; he being the most respected and senior most of all.

(35) Guru Vashisth then permitted other pandits to put tilak to Ram. They were next in seniority/order of precedence.

(36) The mothers then performed the 'Aarti' ceremony of couple on Singhasan. They were happy.

(37) Alms were given to brahmins and others. The gods seeing Ram on Singhasan played their bands and the apsaras (अप्सरा) were dancing.

(38) Bharat and other brothers, Vibheeshan, Hanuman, Angad etc. were holding the sacred umbrella, chanwar etc. as per tradition in respect/submission to the Samrat Ram. This was a way to show that there was absolute cordiality amongst the brothers; and other rajas, vassals to Ram on Ram occupying the throne.

(39) The gods went back to their respective lodges. Then came the four Vedas, who praised Ram and requested to be blessed with his bhakti. They then went back to their lodges.

(40) Then Shiv came. He was very happy and sentimental. He praised Ram as his God and prayed for being blessed with his bhakti—

बार-बार बर माँगउँ हरषि देहु श्रीरंग,
पद सरोज अनपायनी भगति सदा सतसंग।

Here the poet has given importance to satsang. Ram's continuous bhakti can be had by satsang only. Shiv had prayed for being blessed with perpetual bhakti as available through satsang. Shiv then went back to Kailash.

(41) After coronation it would have been evening by now. So Ram arranged for the proper stay of all guests, quite comfortable from all angles.

तब प्रभु कपिन्ह दिवाए सब बिधि सुखप्रद बास।

All people in Awadh lived comfortably and there were festivals all the time showing the magnitude of happiness in Ram rajya. Lots of alms were given to all the people and brahmins at the time of coronation.

(42) Ram after six months had passed, called all vanars etc. and praised for the service done by them and said that they were dearer to him compared to his other brothers, wealth, even Sita, house, family members and other well-wishers. Ram said he was not praising them for praising sake but he actually liked them all as per his temperament/policy.

सब के प्रिय सेवक यह नीति, मोरे अधिक दास पर प्रीती।

That is why Bharat went to bring back Ram from the forests as a sewak and not as a brother because he knew that Ram cared for the sewak more.

अरिहुक अनभल कीन्ह न रामा, मैं सिसु सेवक यद्यपि बामा।

Ram then asked them to go back to their respective houses and to keep themselves devoted to him. Thereby indicating that they must continue to serve Awadh rajya.

अब गृह जाहु सखा सब भजेहु मोहि दृढ़ नेम।

All were happy to hear Ram praising them. Ram then, as per tradition, called for valuable ornaments, clothes etc. At first Sugreev was helped in wearing those by Bharat. This was all being done as per protocol. Sugreev being senior most, he was first entertained by Bharat, who was senior most in brothers; Lakshman helped Vibheeshan in wearing them. Jamvant, Neel, Nal were helped in wearing clothes etc. by Ram himself, again showing that he cared for his persons more. When Angad's turn came, he requested Ram to keep him with himself as Bali had entrusted him to Ram at the time of his death and he had no place to go to now. He had fear that Sugreev, who had personal vendetta against Bali, might not treat him well after he had gone back as so far he was having the protection of Ram. Ram picked him up and embraced him and he himself put the pearl necklace in his neck. Ram persuaded and offered all kinds of protection to him and then bade him farewell. Shatrughan escorted them out of the town as according to protocol they had to be escorted by some one from the royal family. After bidding farewell to all, Bharat and others returned. Hanuman requested Sugreev to permit him to stay to serve Ram for some days. While going out, Angad requested Hanuman to remember him to Ram. This is again as per protocol. He knew Hanuman was closest to Ram and, therefore, any request to him would carry weight to reach Ram. Also Angad had some influence over Hanuman only as others, Bharat etc., were beyond his reach. One purpose of requesting Hanuman to mention him to Ram, time and again was that Ram might keep a constant watch on his interests in his kingdom. Ram then called Nishadraj and bade him farewell giving lot of ornaments etc. to him and again asked him to keep Ram in mind as per his dharam. He was a vassal of Ram and accordingly his dharam was to keep Awadh Raja's interest in view all the time.

Ram was on throne and his rule started after all these formalities were over. Following of the Varans and Ashrams is the fundamental in Hindu way of life. Whenever these were followed, there was all peace and pleasure in the kingdom and whenever there was departure, there was chaos and anarchy. In Ram's rule, all these were followed and, therefore, there was no fear, no sadness and no diseases at all.

वरणाश्रम निज निज धरम निरत वेद पथ लोग

चलहिं सदा पावहिं सुखहि नहिं भय सोक न रोग।

This couplet draws the entire picture of protocol followed in Ram's rule e.g.

(1) Every one was following varan and ashram.

(2) Every one was following his religion (निज निज धर्म). This would indicate that there were more than one religion

(dharam), in Ram's period and as in the present day concept of secularism, at that time too, there was absolute secular set up.

(3) Everyone was learned and knew the path of vedas. Vedas tell the way of life in each situation, in society, religion, household, war, peace, international relation etc. This would show that all modalitics and ways were followed as laid down in vedas. That is why even Ravan did not kill Hanuman inspite of his having killed his son and many others and having destroyed the Ashok garden only because he was Ram's doot (Ram's representative) and Ram was another king for Ravan and killing of the representative of a raja was against the vedic tenets.

(4) Since all were following the vedic and other religious tenets, they were all happy.

(5) If all these are followed, then there would be no fear in anyone's mind that is how even a washerman could criticise Ram resulting in Sita's exile from Awadh. There was no sadness in anyone's mind as the raja was there to redress all grievances as per rule and his dharam. In such a situation, no one would be suffering from serious diseases. All diseases arise out of the pollution—polluted thinking, polluted environ, polluted behaviour and polluted social dealings. If there was no pollution since all were living as per tenets of dharam, the diseases would not crop up. If the religious concepts are followed then as in Ram's rule there would be no bodily, worldly or spiritual ailments.

दैहिक दैविक भौतिक तापा, राम राज नहिं काहुहि व्यापा।

(6) Further since all were devoted to Ram, they became entitled to mukti. None died young and none suffered from any ailment.

(7) There was none poor or in distress. None was illiterate and everyone was with all virtues.

नहिं कोउ अबुध न लच्छन हीना।

(8) None felt proud; all were religious minded; and pure souls; and none was deceptive toward anyone. This

would indicate that there was strict law and order management.

(9) Ram was the Chakarvarti Samrat of the entire universe. The rule of the universe is nothing to Ram, who is the administrator of all the lokas.

(10) All—men and women—respected the brahmins. One wife rule was followed by all.

(11) Rains were in time. All crops were well.

(12) There was lot of wealth in Awadh. Since Ram was Chakarvarti Samrat and all rajas were his vassals, they used to present a lot of wealth to the Samrat making Awadh very rich.

(13) There was no crime due to the people being religious minded and well-wishers of others.

(14) The oceans had been throwing pearls etc. at their beaches.

(15) Ram had performed many Aswamedh yagyas.

(16) Although there were many servants in the house, yet Maharani Sita had herself been doing the house-hold jobs and had been following Ram's orders. This shows the pride in self-help in that period and even the kings were not above this rule.

(17) All in public had been in for praise for Ram and Ram's katha was held in all houses. It was not like the communists' regime but as per the will and devotion of the public for Ram.

(18) All brothers were quite cordial to Ram and Ram too was extra affectionate to the brothers.

(19) Ram used to hold his court along with pandits and elders. This would indicate that the king was advised by the council of ministers as per present institution of government.

(20) In the markets, which were full of all commodities, the things were available without any cost. This is not understood how it was possible in the capitalistic way of society unless all the supplies were controlled by

government and there was some system of public distribution, or "without any cost" might be meaning without high profits.

(21) On Saryu river, there were ghats for horses and elephants to take water and there was one ghat for ladies, where gents had no approach. There was also one Rajghat where the four brothers used to take bath along with others. There was a place for rishis too. There were gardens and parks all through. All people were appreciative of Ram.

(22) There was mutual cordiality between Raja Ram and the people. The people served devotedly the raja and the raja in turn kept everyone comfortable.

एहि विधि नगर नारि नर करहिं राम गुनगान,
सानुकूल सब पर रहहिं सतंत कृपानिधान।

Ram had been going for a walk etc. along with other brothers and Hanuman and had been discussing many things, worldly, as well as, spiritual. On a similar visit to a garden, once Ram and brothers with Hanuman had gone where Sankadik rishi had come too. Sankadik rishi used to visit the place where Ram katha was held. Seeing the muni coming, Ram, as per protocol, paid respects, although he knew that the muni had come to him as a bhakta; enquired about the well being and spread out his yellow cloth and requested muni to sit. All the three brothers and Hanuman also paid respects. The muni became very sentimental seeing the brothers. Ram felt obliged for the muni having come there. The muni too praised Ram and requested for being blessed with his bhakti. He got his wish fulfilled and went back. Now all brothers, having seen Ram coming to him for his blessings, wished to ask him something as God but they were hesitant in asking the same directly. They, therefore, proceeded through proper channel. They requested Hanuman, who had been acting as Ram's private secretary. In modern institution of management too, the people can approach the boss through his private secretary only. Some such procedure was in vogue at that time too. Hanuman, therefore, requested Ram that Bharat had desired to ask something. Ram immediately said that there was no difference between Bharat and him and, therefore, no formality needed be observed by him. Presently also some people have direct access to the ruler and do not have to go through proper channel. Ram had been hinting of the same immunity being available to Bharat too. Bharat felt obliged but Bharat mentioned himself as a sewak and as a sewak only (not as a brother, who had direct access to him) requested Ram to tell him the difference between the saint and non-saint (सन्त और असन्त).

संत असंत भेद बिलगाई, प्रनतपाल मोहिं कहहु बुझाई।

The poet through the medium of Bharat has from Ram himself managed to tell the difference between a saint and a non-saint as such definition can, with authority, be told by Ram as God only. As already indicated, the poet has, as a matter of protocol, and abundant caution of its being bonafide, been picking up the correct character for defining a thing. For defining the spiritual matters, he has always got hold of Ram, Shiv or a learned muni like Guru Vashisth/Vishwamitra etc. Ram accordingly narrated the difference between the saints and non-saints.

Saints and non-saints are like the sandal (चन्दन) and axe. The axe cuts the sandal tree but sandal vanishes giving its flavour/smell to the axe. That is why because of this temperament of passing on the virtues to others, sandal is used in worshipping God and axe is beaten with a hammer after warming it in fire.

(i) The saints are :

(a) Above all worldly vices.

(b) They are modest and with all virtues.

(c) They become sad seeing others unwell and become happy in others happiness.

(d) They keep themselves composed in good and bad times. They have no enemies and are above the effect of worldly life.

(e) They have no greed; are always happy and have no fear from anyone. They donot get enraged.

(f) They are soft; have pity on the poors and on bhaktas with heart, action and speech without any consideration.

(g) They respect all and do not expect any respect from others and are not proud.

(h) They are always Ram's bhaktas. They respect the brahmins and follow religious tenets.

(ii) All the above ingredients goes in making a person a saint. The ingredients of the non-saints are :

(a) Nobody likes their company; and if anybody comes in their contact, he is always a loser.

(b) They feel jealous seeing others prosper and take interest in listening to the ills of others.

(c) They are full of vices like enragement; have passion, arrogance, and greed.

(d) They have no sympathy for others and are deceptive; develop enmity with others without any reason; are not obliged to even those, who are good to them.

(e) They believe in lies and deception; they speak soft but do harm to others.

(f) They are malicious to others; have love with others' wives; snatch others wealth; and speak ill of others.

(g) They are very greedy; they live like beasts, and cannot tolerate anyone else's praise. They are happy in seeing others in distress.

(h) They are always in rage, greed, passion, and deception.

(i) They do not respect their parents or gurus.

The persons with these vices are non-saints. They were not to be seen in Satyug and Tretayug; there were a few in Duapur and a lot in Kalyug.

ऐसे अधम मनुज खल कृतजुग त्रेता नाहिं
द्वापुर कछुक वृंदं बहु होहहिं कलियुग माहिं।

(iii) Caring for others is the best dharam.

(iv) There is no sin greater than harming others.

The brothers alongwith Hanuman were happy hearing these fundamentals. They then went to rajmahal. Such incidents took place from time to time. Narad had been visiting Ram rajya time and again and telling all that he saw there, to persons in Brahmlok.

Ram had a system of holding regular darbar with pandits, elders, senior citizens, his brothers, rishis etc. to listen to public grievances. This is like the present system of listening to public grievances organised by certain authorities. The system of holding darbar for listening to public grievances and conveying his messages to public, had been in vogue in our Satyug, Ram period, Krishan period and continued in Maurya, Gupta and in Rajput periods and subsequently Muslim rulers (Jahangir was famous for it) had also been following the system, which has come down to even today. This democratic system of holding darbars, where not only public grievances were sympathetically heard and redressed but was a lesson to wrong doers—whether in public or government job and such wrong doers were adequately punished so that such wrong doings were not repeated either by them or by others. In one of such darbar, held with the guru, pandits and other public men, Ram said, that he wanted to tell all—whether they follow or not is their sweet will—

नहिं अनीति नहिं कछु प्रभुताई, सुनहु करहु जो तुम्हहि सुहाई।

This shows that—

(1) The raja did not speak anything not covered by rules.

(2) He did not say anything to show his supremacy over others.

(3) They may listen but were not bound to do what was told and were free to do according to what they felt like doing.

(4) If he talked anything not correct then he wanted to be told so.

(5) For telling him his wrong sayings, they needed not have any fear of the raj.

(6) Thus the rajas desired people to express their feelings freely or as per modern ethics of fundamentals—freedom of expression and speech was granted at that time to the public even in the monarchy system of government—unlike muslim rulers, who were more of autocrats.

जौ अनीति कछु भाषौं भाई, तौ मोहिं बरजहु भय बिसराई।

The raja is able to know his shortcomings only if the public have free and fearless right of expression.

(7) Ram propounded the theory of rebirth and that too through eighty-four lac species.

आकर चारि लच्छ चौरासी, जोनि भ्रमत यह जिव अविनासी,

फिरत सदा माया कर प्रेरा, काल कर्म सुभाव गुन घेरा।

कबहुंक करि करुना नर देही, देत ईस बिनु हेतु सनेही।

(8) The specie of human being is attained with God's grace by a few only.

(9) The only aim of having attained the human being specie, should be to have mukti.

जो न तरै भव सागर नर समाज अस पाइ,

सो कृत निदंक मदंमति आत्माहन गति जाइ।

And for this purpose, the easiest way is Ram's bhakti as the other procedure through gyan (ज्ञान) is full of difficulties.

सुलभ सुखद मारग यह भाई, भगति मोरि पुरान श्रुति गाई।

(10) For attaining bhakti one should resort to attending to satsang and serving the brahmins.

(11) Ram also told a secret that one could not have Ram's bhakti without worshipping Shiv too.

औरउ एक गुपुत मत सबहि कहउँ कर जोरि,

शंकर भजन बिना नर भगति न पावइ मोरि।

Here the poet has narrated : (i) That for attaining Ram's bhakti, one should worship Shiv too. Ram told this as a disclosure of secret so that the people could believe it fully. (ii) There was at that time in 16th century difference in the thinking of Shaivites and Vaishnavites—each considering his sect as a distinct from the other. The poet by having told that Ram bhakti is possible only with Shiv bhakti, has eliminated the difference between the two. (iii) To make the message more sacrosanct, the poet has managed to send this message through Ram himself to the public at large. Ram had so far been presenting himself in public as an ordinary human being doing 'manuj leela' but here he has presented himself as God's incarnate. The message, therefore, is taken as more authoritative; having been conveyed by God himself.

(12) Ram told that once a person is fully devoted to him, he would not be involved in worldly affection, pride and other worldly affairs and if once he is absolved of all these, he is sure to attain mukti.

(13) After hearing all this from Ram himself, people accepted him as their all-in-all and offered their full devotion to him. This is how a raja is to behave with his praja. He is not only to care for the worldly management and administration but also to care for their nirvan/mukti. The modern concept of goverment is bereft of the spiritual aspect completely rather such utterances are considered non-secular or void of the constitution and accordingly a crime. That is why the government in present days is not able to carry the public with them. They also do actions against the rules leading to so many court cases against the government. Such a situation was unthinkable in Ram's rule. The public accepted that such teachings could be given by the raja only as the mother, father etc. were all selfish and would teach as is to their advantage only.

असि सिख तुम्ह बिन देइ न कोऊ, मात पिता स्वारथ रत ओऊ।

Then all went to their houses after having been permitted by Rạm to go. Such was the political as also spiritual protocol amongst the raja and the public (प्रजा).

Here Ram having described himself as a God incarnate (which fact Guru Vashisth knew but had not been disclosing as Ram had come as God's incarnate to act and live like ordinary human beings) Muni Vashisth came to him. Ram, as a matter of protocol, respected him as a guru and washing his feet took charanamrit (चरणामृत). Guru took his seat and then told Ram folding his hands. The guru folded his hands before Ram because now the guru wanted to speak to Ram as God and, therefore, had to observe the requisite protocol meant for that situation.

राम सुनहु मुनि कह कर जोरी, कृपा सिंधु बिनती कछु मोरी।

The muni said that he was surprised to see Ram acting as a human being but still with spiritual (Godly) zeal. This had put him in a dilemma whether he only was the God as told by Brahma to him, when Vashisth had been deputed by Brahma to work as 'Purohit' for the Awadh dynasty and told him that in course of time Vishnu would come as incarnate in that dynasty and he, acting as his guru at that time, would, attain moxa and on that assurance by Brahma he accepted this rather mean job of a purohit in the hope of seeing him in this universe as his disciple.

उपरोहित कर्म अति मंदा वेद पुरान सुमृति कर निंदा।

Now he had got that fulfilment. Guru Vashisth accepted that he had read all vedas, shastras etc. and their conclusion is that the salvation lies in Ram's bhakti only.

तव पद पकंज प्रीति निरतंर, सब साधन कर यह फल सुन्दर।

Even Guru Vashisth requested Ram to be blessed with his bhakti in each birth.

नाथ एक वर मागँउ राम कृपा करि देहु,
जन्म जन्म प्रभु पद कमल कबहुँ घटै जनि नेहु।

Here :

(1) Guru Vashist accepted Ram as God incarnate, whose bhakti was essential rather bhakti is more joyful than even the mukti;

(2) The theory of death and rebirth; and

(3) With Gods blessings, one could remember the things of the previous specie (योनी) in the next yoni.

Saying this and having got his wish fulfilled, the guru came to his house.

On an outing, Ram, while going, took Bharat, Hanuman etc. with him and gave many horses, jewels, dresses etc. in alm to the deserving people. He then went to a park. Bharat spread his cloth there and Ram and others sat.

भरत दीन्ह निज बसन डसाई, बैठे प्रभु सेवहि सब भाई।

This shows the cordiality in the four brothers and followed the requisite social protocol each one was expected to observe. At that time Narad muni came there and joined them. He praised Ram as usual and went back to his place.

Shiv then told Parvati to whom he had been telling Ram katha to remove her doubts about the bonafides of Ram being the incarnate of Vishnu, that he had completed the entire katha and if she still had anything to ask she could do so. This is the normal protocol to tell everything one wanted to be told and then to ask if anything remained to be told. This is also asked to see whether or not the listener had felt satisfied. Parvati accordingly said that she had felt satisfied and had known the bonafides of Ram.

तुम्हरी कृपा कृपायतन अब कृतकृत्य न मोह,
जानेउँ राम प्रताप प्रभु चिदानंद संदोह।

But then Parvati asked that since Shiv had heard the katha from Kagbhusand, who had all the devotion for Ram then how is it that such a creature having Ram's bhakti was a crow. Her doubt arose in view of the fact that :

(1) Out of thousands of human beings, one became devotee of dharam,
(2) Out of thousands of devotees of dharam, hardly anyone attained vairagya;
(3) Out of crores of vairagis, hardly anyone had real gyan;
(4) Out of crores of gyanis, hardly anyone attained mukti;
(5) Out of thousands of them, hardly anyone got absorbed in Braham; and
(6) Out of many absorbed in Braham, hardly anyone attained Rambhakti.

This shows how difficult it was to have Rambhakti and a crow could have it was surprising. How, therefore, Parvati asked this all happened. Protocol assigns that if one has the able guru, then one should get all his doubts/problems cleared without any hesitation. Shiv had already removed Parvati's doubt about Ram's bonafides and now she considered him capable of removing this doubt as well. She also asked how Garuda, who is quite capable and close to Vishnu could reach Kagbhusand and hear Ram katha. From this, Shiv could adjudge that Parvati had already absorbed herself in Rambhakti.

Shiv told that such question Garud also asked Kagbhusand and Kagbhusand had narrated the entire Ram katha and his life sketch how he got Rambhakti, to Garud. At that time Shiv had also seen the Ram katha being narrated. He also guised himself as a bird and listened to the same. He could not listen to it as Shiv as Kagbhusand would have hesitated in speaking in presence of Shiv and also the bird only could understand the bird's language.

खग जाने खग ही को भाषा।

So Shiv had to sit there as a bird only and returned to Kailash after listening to the entire Ram katha. Garud had gone to Kagbhusand on the advice of Shiv to redress the doubt developed in his mind about the bonafides of Ram being incarnate of God when Ram had been bound in nagpash by Meghnad and Garud had gone to get Ram released from that binding, thinking how the God incarnate as Ram had been lying duly bound there when the persons get absolved of the universal ties with the grace of almighty God. Then Garud had gone to various gods for the redressal, including Narad, Brahma etc. but Shiv only told him to listen to Ram katha narrated by Kagbhusand. Here Shiv could have straightaway told Parvati how Kagbhusand got Ram's bhakti but he wanted to bring in some other creature, who too developed such doubts and the same were redressed by Kagbhusand. So Garud was brought in. But the importance of the fundamentals of satsang where Ram katha is held, were narrated by Shiv himself to make the public at large believe it. He said that one cannot enjoy Ram katha without satsang and without Ram katha, the worldly passions, would not go. Further, without elimination of worldly passions, one cannot have devotion in Ram. Therefore, satsang was at the base of the entire proposition.

बिनु सतसंग न हरि कथा तेहि बिनु मोह न भाग,
मोह गएँ बिनु राम पद होइ न दृढ़ अनुराग।

Here Shiv could have also coached Garud and eliminated the doubt of Garud but he did not want to do so himself as he had known that the doubt had arisen as a result of Ram's maya on Garud having become proud on releasing Ram from nagpash and this should be redressed by satsang only so that the people at large had faith in satsang. This is how even the gods did trust in protocol of entrusting a job to the person/institution, who are fit to do it rather than God himself dispensing, on all such matters. Also Shiv thought it proper for Garud to go to Kagbhusand as again

कछु तेहि ते पुनि मैं नहि राखा, समुझइ खग खगही कै भाषा।

The bird understood the language spoken by birds only.

Here Shiv has also propounded one more matter of principle that one should not talk to anyone on way when he was going on some important job somewhere else as at that time he would not be able to attend to him properly. One should rather approach a person capable of doing the job only after checking up whether he was free to attend to him. This is like the modern system of taking appointment for seeing someone. Such institution existed in Ram period too when Garud mentioned his doubt to Shiv on way, and Shiv was going somewhere else :

मिलेहु गरुड़ मारग महँ मोही, कवन भांति समुझावौं तोही।

Garud went to Kagbhusand's place. On reaching there, itself, the maya, worldly passions and all fears/doubts got eliminated. This is the effect of the environ itself then the effect of the satsang could be well imagined. Garud saw many old birds coming there and listening to Ram katha. Seeing the Garud there, all became happy. They welcomed the Garud; asked his well being and offered a seat to him as required by protocol. Even in birds so much protocol is seen. After respecting him, Kagbhusand felt obliged on his having come there and requested for being told what he could do for him. Garud is the head of all birds. Therefore, the crow (Kagbhusand) requested him for orders as to what was required to be done.

"आयसु देहु सो करौं अब प्रभु आयहु केहि काज"

The Garud told that his grievance had already been redressed after coming to that place itself and requested for telling him the Ram katha. Kagbhusand narrated the entire Ram katha as a result of which, all doubts about the bonafides of Ram got eliminated.

गयउ मोर संदेह सुनेउँ सकल रघुपति चरित,
भयउ राम पद नेह तव प्रसाद वायस तिलक।

He also felt obliged to Ram for having developed the doubt with his maya, so that Garud could come there for redressal of doubts and hear the Ram katha.

जौ नहिं होत मोह अति मोही, मिलतेउ तात कवन विधि तोही।

On the other side, Kagbhusand expressed his obligation for Garud having come there and having given him a chance to narrate Ram katha to him. This is the mentality of the great people that they rather than feeling greatness on listening to their praise by others, for the services rendered, feel obliged to them for having given a chance to serve. Kagbhusand saw that Garud was feeling regret over his having developed the doubt. To pacify him, Kagbhusand told him that it was all Ram's maya which created such doubts. For ordinary persons, the doubts get redressed in the daily life but for Ram's bhakta any doubt about Ram's bonafides can be redressed only through Ram katha and that too if narrated by a capable person. Here Kagbhusand was all capable to narrate Ram katha and to remove any doubts on Ram's bonafides, even Shiv was in praise for the same. To encourage Garud, therefore, Kagbhusand told him that he could not be blamed for having doubted Ram's bonafides. Doubts of various kinds through Ram's maya have been developing in the minds of Shiv, Brahma and other gods too. Even Narad was involved in maya due to which he became proud after having won 'Kama'. Although Shiv had at that time warned Narad not to narrate the incident of his having won 'Kama' before Vishnu as it would not be in his interest to do so but when one has bad time, he takes good advice too with biased mind and acts for the forbidden job. Narad did go to Vishnu; narrated his victory over Kama and appeared having felt proud of this achievement. Vishnu could not tolerate his bhakta becoming proud. He, therefore, with a view to eliminate Narad's pride, created a town; a swayambar of rajkanya on way of Narad; made Narad go there; see the girl (kanya), and getting trapped in her charm. Then to get her married, Narad went to Vishnu to grant him a beautiful figure so that the girl wooed him in the swayambar. Since it was all creation of Vishnu himself, he granted him the shape of a vanar which Narad did not know. Having thought that he occupied the best figure, Narad was certain of marriage but the girl wooed Vishnu Bhagwan, who too was there and the girl was none else but Lakshmi herself. The two persons sitting by his side told Narad to see his face. When Narad saw his face of a vanar, he got enraged, went to Vishnu and cursed him that he too would cry on the separation from his wife, when he went incarnate in the world. Vishnu accepted the curse. Vishnu knew that in the entire episode, he would have to face the curse of Narad but even at this cost, he wanted to mend Narad, who had become proud after winning Kama as the same Narad fell for a girl. After that Vishnu removed his 'maya' and Narad became a sanyasi as usual but he still was not convinced why Vishnu did not permit him to get married. His doubt was subsequently redressed when he went to Ram at the time of Sita having been kidnapped and Ram had been wandering in forests in search of Sita. Ram then satisfied him that he could not allow his man to go astray under the influence of any vice. Then Narad was convinced of Ram's greatness and his benevolence for his bhaktas. So here too Kagbhusand removed the doubt in the mind of Garud and still showed his obligation for the Garud having come there and Kagbhusand could be of any help to a Ram's person. He said :

तुम्हहिं न संसंय न मोह न माया, मो पर नाथ कीन्हि तुम्ह दाया।

Kagbhusand also consoled Garud that he was not an exception; even the munis like Narad, Sati, etc had been the victim of Ram's maya. He told there was none, who had not been under the influence of worldly affection, and there was none, who had not been influenced by passion. Greed too had influenced every one and none was above being enraged. Even Ram, doing manuj leela got enraged when inspite of having been worshipped by Ram for several days, the ocean did not give his army a passage. In this world there was none even a learned, a tapasvi, a brave, a poet or a pandit, who are full of all virtues, are influenced by worldly capitalistic greed. There was none, who did not yield to the charm of wealth and women. Such a maya is the maid servant of Ram. Although apparently this all appeared a farce but everyone was influenced by one vice of maya or the other and one cannot get rid of it without the blessings of Ram. This is how the poet, through the medium of Garud and Kagbhusand, has told the universe the influence of maya which can be overcome with the grace of Ram's bhakti only. Kagbhusand also told that for the sake of his bhaktas only Vishnu came incarnate as Ram and conducted himself as an ordinary person. This had put many in doubt about the bonafides of Ram as incarnate of God. Even Sati, Shiv's wife could not escape it and had to pay very heavily for it losing Shiv and then her life also. Those who understand this enjoy Ram's katha and others raising doubts, spoil their minds only. Kagbhusand then narrated how he himself had been influenced by Ram's maya. This fact he was telling Garud as he was Ram's man and nothing could be concealed from him. This shows the frankness of a person to another person, in whom he has developed confidence. Nothing should be kept secret from such a person. He said Ram does not allow pride to enter the mind of his men.

सुनहु राम कर सहज सुभाऊ, जन अभिमान न राखहिं काऊ।

Even though elimination of such vice involves some pain initially but it is for the ultimate gain of the person as a child having developed ulcer, the mother gets it operated. Though the child cries at the time of operation yet the mother is not shaken as she knows that ultimately the child would get rid of the ailment.

जदपि प्रथम दुख पावइ रोवइ बाल अधीर,
व्याधि नास हित जननी गनति न सो सिसु पीर।

Here Kagbhusand tells that whenever Vishnu, for the sake of his bhaktas, came incarnate as Ram and conducted himself as an ordinary human being, he used to go and enjoy Ram's conduct, particularly in childhood as Ram, as a child, was his God. When Ram was born in Awadh once, he went there as a baby crow. He would remain with Ram, wherever he went and used to eat the remains left over by Ram after his meals. This was the spiritual protocol between Ram and the bhakta.

लरिकाई जहँ जहँ फिरहि तहँ तहँ संग उड़ाऊँ,
जूठनि परइ अजिर महँ सो उठाइ करि खाउँ।

Ram too had been doing some humorous action to please the bhakta and also to keep him reminded that he was not a mere child but almighty God. Since people sometimes got doubt about Ram's bonafides as Sati, Garud etc. so was the case with Kagbhusand too, when once having seen Ram playing like a child, Kagbhusand developed doubt how he could be almighty Chidanand.

प्राकृत सिसु इव लीला देखि भयउ मोहि मोह,
कवन चरित्र करत प्रभु चिदानंद संदोह।

Infact Ram had been conducting such lila only to test the other person if he fell under the influence of Ram's maya and started doubting his bonafides itself. In other words such actions were only to establish in a stricter way the bonafides of Ram. Poet too has mentioned of such conduct of Ram and then by redressal of such doubt with a view to tell the readers that on so many actions of Ram (who had incarnated to live like ordinary human being), people would ordinarily develop doubts and then the redressal of such doubts would lead to greater understanding of Ram by his bhakta. This happened in the case of Sati, Narad, Garud, Kagbhusand, Jayant, Nishadraj, Raja Dasrath, Guru Vashisth etc.

माया वस्य जीव अभिमानी, ईस वस्य माया गुन खानी।

And one can get rid of the Ram's maya only by becoming Ram's bhakta.

रामचन्द्र के भजन बिनु जो चह पद निर्वान,
ग्यानवंत अपि सो नर पसु बिनु पूँछ विषान।

As without sun, the darkness of night does not disappear inspite of there being crores of stars as also the moon, so Ram's maya cannot he eliminated without Ram's bhakti. One more thing, particularly in the relations of Ram and his bhakta, is that Ram's bhakta does not fall pray to ignorance but to knowledge only according to Ram's grace.

हरि सेवकहि न व्याप अविद्या, प्रभु प्रेरित व्यापइ तेहि विद्या।

Ram's display of maya on Kagbhusand could not be known by his parents and other brothers. Ram ran to catch Kagbhusand but under influence of Ram's 'maya', undermining Ram's power to catch him wherever he went, Kagbhusand flew above. But wherever Kaghbusand went, Ram's arm to catch him followed him. Kagbhusand tried to fly to the extent he could but Ram's arm followed him.

Ultimately Kagbhusand became unconscious and fell on earth. On gaining consciousness, he found himself in Awadh in front of Ram. Seeing him, Ram smiled and Kagbhusand went into his mouth. There Kagbhusand saw many brahmands in Ram's abdomen. He saw crores of Brahmas, Shivs, suns, moons, earths, oceans, human beings establishments, which Kagbhusand had never known or heard or seen nor apt for being understood. In each Lok, Kagbhusand saw separate Brahma, Shiv, Vishnu, human beings, gandharva, pisachas, nisacharas, the God's other creatures etc. even Raja Dasrath, Bharat and other brothers and Kausalya mother were seen in various forms. He wandered about in all the Lokas but could see only one Ram. This shows only Ram is Akhand (अखंड) and all others have many forms.

अगनित भुवन फिरेउँ प्रभु राम न देखेउ आन।

The poet has tried to establish here that for Ram bhakta, he has to know one Ram only whereas in the case of others, Shiv, Brahma etc. one has to worship so many, creating confusion. Therefore, to avoid confusion and from the protocol angle too, one can serve one master and not many. Therefore, Ram alone is to be served by Ram's bhakta in which case there would be no ambiguity. Any principle, tanet, ethical discourse etc. should be without any ambiguity—this is the fundamental of spiritual protocol and that aspect is fulfilled by worshipping Ram alone. When he became upset after seeing many Brahmands etc. Ram laughed enabling Kagbhusand to come out and Ram again started behaving with Kagbhusand as a child as before. By showing other brahmands etc., Ram proved to him that he was doing manuj leela only to show the people at large that he was an ordinary human being but he had at the same time cared to redress the doubts of his men, if any. Kagbhusand after coming out of Ram's month still continued to be upset and requested Ram to protect him. Ram withdrew his maya and Kagbhusand was alright—

प्रेमाकुल प्रभु मोहि विलोकी, निज माया प्रभुता तब रोकी।

और

कीन्ह राम मोहि विगत विमोहा।

Kagbhusand then praised Ram and Ram in turn asked him to ask for any boon. This is the normal protocol between bhakta and Bhagwan. Where Bhagwan is pleased, he desires to fulfil the wishes of the bhakta because after all for every action of the human being there is always some desire. In such a situation, Ram offered to bless him with gyan, intelligence, vigyan or sanyas, whatever he wanted but Kagbhusand thought that Ram had not offered to bless him with his bhakti which was most important of all the other things as all other things were dependent on bhakti only. Kagbhusand said—

भगत कल्पतरू प्रनत हित कृपा सिंधु सुख धाम,
सोइ निज भगति मोहि प्रभु देहु दया करि राम।

Ram said 'सवमस्तु' – 'you get it'.

Ram, in addition, of his own, blessed Kagbhusand also with all virtues and said that maya will never confuse him any more. Ram also told Kagbhusand the ethics of Brahmgyan. He told that all creatures and various kinds of mortals and immortals were his creation and were managed by his maya only. All had been created by him and were brought up by him but out of all, human beings were closer to him. Within human beings too, brahmin were dearer; within brahmins the pandits of vedas were more dear; within pandits too, those pandits were closer, who led their lives as per the verdict of religion and vedas; within such pandits too, those detached from worldly life were dearer; within such detached the gyanis were closer; within gyanis the vigyanis were closer; and within the vigyanis too, his bhaktas were still closer to him as they had no one else to depend upon. He said—

"मोहि सेवक सम प्रिय कोउ नाहीं"।

Such ethics of Vedas have been narrated by the poet through Ram only to seem more authentic. Here Ram had also indicated that a person, who was without bhakti was like any other person to him even if he was Brahma himself and even a very mean person, who was Ram bhakta, was dearer to Ram even more than himself :

भगति हीन बिरँचि किन होई, सब जीवहु सम प्रिय मोहि सोई,
भगतिवँत अति नीचउ प्रानी, मोहि प्रान प्रिय असि मम बानी।

Here the poet through Ram, almighty God himself, have pronounced that the varan/ashram etc. institutions were the creation of mankind and these had no recognition in the realm of God, where God recognised his own bhaktas only as against the non-bhaktas irrespective of the caste and creed, they might be belonging to. At the time of Sita swayambar too the poet although all through has recognised the institution of varan/ashram and has indicated that broadly the people were divided according to the varans, yet there could be exceptional cases like Vishwamitra, although a kshatriya, had become tapasvi and was counted in rishis. Similarly Nishadraj, belonging a mean class became closer to Ram by dint of Ram's bhakti alone so much so that even guru Vashisth gave him that much recognition. In the swayambar, the arrangement for the seating of the persons was not according to varans—brahmin, kshatriyas, vaish, shudra etc., but by their capability.

उत्तम मध्यम नीच लघु, निज निज थल अनुहारि।

Also here Ram has made the Kagbhusand with all virtues and also with his uninterrupted and continuous bhakti although not even a human being. In confirmation of what Ram said (even though not so required from the social protocol), Ram further elaborated that a father although has several sons with their different kinds of virtues like one is pandit; one tapasvi; one gyani; one very wealthy; one very brave; one donor; one very intelligent knowing everything; one of religious mind but father's affection for all would be the same. But if one of them is father's devotee by heart, actions and speech and does not depend on another person, such a son would be dearer to the father compared to all others although he might be least learned of all. Likewise Ram has equal affection for all mortals and immortals but out of them, those, who worship Ram without any consideration, are dearer to him.

पुरुष, नपुसंक नारि वा जीव चराचर कोई,
सर्व भाव, भज कपट तजि मोहि परम प्रिय सोई।

Here Ram has removed the distinction between brahmin, kshatriya, vaish, shudra etc. and even between the mortals and immortals but has recognised one, who worshipped him without any consideration. The distinction of varans has been made by the 'man' as a social system of governance of mankind. Kagbhusand was happy to learn it and after having coached the Kagbhusand in this way, Ram became a child and started crying on the mother calling him. After that Kagbhusand never had been influenced by maya as booned by Ram. But this all could be attained by Ram's mercy only.

राम कृपा बिनु सुनु खगराई, जानि न जाइ राम प्रभुताई।

Without Ram's mercy one cannot know the greatness of Ram and without knowing that greatness, one cannot have faith and without faith, one cannot have affection for Ram and without affection, one cannot have Ram's bhakti and without bhakti, one cannot have full attainment.

बिनु विश्वास भगति नहिं तेहि बिनु द्रवहिं न राम,
राम कृपा बिनु सपनेहुँ जीव न लह विश्राम।

Kagbhusand also told that Ram had the strength of crores of winds, (here from the poet's assertion, it appears that the wind is considered to be most powerful and this fact has been scientifically proved too in present days); he has the light of crores of suns; he is cool like crores of moons and is one who can redress all worldly agonies. In the end Kagbhusand said—

रामु अमित गुन सागर थाह कि पावई कोइ।

Here Kagbhusand had acted as a guru to Garud and the doubts could be redressed where one got a capable guru.

"गुरु बिन होई न ज्ञान"

Garud got all the enlightenment so far as his doubt about Ram's bonafides was concerned. But now he had one doubt in his mind as to how, inspite of his being Rambhakta, learned, simple, gyanwan, sanyasi, vairagi, he was having the specie of a Kagbhusand, which is not so much appreciated by anyone.

कारन कवन देह यह पाई, तात सकल मोहि कहहु बुझाई।

This very doubt had arisen in the mind of Parvati, when Shiv told her the entire Ram katha, which he had heard as a bird from Kagbhusand. We are now back to the same place of the topic. And since Kagbhusand had acted as Garud's guru here and nothing doubtful should be kept when a guru is available so Garud broached this subject too to get enlightement. Also Kagbhusand was not to have an end of his life as per Ram's boon. This too had surprised the Garud. He, therefore, sought clarification in that regard too.

"तुम्हहि न व्यापत काल अति कराल कारन कवन"

Kagbhusand was capable of remembering all his previous lives too. This was possible by virtue of his having attained the enlightenment of Braham. So recollecting the same, Kagbhusand narrated the entire history to Garud. Kagbhusand told that this specie of Kagbhusand had been of great importance to him as he had attained Ram's bhakti with this specie only.

एहि तन राम भगति मैं पाई, ताते मोहि ममता अधिकाई।
और
अति नीचहु सन प्रीति करिअ जानि निज परम हित।

This is the tenet of protocol and in one's own interest that if one sees some benefit to oneself, one should not hesitate even to love a mean person. Even otherwise one should love the specie which can make him reach the almighty and if any specie carries one away from God, then one should not even accept the species of Brahma. Kagbhusand also told that he could die if he wished but he would not as even Mukti could not give him the pleasure which he was having as Kagbhusand and going through Ramkatha daily.

देखेउँ करि सब करम गोसाईं, सुखी न भयउँ अबहिं की नाईं।

This shows that the pleasure lies in contentment in what one has rather than wishing for what cannot be available. Kagbhusand then explained the previous lives, which started in pre-Satyug period, when again there was Kalyug and everyone was against dharam. According to Hindu Mythology, the universe has four yugs— Satyug, Tretayug, Duaparyug and Kalyug. The cycle of these yugs is a continuous process. At present we are in Kalyug. Ramcharitmanas was also written in Kalyug. This yug is about 5000 years old. Prior to this, there was Duapuryug in which Krishna incarnation took place. In that yug, there was Kans killing, Mahabharat war etc. This yug lasted for lacs of years. Prior to this, there was Tretayug in which Ram incarnation took place. Ram killed Ravan etc. rakshasas and established Ram rajya, completely free of all ailments, shocks and worries. But in that period too rakshasas marred the show for many years necessitating Vishnu to come as incarnate Ram to kill rakshasas and establish Ram rajya— a symbol of peace and prosperity. Prior to Tretayug, there was Satyug, when kings like Harishchander, Manu etc. had born and vedas originated along with other shastras and smrities followed by Hindus in their social, political, and spiritual governance. The varans and ashrams also started in that period. Prior to Satyug again there was Kalyug and so on. Now we are awaiting the fall of Kalyug by the Kalki Avtar yielding place to Satyug etc. It is also said that there was Ramkal in each Tretayug and Krishankal in each Duaparyug. So the Kagbhusand was narrating his story when he was born in Kalyug prior to Satyug. He was born in a shudra family, indicating thereby that prior to Satyug too there was the concept of varans/ashrams etc. and the change of yugas is a cycle of historical evolution. He was Shiv follower and used to speak ill of other gods. He lived in Awadh but did not know the importance of Ram then. Like the present Kalyug, in the previous Kalyug too there was all religious anarchy and people were afflicted with worldly ambitions and vices.

भए लोग सब मोहबस लोभ ग्रसे सुभ कर्म,
सुनु हरिजान ग्यान निधि कहउँ कछुक कलिधर्म।

Some of the vices of Kalyug have been indicated by the poet. Although manas was written in 16-17th century A.D. (in Kalyug itself), some of the fundamentals of the Kalyug existing in 20th century appear to be a prediction as these cannot be from any other book which could explain what existed in the previous Kalyug. Some of these are :

(1) All people would be ambitious of worldly life;

(2) People would be involved in greed and even one would expect some consideration out of the good jobs done.

(3) There would be no following of the varans and ashrams.

(4) All men and women would act against the ethics of shastras.

(5) The brahmins would be sellers of vedas i.e. they would teach the religion discourses on consideration only. The raja would eat away public money i.e. there would be most political corruption.

(6) Everyone would follow his own dharam.

(7) One, who boasts would be pandit.

(8) Most ostentatious and viceous persons would be considered sants.

(9) One who could snatch others wealth would be considered intelligent.

(10) A liar would be considered the most learned.

(11) Immoral and irreligious people would be considered as gyani and vairagi in Kalyug.

(12) People with long hairs would be considered tapasvi.

(13) Those having horrific dresses and eating everything—eatable or non eatable—would be considered as sidha and would be honoured in Kalyug.

(14) All people would be under the thumb of women and would act as their puppets.

(15) Shudras would be learned and would teach the brahmins.

(16) All people would be involved in passion and greed.

(17) The divorcees would be honoured by other persons for the sake of quenching their passions and on the contrary the married would have no ornaments to adorn themselves.

(18) The pupils would be stealing the wealth of their teachers rather than respecting them.

(19) The parents would coach their wards only to prepare them to earn wealth.

(20) The ladies and gents would be ignorant of brahmgyan and would not hesitate in killing the brahmin or the guru for the sake of money.

(21) Those involved in others' wives; clever in deceptive tactics; having malicious habits, would be considered as very intelligent.

(22) The sanyasis would comprise of the persons of mean castes such as तेली, कुम्हार, किरात, कोल etc. or those whose either wives die or who lose all their wealth. After this they would get their hairs cut and become sanyasis.

(23) Shudras would be indulged in tapsya, vrat, worship and pronounce religious discourses.

(24) People would mostly be mongrels.

(25) People would start a new panth every now and then rather than following the already laid down tenets of religions.

(26) The sanyasis would be rich and live in luxurious homes. They would be involved in all sorts of vices and the family men would be comparatively poorer.

(27) The people would divorce the pious and faithful (पतिव्रत) ladies and would bring the professionals in their houses.

(28) The sons would recognise the parents till they are married and the moment they meet their in-laws, their own family men would appear to be their enemies.

ससुरारि पिआरि लगी जबतें, रिपुरूप कुटुंब भए तब तें।

(29) The king shall be follower of irreligious tactics and punish the people without any crime and those who are criminals would be honoured and would be closer to the rulers.

(30) The rich, even from mean castes would be considered honourable and those who do not follow vedas would be considered as the God's bhaktas.

(31) The poets and writers would not be honoured and would die of hunger etc. There would be frequent famines in Kalyug as rain etc. take place only when all tenets of dharam are followed as in Ram rajya. There would be no rains and so no crops.

(32) The ladies would have no ornaments. They would never feel satisfied. They would be poor and lost in worldly affections.

(33) People would be having all kinds of ailments with no pleasure. They would feel proud and would get enraged without any reason.

(34) The life span would be shorter.

(35) People would be immoral. They would have no respects even for their daughters and sisters (i.e. they would indulge in illicit relations with them).

(36) There would be no donors and no suppression of worldly ambitions.

These are some of the vices of the Kalyug, but there are good things too in Kalyug such as one can attain mukti with least hardship. The attainment which in Satyug, Treta and Duapur could be had by lots of yagya, tap, yog etc. can be had in Kalyug only by Hari name. In Satyug, people had been yogis and sanyasis to attain mukti; in Treta only performance of yagya would grant mukti to people; in Duapur, people would have attainment with Ram puja only, whereas in Kalyug by uttering Hari name only, people would attain mukti. In Kalyug there is no need of performing yog and yagya, only Ram's name would grant them mukti if he is worshipped without any consideration. One evident virtue of Kalyug is that people are not sinners by heart and are rather righteous. With these good things being available in Kalyug, Kagbhusand admired Kalyug saying—

कलियुग सम जुग आन नहिं जौं नर कर विश्वास,

गाइ राम गुन गन विमल भव तर बिनहिं प्रयास।

Kagbhusand further told that once there was famine in Awadh. So he shifted to Ujjain as a very poor person and after earning something after some time, he started worshipping Shiv. He had been serving a pandit, who used to worship Shiv. He was a sadhu but Kagbhusand's services were deceptive. The sadhu had been coaching Kagbhusand like his son but Kagbhusand would always feel proud of himself and would not honour the Ram bhaktas and brahmins inspite of all efforts made by the sadhu. Once that sadhu called Kagbhusand and told him the importance of Shiv pooja and Ram bhakti. The sadhu was quite gentle but it is a fundamental that the mean person after attaining greatness would like to kill the person through whom he attained greatness. Seeing this only the intelligent persons do not have company of the mean persons. They say—

"खल सन कलह न भल नहिं प्रीती।"

One should neither have enmity nor friendship with a bad man. Once, Kagbhusand said, he was worshipping Shiv when guru arrived but he did not stand up in his honour. The guru did not feel it nor said anything but there was an Akaswani saying that although the guru did not mind his rudeness but there was a curse for the Kagbhusand to become a serpent. To honour the guru by standing up in his respect was a social protocol even honoured to date. But wherever there is a breach of such protocol, the breach in punished temporally. The guru, however, worshipped Shiv and requested him to calm down and begged him to excuse the pupil. Through the sadhu, the poet has taught the public at large as to how to praise Lord Shiva as also to give a place to Shiv pooja along with Ram pooja with a view to bring about cordiality amongst the Shaivites and Vaisnavites not exiting in 16th century when Manas was written. Hearing Shiv stuti, there was again an Akaswani asking the guru to seek any boon as desired. As per normal spiritual protocol on the bhakti having been fulfilled and God offering for any boon, the bhakta asks for the continuous/perpetual bhakti. The guru also asked for the same and further requested for the curse being reduced. Shiv said that although the pupil had done a great sin and even inspite of the request of the guru, the curse could not be withdrawn totally and the pupil would have to suffer for it for thousands of lives, yet in each life he would die without any discomfort or difficulty and have rebirth without difficulty. Also he would remember the attainments of this life in whatever specie he might be and also he would have the Ram bhakti in his mind. He should not hereafter insult the brahmins and should always be respectful to them. Shiv also blessed him that he would be able to go wherever he wanted to go without any hesitation or checking. Guruji went to his home and the pupil became a serpent. He would die comfortably and have another specie; again die and have another specie and so on. He, however, as booned by Shiv, did not lose the gyan, he had already attained.

त्रिजग देव नर जोइ तनु धरऊँ तहँ तहँ राम भजन अनुसरऊँ।

Animal, bird, human being or the god, in whatever specie he was born, he continued Ram bhakti. Here the Kagbhusand, through Ram, whose bhakta he was, and through Shiv, who granted him the boon that in whatever specie he was born, he would change the specie (die and reborn without any difficulty) and would continue to have Ram bhakti on each birth, has conveyed and confirmed the Hindus' concept of transmigration of soul and the rebirth in any of the species of the creatures. Since this was a controversal subject during the period Manas was written in 16th century, when there was Mohammedan rule in India and Muslims did not believe in the concept of rebirth/transmigration of souls, the poet wanted to put the controversy to an end by confirming it by Ram/Shiv himself. After transmigrating from many species, the last one he got was that of a brahmin, which was difficult to have. In the childhood, he had been performing Ramlilas; in the youth, he was sent to school but he would not learn anything except Ram bhakti. When his parents died in course of time, he went to forest to do Ram bhakti. He consulted many rishis/munis but could not get convincing reply about Ram bhakti. Many coached him to believe in nirguna bhakti but he could think of none else than Ram. Ultimately he reached Lomas Rishi on a hill top. He accepted Kagbhusand as his pupil and taught him somewhat of Ram bhakti and then shifted to Brahmgyan (निर्गुण ब्रह्म), which Kagbhusand did not like. A dispute arose between Kagbhusand and the Rishi Lomas. Rishi got enraged :

बारम्बार सकोप मुनि करइ निरूपन ज्ञान,
मैं अपने मन बैठ तब करउँ विविध अनुमान।

Kagbhusand then attained gyan and thought—

(1) Human being under the influence of maya cannot have Bhagwat darshan.
(2) A well wisher cannot do harm.
(3) A man with parasmani cannot be poor.
(4) A jealous person can never be happy.
(5) A family cannot prosper with ill-feelings for brahmins.
(6) One would not be involved in worldly ambitions after one has known self.
(7) One cannot be a good man in bad company.
(8) Visitors to others' wives cannot remain happy.
(9) An atheist cannot attain salvation or have any happiness in life.
(10) One cannot be a successful raja without knowing the ethics of governance.
(11) A Ram bhakta cannot be a sinner.
(12) One cannot get appreciation without doing good deeds and conversely one cannot be appreciated and at the same time doing wrong things.
(13) Hari bhakti is the ultimate attainment.
(14) A human being not involved in Ram bhakti is the greatest loser.

Like this Kagbhusand had been thinking in above terms and not listening to what the rishi preached. The rishi ultimately failed in his efforts to persuade Kagbhusand to learn what he preached and cursed him to become a 'Kagbhusand', who would always utter his 'kaw' 'kaw'. Kagbhusand accepted the curse unhesitatingly. He became Kagbhusand and after paying respects to the rishi and remembering Ram, he departed from the rishi's ashram. The rishi cannot be blamed for it as it was all the creation of Ram only. By diversifying muni, Ram wanted to test Kagbhusand's bhakti for him. Ram having found Kagbhusand his own by heart, action and speech, again brought muni to his self. The rishi too having seen Kagbhusand as staunch believer of Ram repented on having passed curse on Kagbhusand. He called him back and gave him 'Ram mantra' to remember Ram as a child. Muni kept him in his ashram for sometime and taught him Ramayan and told that he had taught him Ramayan having found him a Ram bhakta through and through. The muni gave him the boon of attainment of Ram bhakti by him always. Kagbhusand paid his respects and departed from that place.

सदा राम प्रिय होहु तुम्ह शुभ गुन भवन अमान,
कामरूप इच्छामरन ग्यान विराग निधान।

The rishi also gave the boon of attaining anything he desired but since he got Ram mantra only after becoming Kagbhusand, he had developed affinity to that specie and inspite of rishi's boon of changing from this specie, Kagbhusand did not leave that specie and without his wish he would not die too. So he had been living as Kagbhusand only doing Ram katha in the mountain near the sarovar which was the place without any sins. As there could not be any sin/sinner in a diametre of 10 kms., anyone who entered that campus would be absolved of all sins and doubts. So did the Garud too. The rishi's boons had been confirmed by the almighty God.

एवमस्तु तव वच मुनि ग्यानी, यह मम भगत कर्म मन बानी।

Ram confirmed the boon of the rishi and also confirmed that Kagbhusand was his bhakta by heart, action and speech. Eversince then he had been living in the ashram doing Ram bhakti and visiting, Awadh, whenever Ram came as incarnate of Vishnu.

तातें यह तन मोहि प्रिय भयउ राम पद नेह,
निज प्रभु दरसन पायउँ गए सकल सन्देह।

Kagbhusand, therefore, told and confirmed that Ram bhakti was the only way to attain salvation and there was no other way/method to reach him.

Having heard the biography of Kagbhusand that he having been deeply involved in Ram bhakti i.e. Sagun bhakti, and the muni wanting to teach him Nirgun bhakti, a doubt arose as to why he was so much insistent on Sagun bhakti only and what is the great difference between the Sagun and Nirgun bhakti. Now since Garud had a capable guru, he thought it proper to get this doubt too redressed. Infact it is the off shoot of the period when Manas was written in 16th century when there was peace in Mughal rule and many Nirgun (Kabir, Nanak etc.) and Sagun (Ram and Krishan bhaktas like Tulsidas, Surdas, Nanddas, Meera) had born and since each one considered his own way of attainment as fool-proof, there was generally a dispute between them too more so as Hindus were, by and large Sagun bhaktas and Muslims did not believe in idol worship and at that time there being Muslim rule, the Hindus had been facing difficulty in reconciling to the Nirgun Brahm concept. The poet, therefore, thought it proper to enlighten the Hindus in this regard by telling that there was not much difference between the two methods of attaining salvation as the goal of both was the attainment only and people with either belief had been having such attainment, the poet precisely narrated that both of these were the ways in that direction but with different methodology. The teachers (guru) too felt pleasure in redressing the doubts of the pupils. It was only when the pupil did not listen to the guru's preaching at all that the guru gets enraged as Lomas rishi got enraged on Kagbhusand not being prepared to listen to Brahmgyan. Kagbhusand having experienced this difficulty and having now realised that both methods led to attainment of salvation, he was happy to remove the doubts in the mind of the people at large through the media of his pupil Garud. He told that in as much as both led to salvation, there was no difference between the two but the rishis narrated some difference in their application which he would explain.

भगतिहि ज्ञानहि नहिं कहु भेदा, उभय हरहिं भव संभव खेदा।
नाथ मुनीस कहहिं कछु अन्तर, सावधान सोउ सुनु विहगंवर।

Gyan, vigyan, vairagya and jog are all males, and forceful and 'maya' is female. When one attains the male, the female, vanishes. Therefore, the function of all these is to eliminate the 'maya'. But till one attains any of these, one is constantly under the influence of female 'maya' like an ordinary human being remaining under the influence of women. Even the munis/rishis cannot escape the influence of females, that is why they live like hermits in forests.

Apart from the four males (ज्ञान, विज्ञान, वैराज्ञ और जोग) which can influence maya, the female, by dint of their being forceful maya is also put off by bhakti (भगति). This is based on the principle :

"मोह न नारि नारि कैं रूपा"

A lady is not attracted towards the beauty of another lady but feels jealous of the same. So when bhakti is attained then too one gets rid of maya and consequently the attainment of salvation. Now maya and bhakti both are relevant to God. One is controlled and under his direction, influences the universe, but the other influences the God himself and consequently no effect on universe. Ram, therefore, likes bhakti only. This, it was stated, is the secret of Ram himself, which is not known ordinarily to all but one who has known it, he gets closer to Ram.

यह रहस्य रघुनाथ कर वेगि न जानइ कोई,
जो जानइ रघुपति कृपा सपनेहु मोह न होई।

The human being is, however, involved in maya and the more he tries to get rid of it, the more he gets involved in it. One, therefore, have to lead a very controlled life to get over 'maya'. For this purpose, apart from the lot of Jap, Tap, etc. performed by one, one has to eliminate the influence of kam (passion) by leaving the lady; rage by leaving the worldly involvements; pride by leaving the worldly attainments and greed by leaving the materialistic world. For all this, one has to control the sensual pleasures. The sensual pleasures are all very weak points in the human beings. As soon as a human being falls prey to the influence of any sensual pleasure, he loses his self and control of the sensual elements and gets trapped in. One can, after this entrapping, get out of it only by gyan, vairagya etc. or alternatively by bhakti. Gyan, vairagya etc. are very tough paths to be followed for eradication of maya and a lot of sensual control is required which is beyond a human being's normal administration whereas it is easier to be attained through the path of bhakti.

राम भजन सोइ मुकति गोसाईं, अनइच्छित आवइ बरि आई।

Such is the protocol, the poet has depicted, even in the spiritual matters and spiritual relation of creature and God. Once the bhakti enters one's mind then it does not permit any worldly passions etc. to get into that mind and consequently one gets rid of the influence of maya resulting in attainment of salvation. Further, for reaching Ram, who is not to be seen or is not visible, one has to reach him through his bhaktas because Ram cares more for his bhaktas.

मोरें मन प्रभु अस विश्वासा, राम तें अधिक राम कर दासा।

Therefore Ram's bhakti can be attained by satsang or the company of Ram's bhaktas.

अस विचारि जोइ कर सतसंगा, राम भगति तेहि सुलभ विहंगा।

It is like our present protocol of reaching a higher authority. If one tries to reach the higher authority independently, it becomes very difficult because the access to him directly is not possible. One, therefore, has to find an easier way of reaching him through his lieutenants (P.As.). Similarly, it is very difficult to reach the almighty directly, but becomes easier to reach him through his persons (भक्त)/bhaktas or through satsang.

For the sake of further clarification for mankind, Garud puts forth seven doubts for clarification :

(1) Which is the toughest specie to be attained?
(2) Which is greatest grief?
(3) Which is greatest relief?
(4) Who is a saint?
(5) Who is a non-saint?
(6) Which is the best deed?
(7) Which is the worst deed?

Kagbhusand gave the replies seriatim as under :

(1) Human being is the best specie but can be attained with great difficulty. In this specie one can have the knowledge, gyan, vairagya, bhakti etc. and if one does not perform bhakti etc. even after attaining human specie, one has wasted this life.
(2) Being a poor is the greatest grief. One resorts to all sorts of bad deeds in poverty to come over it and consequently gets involved in it more.
(3) Company of a saint is the biggest achievement and consequent relief for any creature.
(4) A saint is one, who generally helps all others by heart, action and speech. He even suffers because of other's ailment to get him relief.
(5) On the contrary, the non-saints try to harm others even without any gain to themselves. They try to destroy others physically, mentally, and materialistically and in the process get themselves destroyed.
(6) Helping others is the best deed.
(7) Thinking bad of others is the worst deed.

Then the spiritual/sensual ingredients also cause ailments to the human beings such as involvement in worldly ambitions (मोह)is the root cause of all ailments :

मोहु सकल व्याधिन्ह कर मूला।

Passion creates all ailments pertaining to wind (वायु) greed leads to ailments of cough (कफ) and rage leads to all bilious (पित्त) ailments and if one is involved in all these at a time then one loses senses/consciousness and consequently dies. In other words, the poet wants to tell the people that for proper health, as scientifically proved, one should have control over these worldly passions of greed, rage, passion etc. because all ailments are caused due to anger, blood pressure, over thinking, etc. The institutions of jap, tap, samadhi etc. relieve the person from worldly involvements and to that extent he is sensually alert and free. They also change the man's mind so much that a person after attaining bhakti, is absolved of all worldly passions and accordingly all worries, anxieties etc. too. So bhakti is the real panacea for all ailments.

और राम कृपा नासहिं सब रोगा, जौं एहि भान्ति बनै सँजोगा।

रघुपति भक्ति सजीवन मूरी, अनुपान श्रद्धा मति पूरी।

In the end Garud felt satisfied and was thankful to Lord Ram that for his better understanding of Ram, he was made to have the doubt about Ram's bonafides as an incarnate of Vishnu leading to his meeting Kagbhusand and consequent redressal of all his doubts. In other words, through the medium of Kagbhusand and Garud, the poet has brought home to the people at large the protocol between Brahma and his creatures; amongst the gods themselves. It has also been shown that a person is not great because of the caste in which he is born but because of his deeds. Kagbhusand was happy as a Kagbhusand only and in fact did not want to give up that form inspite of his having the boon from Rishi Lomas as also from Ram himself for change of specie or for complete mukti. He felt as a Kagbhusand he was better off as he was able to indulge in Ram's bhakti and teaching the same to others too rather than attaining ultimate salvation and get dumped in Swarag for good. The poet has tried to show that—

(1) bhakti is a better device for reaching the almighty compared to the other tougher routes through gyan, vairagya etc.

(2) The bhakti or for that matter the other methods too require the person to get rid of the worldly involvements causing rage, worry, greed, affection, pride etc.

(3) Bhakti is the easiest and surest way of attaining salvation in Kalyug.

(4) At the time Ramcharitmanas was written by Tulsidas, it was 16th century A.D. and there was Mughal rule in India. Mughal rule was comparatively peaceful compared to the previous Muslim rules of Slave, Khilji, Tughlak, Suri etc. dynasties. This peaceful atmosphere produced many poets and bhaktas having belief in Ram, Krishan, Shiv, Nirgun, Sagun etc. and there was no cordiality between various such sects. Tulsidas as Ram bhakta was initially not prepared to bow before Krishan. Similarly Shaivites did not recognise Ram as a God and vice versa. Above all with the advent of Muslims, who neither believed in idol-worship nor in Sagun Braham, there was further disparity of views and Muslims being the rulers of the country, considered their thinking as supreme and enforced the same on Hindus leading to many conversions from Hindus to Islam. At such a period, Tulsidas having known all these disparities had tried through Manas to redress these mostly. He showed Ram as Shiv bhakta and Shiv as Ram bhakta. Similarly Krishan and Ram both have been shown as incarnates of God Vishnu and, therefore, both were one and the same. Infact the staunch Ram bhakta like Tulsidas too bowed before Krishna and also subsequently wrote Geetavali or Krishan-Charitam. To remove disparity between Hindus and Muslims as also between Nirgun (like Kabir) and Sagun devotees, Tulsidas has in the dialogue of Garud and Kagbhusand said that there was no difference in Nirgun and Sagun bhakti as through

both one attains salvation. It is only the difference of process and methodology that has to be followed in these two beliefs suiting one's conscience. The effort made by the poet in this book has helped in a long way in eradicating the differences between various sects. This itself was an accomplishment by any poetic attempt.

(5) Wherever there developed any doubt, the poet has given the clarification/confirmation through the medium of Ram, Vishwamitra, Guru Vashisth, Shiv etc. so that it appeared authentic and believed by all. In other words through this book, the poet has redressed all possible doubts arising in bhakti.

(6) Bhakti is not the monopoly of a few persons belonging to particular castes of brahmin, kshatriya and vaish only. Persons of any caste including shudras, can resort to it. Ram has even gone further to give right of his bhakti to non-human beings and even the immortals. That is why the poet has brought in the dialogue of Kagbhusand and Garud to impress upon the public that in those species too, they could understand Ram better and were not now prepared to leave that form and have that of human being knowing fully well that the specie of human being is best of all species.

(7) Even when involved in bhakti, the bhakta should not cause disrespect to the brahmin, guru etc. as one cannot be pardoned for such omissions even by God in whose bhakti he remained lost. In other words having been following the spiritual protocol, one should not sacrifice the social and religious protocol for that purpose. In that situation one gets neither of these fulfilled and ultimately gets curse of God.

(8) While in bhakti, one should perform it with full devotion and belief and should not give place to any doubt.

(9) If one develops any doubt then he should find out a capable guru and get all his doubts redressed rather than carrying those doubts with him and allowing them

to multiply. Once a capable guru is found, one should get all his doubts redressed unhesitatingly.

(10) After having found a capable guru, who is able to redress the grievances, one should not be very stubborn in his thinking only and placing his thinking above that of guru itself because in such a situation, he would only get the curse of the guru, which leaves him good for nothing. The guru should also be like Kagbhusand, who should not keep anything secret from the pupil; once having accepted him as such Kagbhusand had in the end said—

नाथ यथामति भाषेउँ राखेउँ नहिं कछु गोइ,
चरित सिंधु रघुनायक थाह कि पावइ कोइ।

This also brings us to an end of this writing making an effort to find out the element of protocol in Ramcharitmanas—social, religious, political and spiritual. This might also serve the purpose of annihilating some of the doubts in the minds of readers of Manas.

जासु नाम भव भेषज हरन घोर त्रय सूल
सो कृपाल मोहि तो पर सदा रहउ अनुकूल।

Glossary

Arti : Worship with lighted lamp
Ahutis : Oblation
Agani preeksha : Fire trial
Amrit kund : Nectar tank
Apsaras : Divine dancer
Asan : Stage
Asheesh : Blessing
Ashok Vatika : A garden
Ashirwad : Blessing
Ashram : Hermitage
Ashwamedh Yagya : Horse sacrifice
Awadhwasis : Residents of Awadh
Barat : Marriage party
Baratis : Members of marriage party
Basant : Spring
Bhakta : Devotee
Bhagwan : God
Bhagya : Fate
Bhed : Division/secrecy
Bheels : Tribals
Bhiksha : Alms
Bhoomi : Land
Bhoot : Past/evil spirit
Booty : Plant
Brahmchari : A celibate
Brahmacharya : First of four stages in man's life
Brahmand : Universe
Brahmgyan : Divine knowledge
Brahmin : One of four castes in Hindus
Brahm-jiv bhed : God and creature relation
Chanchal : Unsteady
Charanamrit : Foot ambrosia
Chita : Funeral pier
Chudamani : Head jewel
Dakshina : Remuneration to priest
Dam : Value
Dand : Punishment
Darbar : Royal court
Darbaris : Courtiers
Darshan : Glimpse
Dera : A camp
Dev pooja : God worship
Dham : Abode (of deity)
Dhanush : Bow
Dhanush-ban : Bow and arrow
Dharmatma : Devout

Digpal : Protecting deity in each direction
Doot : Representative
Dupatta : Turban
Dwara : Door
Ganas :Communities
Geetawali : A book
Ghat : Bank
Grahas : Planets
Guru : Teacher
Gyan : Knowledge
Gyanis : Learned
Hari : God
Havan : Fire sacrifice
Ishwar : God
Jap : Remembering deity's names
Jatayu : An eagle
Jawans : Youths
Jay : Victory
Jayakara : Cheers hailing victory
Jayamala : Garlands by bride in groom's neck
Jeeva : Creature
Jog : Concentrated meditation
Jogi : Ascetic
Jungle : Forest
Jyotish : Astrology
Kali Avtar : God's incarnation
Kam : Passion
Karma : Deed
Katha : Religious discourse
Kaw Kaw : Crow's voice
Keshav Raj : God Krishan's reign
Khazana : Treasury
Kripa : Grace
Krishan-Charitam : God Krishan's life sketch
Kshatriya : One of four castes of Hindus who rules
Ksheer: A dish prepared with milk and rice
Leela : Deeds of god incarnation
Lokas : The three worlds
Machan : A raised platform
Mahabharat Kal : Period when Mahabharat was enacted
Mahal : Palace
Maharani : Empress
Mala : Garland
Manas : Man
Mandap : A pavilion
Manglacharan : Benediction
Manaskar : Writer of Ramcharitmanas
Mantra : A vedic hymn
Mantri : Minister
Manuj leela : God's deads as human being
Marg : Way/Path
Maya : Illusion
Mayavi : Illusive
Milap : Meeting
Mukti : Salvation

Munis : Ascetics/Hermits
Naridharma : Wife's religious pledge
Navada Bhakti : Meditation of nine kinds
Nirgun : Formless god/god without qualities
Nirvan : Salvation
Niti : Policy
Paduka : Wooden slippers
Palki : Chariot
Pandal : Pavilion
Pandits : Priests
Paramgati : Salvation
Parasmani : A mythical stone which converts iron into gold
Patal : Nethermost world
Pativrata : Faithful wife
Pativrata Dharam : Faithful wife's conduct
Pauranic : Mythological
Pisach : Evil spirit
Praja : Subjects
Prasada : Offerings to idol
Prayag : Junction of rivers Ganga, Yamuna and Saraswati
Pucca : Strong/firm
Puja Archana : Worship
Puranas : Mythological books
Purohit : Priest
Putresthi Yagya : Worship to be blessed with son
Raghukul : God Ram's dynasty
Raja : The King
Rajbhag : King's share of produce
Rajguru : King's priest
Raja-praja : Ruler-ruled
Rajkanya : Princess
Rajkumar : Prince
Rajkumari : Princess
Rajmahal : King's Palace
Rajmata : King's Mother
Rajneeti : Politics/diplomacy
Raj-tilak samagri : Coronation material
Rakshasas : Monsters/demons
Rakshasasni : Monstress
Ramayan : Biography of god Ram
Ramayan Kal : God Ram's period
Ram Kal : God Ram's period
Ramlilas : Deeds of god Ram
Ram-nam : Memorising god Ram's name
Ram Rajya : Reign of God Ram
Rani : Queen
Ridhi : Goddess of wealth
Rishis : Hermits
Sabha : Council/meeting
Sadhu : Hermit
Sagun : Good Omen/god in form/god possessed of atributes
Sainiks : Soldiers/sepoys
Sakha : Friend

Samadhi : Intense meditation
Samaj : Society
Samarpan : Devotion
Sam : Conciliation by peaceful means
Samagri : Material
Sampati : Wealth
Samrat : Emperor
Samvat : Hindu era
Sanskar : Mental impression
Sant : Saint
Santhri : A mat
Sanyas : Asceticism/renunciation
Sanyasi : An ascetic/one who has renounced world
Sapath : Oath
Saptpadi : Ceremony of seven circumambulation
Saraj-ud-daula : A nawab
Sarovar : Water tank
Sarthi : A charioteer
Sasural : In-laws
Satsang : Association with pious men
Satya Yug : Mythological period/first of four Hindu periods
Sena : Army
Sevak : A servant
Sewa : Service
Sewakdharam : Servant's duties
Shaloka : Couplet in Sanskrit poetry
Shastras : Hindu's religious treatise
Shivling : Symbol of lord Shiv
Shudra : One of Hindu's four castes (who serves other three castes)
Sidha : A saint
Sidhi : Supernatural power
Singhasan : Throne
Smrities : Books of traditional codes of Hindu laws
Stuti : Praise
Sudh : Pure
Suhagin : A woman whose husband is alive
Swami : Master
Swami-bhakta : Devotee of one's master
Swarga : Heaven
Swayambar : Choice by bride of her husband
Tap : Meditation
Tapasvi : Medidator
Tapasya : Meditation
Tilak : A religious mark over forehead
Tirath : A place of pilgrimage
Tretayug : Second of the four periods in Hindu mythology
Tulsi : A holy basic plant/ ocymum sanctum
Tyaga : Sacrifice
Vairagya : Renunciation
Vaish : Third of the four Hindu castes (dealing in trade & agriculture)

Vaishyas : Persons belonging to third Hindu castes (traders & agriculturists)

Vanars : Monkeys

Vanar Vesh : Monkey's guise

Varan : The four castes in Hindus (Brahmin, Kshatriya, Vaish & Shudra)

Vedas : Ancient sacred scripture of Hindus (Rigved, Yajurved, Samved, Atharvaved)

Vedi : An altar

Videh : State of being beyond physical bonds

Vigyan : Divine knowledge/ science

Vigyanis : Persons having divine knowledge/scientists

Vimans : Aeroplanes

Viswas : Trust/confidence

Vrat : A fast

Yagya : Hindu institution of religious oblation

Yagya-avshesh : Remaining of religious oblation

Yagyashala : Oblation enclosure

Yavan Kal : Muslim period

Yogagni : A lady ascetic

Yugs : Four periods in Hindu mythology (Satyug, Tretayug, Duapur & Kalyug)

Yuvraj : Successor to Throne